Parenting Other People's Children

Parenting Other People's Children

Understanding and Repairing Reactive Attachment Disorder

John L. Stoller

VANTAGE PRESS
New York

Cover art by Peter Gerhart, age 10, winter 2002

FIRST EDITION

Published by Vantage Press, Inc.
419 Park Ave. South, New York, NY 10016

Manufactured in the United States of America

ISBN: 978-0-533-15322-0

Library of Congress Catalog Card No.: 2005907269

0 9 8 7 6 5 4

To Peter and Martin

Contents

Preface   ix
Acknowledgments   xvii
Introduction   xix

Section I: Theory
  1 Bowlby's Attachment Mechanism Paradigm   3
  2 Maslow's Hierarchy of Needs Paradigm   10
  3 What Is Trust?   18
  4 Trust Mechanism and Trust Disorder Paradigms   25
  5 Evaluating Behavioral Motivation   40
  6 Behavioral Characteristics of Transferal Trust Disorder   60
  7 Anger   79
  8 Addictive Personality Paradigm   85

Section II: Practice
  9 Introduction to Practice   109
 10 The Four Rules of the Push-Pull Technique   118
 11 The Repair Cycle   128
 12 Touching and Holding   149
 13 Behavior Management   152
 14 Battles   167
 15 Structure (Situational Trust)   178
 16 Kidding   181
 17 Esteem   185
 18 School Issues   190
 19 The Brat   198
 20 Misconceptions Revisited   207
 21 Conclusions   220

Appendixes
Appendix A: CAIS   231
Appendix B: Model Factors Overview   233

Appendix C: The Related Disorders   235
Appendix D: Goal Sheet   239

Bibliography   241

Preface

Reactive attachment disorder (RAD) occurs in children that suffer from the effects of bad parenting in their first years of life. When older, these children become aggressive, controlling, defiant and self-centered. I am a foster parent, and my experience has been that RAD-like symptoms are indeed very common in foster children. I have also found that I have a knack for helping these children to grow toward normalcy.

RAD is a poorly understood, poorly diagnosed and poorly treated malady. Depending on which expert you consult, the prevalence of RAD varies from ten percent to seventy percent in older foster children. Such a vast discrepancy in the numbers can only be accounted for by different clinicians using different criteria for making the diagnosis.

Depending on which expert you consult, RAD can be different things. Clearly, RAD is caused by pathogenic care in early childhood; all agree on that. The official description from the American Psychiatric Association's manual *Diagnostic and Statistical Manual of Mental Disorders* requires RAD to manifest itself before the age of five. Pathogenic care can vary from the extreme of having the child lie in a crib all day long with no emotional stimulation, just having its basic physiological needs satisfied, to a colicky baby with a basically good mother who is just too stressed to be able to meet the additional care that a baby with colic requires. In extreme cases, the child will withdraw into a frozen watchfulness and will be afraid to interact on almost any level with other human beings. On the other end of the spectrum, the child will be defiant, controlling and self-centered. Children do not have to have RAD to be defiant, controlling and self-centered, but if they do have RAD, the etiology (set of factors or cause of a disease) for their behavior is pathogenic care in infancy, and repairing the child is definitely going to be more difficult.

There is no book currently available that tells definitively how to repair a RAD child. While the elements of repair are seeded throughout the RAD literature, no one puts it all together into a comprehensive treatment program, nor does anybody accurately tie the treatment of RAD back to the underlying cause and thereby help the reader understand the rationale for treatment. Most books present Bowlby's attachment theory then skip immediately forward to treatment. Many rely too heavily on behavior management techniques designed primarily to benefit the caregiver, not the child. These books tell you how to win control battles and manage a RAD child's behavior; but managing behavior is not repair.

The word "reactive" in the phrase "reactive attachment disorder" means that the condition is a reaction to the pathogenic care. Contrast this to attention deficit hyperactivity disorder (ADHD) which appears to be a genetically induced chemical imbalance in the child. Unlike the ADHD child, the RAD child's behavior is learned. His behavior is motivated from basic survival needs. Look at it from the child's point of view. It has to be very unsettling to have the fulfillment of your basic survival needs at the mercy of a capricious or uncaring caregiver. When other people do not take care of you as they should, when other people cannot be trusted to take care of you as they should, your attempts to be in control at all times become instinctively necessary for survival. The RAD child, in many ways, acts the same as many self-centered, defiant, bratty children but the etiology is distinctly different. The bratty child is basically a normal child who, possibly as a result of overindulgent parents, has never been required to relinquish the control that we automatically confer on all infants.

The properly-cared-for baby starts life effectively in control. Ideally when the infant cries, its caregivers come running and tend to its needs. Though the infant is not really in control, from his perspective it may seem that way. The child's demands are always met. The RAD child, on the other hand, starts life knowing he is not in control.

We now know that emotions start developing in the infant long before intellect—probably as early as weeks after birth. Our awareness of the importance of these early emotions in shaping the individual's later emotional health is relatively recent. Previously, it was assumed that if you could not remember it, it was not important. However, intellectual memory is not the only type of memory that we have. There is also emotional memory, and the child, while he cannot bring to mind any of the incidents that occurred in the first year of life, certainly has emotions surfacing throughout life stemming from his emotional memory of that first year.

Normally, at about one year of age, we start to say "no" to the child. The natural progression has the adult eventually in control and the child very much aware of it. The brat is created by allowing the child to be controlling long after he should have relinquished control, by not proceeding into the "no" saying lessons of parenting soon enough. Understandably the brat likes the sensation of power and being the center of attention and is not about to voluntarily give it up.

The RAD child is not going to be so easily repaired as the brat. His desire to be in control is not just because he likes to be in control, but because it is a necessary survival strategy. The brat likes being in control; the RAD child fears not being in control. He does not trust other people to be in control of his life, and he is afraid when they are in control—fear is a strong motivator. Because RAD is not a chemical imbalance, it is not going to be fixed with a pill. Nevertheless the RAD child can be repaired, or at least improved. A good analogy would be malnutrition. Malnourished children after having been fed will often catch up on some of their missing growth, but will never reach the full potential that they would have reached had they enjoyed a good diet from birth. They will always be shorter than they might have been. The younger they are when you correct the malnutrition the better off they will be, and the closer they will grow to their potential adult height. It is the same with RAD children, the earlier you repair them the closer they can get to their emotional growth potential.

The bottom line here is that RAD is learned, so it can be unlearned. The child was taught as a result of receiving pathogenic care not to trust. Consequently, he needs to be in control as a survival mechanism. What is learned can be unlearned, and new lessons can be taught. A RAD child can be repaired. Repairing the child will take time, will take some special skills, and will test your patience.

What prompted my reading and research was not so much my difficulties handling the foster child with RAD entrusted to my care but the school's difficulties. I felt that they were way off base in their handling of the child and that a major control battle had developed between his teachers and him. I was at a loss on finding a way to teach his teachers how to avoid control battles. It seemed like there was no desire on their part to change any of their techniques. So I needed to do some research in a battle to try to educate them. I could not just tell them my ideas because, other than my experience, I seemingly had no credentials. In the beginning, I wrote a few emails to his teacher and the school guidance counselor, but they were basically ignored.

It is tragic that there are so many times when RAD is misdiagnosed. Without a correct diagnosis, both the child and the caregiver suffer. With their charming nature, RAD children are often capable of conning the world into thinking that they are the unfortunate innocent victims of malicious and/or bad parenting. A common scenario would be an unsuspecting stepmother's taking on the parenting responsibilities for her new husband's RAD child from a previous failed marriage. Not only does she not get the support that a correct diagnosis would provide, but everybody points the finger of culpability at her as if she were the source of the problem. The marriage and the family are destroyed, other children in the marriage suffer, and the RAD child gets no better.

The prevailing thought prior to 1950 was that children could not be emotionally damaged as infants, that emotions developed later. Then, in the early 1950's, John Bowlby proposed the Attachment Mechanism: the baby has a need and cries, the mother comes and satisfies that need, and that cycle repeats itself numerous times each day. As a result of this cycle, attachment forms. Mary Ainsworth did the studies in the 1960's that turned Bowlby's Attachment Mechanism from theory to fact. Nevertheless it was not until the late 1970's that the general psychological community came to appreciate and accept the Attachment Mechanism and its importance to future emotional health. The diagnosis reactive attachment disorder was not established until 1980. RAD is a very new diagnosis, only twenty-four years old at the writing of this book. No clinician over fifty years of age has studied it in school. Most of the rest of the clinicians were educated by teachers that had not studied it in school.

ADHD, also, is a relatively new diagnosis. However, there is a huge difference between the two: there are good drugs available for ADHD, and these drugs are very expensive (over three dollars a pill) so ADHD has the advantage of drug companies spending big money to promote the diagnosis, and of course, their medication.

There are no drugs for RAD. Consequently, no big money goes into doing research and promoting the diagnosis. RAD is a reactive disorder, which means that it is learned (reactive means a reaction to or produced by the environment) as opposed to a chemical imbalance, which is not learned but intrinsic to the individual. Right now the only cure for RAD is to unlearn the negative lesson taught to the child in its first year, the lesson that caregivers are not to be trusted; and as of yet learning and unlearning do not come out of a pill and it is unlikely that they ever will.

We are a product of our environment. We learn to adapt in order to survive. Touch a hot iron once and we know not to do it again. Have somebody mistreat us once and we avoid that person. If that person is our caregiver, and we are an infant, avoidance is impossible; then as soon as we have some intellectual capacity we try to take control of our lives rather than voluntarily submitting our fate to the vicissitudes of an aberrant caregiver. We declare independence, we become oppositional and defiant. Because of our experience having somebody else in control is fraught with fear and anxiety.

The ability to trust or mistrust as appropriate is a survival technique. The RAD child learns to mistrust his caregiver as a survival technique, and this negative lesson learned at an early age becomes deeply entrenched in his emotional core. Once learned, it is very difficult to unlearn. It is very difficult to retrain a child to trust. It takes years of quality parenting to rebuild the lost trust. It is an onerous, time consuming and expensive task. A task, more often than not, never completed. RAD is not so much a psychiatric disease as it is just a normal and appropriate response to being in a very scary situation: being totally at the mercy of and having your fate placed in the hands of an incompetent caregiver.

Many clinicians would rather find a diagnosis of ADHD because it is easily treated with drugs. Unfortunately, we cannot bend reality to suit more convenient and less expensive treatment tools. We need to use the right tool for the job.

Foster children, possibly the largest group of children with a high prevalence of RAD, generally do not have the financial resources to afford the older (more experienced) psychologists. Consequently, the older, more experienced psychologists do not specialize in RAD.

I took my RAD child to a psychologist. When I suggested that the child might have RAD, he asked me, "What's that?" When I spelled it out as "reactive attachment disorder" he said, "Oh!" I have had a psychologist tell me that my child did not have RAD, as RAD children are passive and do not interact. I have had a psychologist get upset with me because I was persistent in wanting a diagnosis (*any* diagnosis); she did not see the need for putting a label on the child.

There is no universally accepted treatment for RAD. Once you decide upon the diagnosis of RAD, most psychologists will still want to do traditional therapy on the child, even though the few psychologists who have specialized training and are successful in treating RAD tell us that these techniques are inappropriate for RAD children.[1] Most psychologists will use the traditional techniques that they learned in their formal training, because that is what they know and are familiar with. They do play therapy. They try to develop a trusting relationship with the child and then work through the child's emotional issues. RAD children are master manipulators. They are very good at controlling and directing therapy sessions, which can turn into very expensive playtime for the child. It is frustrating.

Let me summarize:

1) The psychological community is poorly trained in RAD.
2) The psychological community has little experience in identifying RAD and has not reached a general consensus on what constitutes a RAD diagnosis.
3) The psychological community in general does not understand the relationship between the early pathogenic care the child received and the child's symptoms.
4) The psychological community has not developed generally accepted treatments specific for RAD.
5) RAD treatment research and development is under funded.

The few experts who are successfully treating RAD all seem to agree that the parent must be present at therapy sessions. Along with the idea that developing the relationship between the parent and the child is more important than developing a relationship between the therapist and the child (after all, that is the attachment relationship in RAD that has never formed and needs to form now), having the parent present keeps the child from lying to and conning the therapist.

Much of what you know about raising children—the rules, rewards, consequences, punishment, and so on—just do not apply or work with RAD children. There are good books that give good ideas and advice; they talk about the basic underlying problems, and in general are helpful. There are also books that are essentially useless, that give advice that is counterproductive. One book suggested that we cross out the word difficult in "difficult child" and change it to "spirited." "Realizing that the traits of intensity, sensitivity, persistence, and perceptiveness really are traits we value in adulthood"[2] the book goes on to suggest that we leave the child as he is and just change our attitude toward the child. The adjectives that I would use to characterize a difficult child do not match nor are they as kind as this author's list of adjectives. Furthermore, the underlying problems do need addressing.

What started as a project to help my foster child's teachers acquire a better understanding of RAD has turned into a fascinating learning and research project for me. I was observing what I considered to be errors in the way his teachers approached handling my child. What followed was frustration about what appeared to be an inability or unwillingness on their part to understand or even to consider what I was saying. I figured that my message would be more powerful if I put it in writing. I have done quite a bit of writing now and find I truly enjoy the writing process.

I have been struggling with my apparent lack of credentials; though I have three college degrees (including a clinical degree) for a total of ten years of full time college attendance, I have no degrees or formal training in child education or psychology. Why would I have more insight than trained mental health care professionals, and why would I have something to offer in the way of advice to individuals who are already trained to understand and help children with psychological problems? They should be giving me advice, giving me insight.

When I was a child, there was no diagnosis of RAD. Looking back, I now appreciate that my brother had RAD. He was five years older than I and had a major impact on my life. I do not want to give away too many details about my private life, but the experience of growing up as the younger sibling of a RAD individual gives one an intuitive understanding of their behavior. For me, learning how to avoid setting off my RAD brother became a survival skill. That, coupled that with years of experience in raising RAD foster children, gives me experience that very few teachers, social workers, or health care providers can even approximate.

When trying to understand the emotions and behaviors of others, we often try to put ourselves in their place and ask ourselves, how would we feel if we were they. Most people, when they do this with a RAD child, misread the true emotions that motivate the child, because most people do not think the way RAD children think. However, I was blessed (more likely damned) with insight into the emotional workings of the RAD individual. Although I am not formally trained in psychology, as a practicing dentist, I do have experience in clinically diagnosing and treating patients. Therefore helping other people with their problems is not foreign to me.

This book originated out of frustration, frustration derived from not getting the answers to my many questions that I needed to help my foster children. The result, though, appears to be anything but frustrating. Intellectualizing the repair process has helped me to understand myself, and the impact that my childhood has on me as an adult. It has also helped me to better serve the foster children in my care. Writing it down and making it available to everyone, it is my hope, will help many others whose journey and commitment are similar to mine in helping their RAD child to better emotional health.

What I have put to paper is less an anecdotal approach and more a model or paradigm approach; a framework that has helped me to understand and respond to a child's behavior. Really, what I gained was perspective; a capacity to step back, lessen my frustration, avoid my own hot buttons, and become a better foster parent.

I do not pretend to understand neurosis and psychosis. The children I describe here are not irrational, not sick, not pathological, they are responding very appropriately to the environment that created them. Our job as their caregivers is first to create a new environment, a gentler more loving and less hostile (therapeutic) environment, then to help them adapt to that new environment. Our reward is helping another person achieve his or her full range of human emotion.

Notes

[1] Hughes, Daniel A., *Facilitating Developmental Attachment,* 1997, p. 7.
[2] Kurcinka, Mary Sheedy, *Raising Your Spirited Child,* 1998, p. 2.

Acknowledgments

I would like to extend my appreciation and thanks to the many authors and individuals who shared their insights with me in my search for pieces of the "creating a therapeutic environment for children with attachment disorder" puzzle, and subsequently went on to write this book. When I first began researching this topic I had no intention of writing a book, so I unfortunately did not keep track of all the early references.

Sir Isaac Newton said about his accomplishments in formulating the mathematics of calculus, "If I have seen further it is by standing on the shoulders of giants."[1] Maslow was a giant, as was Bowlby. It seems logical that the next step was to merge their ideas. To them, and to all the other authors and thinkers of the past, we all hold a special debt, for their tall shoulders give us a high platform from which to advance.

I hold a debt of deep gratitude to the many contributors whose ideas helped lay the foundation for this book; I would like to single out the following for their special inspiration and help (in alphabetical order):

Fred Blankenburg and Stephen Polonsky, my contacts at the Montgomery County Office of Children and Youth were always there for me giving me support all along the way. Their comments and encouragement are much appreciated. In spite of the fact that I was "just another foster parent" they showed respect for my ideas and promoted them within the agency.

I am indebted to Ron Dempsey and Jim Eldridge for their time and effort in reading the manuscript and giving me invaluable pointers on style, word choice, grammar, and format.

I would also like to thank clinical psychologists Dr. Laurie Kennedy and Dr. Linda Shope for reading my manuscript and offering me comments and encouragement.

I would like to thank Natalie Macy who read and reread my manuscript as it evolved into its final form and gave me both a sounding board to test ideas and pushed me to stay with the writing project to the end.

Kathy Pedriani gave me early encouragement and showed interest in the writing throughout the entire project.

I spent many hours in fascinating discussion with clinical psychologist Dr. Robert Rabinowitz, a close friend and traveling companion, bouncing ideas off him and picking his brain as we traveled through Europe examining old churches and the human psyche to the point of his distraction (never mine). His both critical and non-critical input was invaluable in helping me to formulate my ideas. He introduced me to the term "agent for change" and for me he has become just that, an agent for change, and good change at that.

Christopher Veneziale, my nephew, acted as my main copy editor. For months he and I would meet once a week to work on cleaning up my writing and sharpening my arguments. He had me rewrite most of the book. Clearly he had a great influence on the quality of my writing as well as the quality of my arguments. Many a time I could see the relief on his face when he had very diplomatically made me realize that a particular section was basically garbage and needed a total revamping. If I am an improved writer today it is primarily due to Christopher's efforts. Thanks.

I would like to thank my two natural sons Brian and David and my extended family for allowing me over a year and a half of time to write this book that partially came from time that I would have otherwise spent with them.

Lastly, I need to thank the foster children that have allowed me into their lives, who allowed me to better understand both them and, through them, myself. This has been a journey of discovery and understanding and emotional growth for all of us.

Michael Bridge beautifully says, "When our eyes see our hands doing the work of our hearts, the circle of creation is completed inside us, the doors of our souls fly open, and love steps forth to heal everything in sight."

Notes

[1] Sir Isaac Newton, English mathematician & physicist (1642–1727), Letter to Robert Hooke, February 5, 1675.

Introduction

It is the unusual older child in foster care or who is seeking adoption who *has not* experienced some emotional damage in his or her life. These children need some kind of emotional therapy, some kind of emotional support. Within the foster care community, there has emerged a category of foster care families labeled "therapeutic foster homes" that specialize in helping these children.

I have written this book in part for these foster parents, but also for all the other foster parents who take in older foster children. Like it or not, all families with older foster children probably need to have a therapeutic environment, even if they are not officially designated as such. A therapeutic environment is one that allows and encourages the child to heal and grow emotionally. Through the course of this book, I will define emotional growth.

I have written this book for the adoptive parents of many older children as well. Older children who are put up for adoption often come from the foster care system. Because these children come from the same population sample, adoptive parents need the same skills that foster parents need.

I have also written this book for parents who adopt children from institutions or orphanages. This is a practice that is far more common in overseas adoptions since the trend in this country is to place parentless children immediately in foster care rather than in institutions. There now exists irrefutable evidence that institutionalizing infants often leads to severe emotional damage.[1,2]

Lastly, I have written this book for the professionals that work with foster children, foster parents, and even for natural parents and step parents whose children may exhibit symptoms of attachment disorder.

Meeting children's needs during the first few years of their lives will define how they form attachments to others later in life. Unlike children whose needs are satisfied during these critical years, children whose needs are not met form a different perspective on life. Foster children, almost by definition, are children whose needs are not satisfied. If their needs were fulfilled, they would not have been placed in foster care in the first place. Traditionally, older foster children suffer from a history of needs that were never met.

I have written this book because there is a need for caregivers to understand the nature of the damage, and because I am not aware of anybody else having developed as accurate a working emotional model of these children. In the first section of this book, I build a theoretical emotional model that incorporates, merges, and expands upon the pertinent existing models. Section two is more practical, where I use the model I built to predict and understand the behavior of the child, and as a basis for formulating a therapeutic environment conducive to repairing him.

To build a theoretical model, I begin with the Hierarchy of Needs Model developed by Harold Maslow and the Attachment Cycle Model developed by John Bowlby and Mary Ainsworth. I make minor variations and changes in emphasis to both, and then meld them together to create a new model. This new model is helpful in understanding the emotional reactions of children who would have been previously labeled as having "attachment disorder" (AD) or "reactive attachment disorder" (RAD).

The most important variation I make in the Attachment Cycle Model is to emphasize trust as the basic issue, not attachment. I then ascribe the lack of attachment as secondary to a lack of trust. The distinction is more of a change in emphasis rather than a change of definition since attachment as loosely defined by Bowlby includes trust although it is closer to his idea of love.[3]

The modification I make in the Hierarchy of Needs Model is really not a change to the model itself as Maslow presents it, but instead, it is a change in how most people interpret it. I state (or at least emphasize) that individuals can function simultaneously on more than one level, which does not contradict Maslow.[4] I have also developed a useful set of indicators to relate specific behaviors to Maslow's levels.

I use the new model to explain the children's behavior, and to help readers understand the importance and interdependence of different treatment techniques. I also use the model to debunk various myths that we constantly hear regarding these children.

I call the new model that I have developed "trust disorder," or "reactive trust disorder." The title of this book could be *Trust Disorder*, but since this is a new name for a disorder which I coined, I knew that it would confuse people looking for a book to read on the problems often observed in older foster and adopted children. I chose instead to name this book *Parenting Other People's Children.*

I am going to use the term trust disorder (TD) throughout this book. Appreciate that this is my term and that traditionally it would be referred to as attachment disorder or reactive attachment disorder. They are similar in nature, but with two major exceptions: 1) TD has an emphasis on a lack of trust as being the basic problem which leads secondarily to a lack of attachment, and 2) I do not limit TD to only the most severely afflicted children as is the case with RAD.

I do not suggest any radical methods for treating children with TD. I do define four basic rules (The Four Rules) that are necessary to create a therapeutic environment. These are not four bizarre rules concocted to specifically address the special needs of the TD child. They are four basic rules that codify what good parents all over the world do every day to create emotionally healthy children.

I grappled with the word I would use to describe the process of changing the child from his untrusting emotionally immature condition to a more trusting and emotionally developed human being. Trust disorder is really not a disease, so calling the process "curing the child" would be inaccurate. Even though I call the process "treatment" and I describe something I call a "therapeutic environment," I do not want to give the impression that the child is sick in a traditional sense. We will see that RAD is a learned behavioral response and is pretty much an appropriate behavior response, given the child's history. We need to change the child's behavior because the world at large is not nearly so hostile (hopefully) as the world of the child's early emotional experiences as an infant, and for the world at large, the child's behavior is both inappropriate and counterproductive. I have chosen the word "repair" to describe what we are going to do for the child by way of changing him to an adult with the ability to trust and love.

If you have read other books on RAD, you will be aware of a number of techniques that have been suggested for treating your TD child. Some of the techniques seem contradictory. I give a rationale for how much of each technique should be used to achieve optimal results, and why some of the more onerous techniques suggested in the literature might not be necessary. Getting a quick result with less grief is always a nice outcome.

My experience has been exclusively with boys, so I will use the masculine gender when referring to the child. I think that everything here is just as valid for a girl as a boy. As a historical note, both Anna Freud and John Bowlby used the masculine gender to refer to the child, and Bowlby also used the feminine gender when making a reference to the mother.

In my research for this book, I encountered the following statement about another book:

> This book is NOT for everyone, but if you are tired of overcomplicated, "theoretical" approaches, then this IS THE BOOK FOR YOU. [It] gets to the point fast and makes a strong case for common sense and simplicity.[5]

I take exception with this statement. Why is it that people assume a "theoretical" approach is going to be overcomplicated and inconsistent with common sense? Why would understanding the theory behind the child's behavior not simplify creating the optimal therapeutic environment to help him?

I do agree with the author of this statement that the models that have been previously presented are not very helpful. I like to think that the theoretical model that I present here is intuitively obvious, is consistent with common sense, and is quite helpful. In fact, common sense is really a byproduct of having a good intuitive understanding of an accurate working model. This book should help the reader develop a common sense approach to understanding the TD child.

There are two existing models or paradigms for human behavior that are generally accepted and have been proven valid. My model is going to use these existing models as its basis.

I never liked the word paradigms: I thought it sounded pretentious and less meaningful than more direct words. It has been used for years in the psychological community, and has more recently become a common buzzword in the business world, particularly with MBA students. "OK people, listen up! There is a new paradigm for mail delivery here at XYZ Corporation. It will now be placed in a little box with your name on it." Why could they not just say "a new way" or "a new model," since either word would work better than paradigm? I graduated with an MBA from Wharton in 1972, and never once heard the word paradigm at that time.

However, in the context of what I am doing here, paradigm turns out to be the perfect word. I guess that is why the term has been used in psychological circles for years. It may sound like a sophisticated and scientific term, but it is a fairly simple concept and should not scare anyone away. The word paradigm can mean either (a) an example of, or (b) the model of a generally accepted theory on how ideas relate to one another, forming a conceptual framework.[6] This is exactly my goal: to form a conceptual framework for trust, which I have postulated as the basic issue in reactive attachment disorder. In other words, a trust paradigm.

The strength of any model lies in its ability to predict, and in this case we do so by anecdotally considering a vast range of children. We can test the model by inserting each child's parameters and variables into the model. Then we can compare the results predicted by the model with real-world observations. When the model accurately predicts real-world observations, our level of confidence in it increases; when it does not, we know that we have to refine and change the model. Refer to Appendix B for a summary of the parameters that I have used to build my model.

Whenever possible, we break models down into sub-models to make understanding them easier. After developing and mastering the sub-models, we reassemble them (in our minds) to create an overall model that we hope both explains and predicts the real world. The next two chapters, Bowlby's Attachment Mechanism Paradigm and Maslow's Hierarchy of Needs Paradigm, are the two important sub-models that I use to build my overall model.

Notes

[1] Levy & Orlans, *Attachment, Trauma, and Healing*, 1998, p. 15.
[2] Bowlby, John, *Maternal Care and Mental Health*. Geneva: World Health Organization Monograph Series (2), 1951. Cited in Karen, *Becoming Attached*, 1998, p. 64.
[3] Karen, *Becoming Attached*, 1998, p. 90.
[4] Maslow, *Motivation and Personality*, 1970, p. 27.
[5] Hakarian, Edward. Book review of *The Child Whisperer* by Mathew Thomas Pasquinilli on amazon.com web site. June 2, 2003.
[6] Paraphrased from the Microsoft Office computer dictionary.

Parenting Other People's Children

Section I
Theory

1

Bowlby's Attachment Mechanism Paradigm

John Broadus Watson (1878–1959) is the father of the classical behaviorism movement, which started in 1913 and gained acceptance in the wake of the earlier introspective psychology pioneered by Sigmund Freud (1856–1939). Watson commented on children in his book *Psychological Care of Infant and Child* in 1928:[1]

> Treat them as though they were young adults. Dress them, bathe them with care and circumspection. Let your behavior always be objective, kindly, and firm. Never hug and kiss them, never let them sit on your lap. If you must, kiss them once on the forehead when they say goodnight. Shake hands with them in the morning. Give them a pat on the head if they have made an extraordinary good job of a difficult task.[2]

This is professional advice from one of the top psychologists of his day, and 1928 was not that long ago. Is it wrong? Good God, yes!

Our understanding of children and their needs has progressed dramatically in the last half of the twentieth century. We can be thankful that John Bowlby (1907–1990), with help from James Robertson, Mary Ainsworth, and others, brought new direction to child psychology and developed attachment theory. When Bowlby first introduced attachment theory in the early fifties, it was met with hostility from both his colleagues and the general public. It was not until the late nineteen seventies that his theories became commonly accepted.

Bowlby introduced the word "attachment" as something separate from love or bonding. Bonding is a very quick event, as in the case of the baby goose that imprints and bonds to the first thing it sees when it hatches, which is usually the mother. On the other hand, attachment is a "complex developmental process"[3] that takes time to occur. Bowlby primarily viewed attachment as being comprised of love, but it included security and joy as well.[4]

Bowlby did not usually refer to attachment per se, but to something he called "attachment behavior," which consisted of behaviors he attributed to the relationship that develops between the mother and infant. Such behaviors include the infant crying when the mother walks away, or the infant only wanting to be consoled by the mother when under stress. Bowlby and his associates identified a whole set of behaviors, then used them to develop a system to categorize different degrees of attachment.

Though the attachment usually occurs between the mother and the child, Bowlby never said that it *must* occur between the mother and child. Instead, it can occur between anybody who fulfills the traditional role of the mother, be it the father, aunt, or anyone else who takes on the role of primary caregiver for the child.

"Attachment" is the strong emotional link that usually occurs first with the child's mother, but only because she is usually the primary caregiver, the one who consistently and predictably responds to the child's everyday needs. From Bowlby's work, we know attachment occurs early, that it is important for the future development of the child, and that it forms the basis for future relationships the child will have throughout his life. We also know that attachment does not always develop as it should, and when this happens, the child can develop emotional problems that will last throughout his life.

The Attachment Mechanism

Attachment occurs in two phases: the first year "healthy attachment cycle," and the second year "secure attachment cycle."[5] If these cycles are not adequately completed, then attachment problems ensue.

During the first year of life, when the baby signals his needs to the mother by crying or fussing, the mother comes and attends to the baby's need. If this cycle is repeated many times, the baby learns to trust that his needs will be met. The first year "healthy attachment cycle" occurs every time the child experiences a need and cries for attention. The way it is supposed to work is like this:

- The child feels a need, and communicates that need to its primary caregiver (usually the mother) by body language or crying,

4

or perhaps the primary caregiver anticipates the need in advance.
- The primary caregiver comes and attends the child's need.
- The child learns to trust (or at least not to distrust) based on the experiences of how his needs are fulfilled by the primary caregiver.

This cycle repeats itself every time the baby calls for attention. By repeating this cycle over and over again, day after day, by the end of the first year the child should have a strong basis for trusting not only his caregiver, but also the world around him. He learns to trust and depend on his caregiver not only to meet his needs, but also to know what his needs are. Assuming that all goes well, the baby never has to worry that his needs will not be met. The world as he knows it is a safe, secure, and friendly place in which to live.

Sometime during the second year of life, the baby moves from the "healthy attachment cycle" to what is called the "secure attachment cycle"[6] In his second year of life, the child will still have needs just like the first year, and the cycle described above will still occur. But as the infant matures, he will start to add some new demands for attention, demands that perhaps do not fall into the "need" category. These demands will be more along the lines of *wants* rather than *needs*, and the primary caregiver will have to make decisions as to which demands to fulfill and which to ignore. The word "no" will creep into the vocabulary commonly heard by the baby. The way the "secure attachment cycle" works is like this:

- For *needs* it works just like the "healthy attachment cycle" of the infant's first year, as described above.

If it is not a *need* that the child has communicated but a *want*, it works like this:

- The child communicates the *want* to its primary caregiver, just as he would for a *need*.
- The primary caregiver comes to attend to the child.
- The primary caregiver determines that the child does not have a *need*, but instead has a *want*.

5

- The primary caregiver says "no" to the *want* and does not fulfill the request.

A different kind of cycle takes place, one where the demand is terminated with a "no" rather than a fulfillment. If the baby has developed a solid foundation of trust in the first year, then he should accept the caregiver's decisions, and use them to learn the difference between wants and needs. He should come to realize that "no" means that he does not really need what he thinks he does.

By repeating these cycles over and over again, day after day, at the end of the second year the child should have developed strong attachment and have a strong basis for differentiating between wants and needs.

If the baby does not become attached during the first year of life—that is, if he has not learned to trust his caregiver to fulfill his needs reliably and predictably (possibly due to a capricious way that needs were met during the first year of his life)—then this second part of the attachment process will not only fail, it will also serve to make the baby even more poorly attached. The baby has no way to distinguish between needs and wants other than what he is taught by his caregiver. In order to learn that lesson, he first needs to be attached. He has to trust the decisions made by the caregiver. Then, he can learn by copying the caregiver's decisions. If he does not trust the caregiver, what is normally a good lesson for the attached child becomes a bad lesson for the unattached child.

If you say "no" to a well-attached child, rather than shake his foundation of trust, it remains intact, and the child advances toward the ability to differentiate between needs and wants. If you say "no" to a child whose attachment is shaky to begin with, it further weakens his base without teaching him any valuable lessons. He will only see it as another instance of his caregiver being unresponsive.

The attachment mechanism starts almost at birth, certainly within weeks of birth.[7] There appears to be a very small window of time immediately after birth within which a child can be moved between caregivers before the consistency of having one primary caregiver who attends to all the child's needs becomes important in order for the child to become well attached.

Reactive Attachment Disorder Paradigm

"Attachment disorder," "reactive attachment disorder" (RAD), and "reactive attachment disorder of infancy or early childhood"[8] are the currently accepted names for individuals who have social and emotional problems stemming from attachment cycle failure.

The word "reactive" in the term "reactive attachment disorder" means that the basis for the disorder is not internal. The child does not have a genetic or chemical imbalance, but instead, the source of the disorder is external. The child simply reacts to that external source. The child is not irrational, sick or pathological; he is merely reacting in a predictable way to an environment that has been something less than accommodating.

The word "attachment," as used in this term, is derived from Bowlby's research in which he did not actually define attachment, but instead defined a set of behaviors that he called "attachment behavior." He avoided rigorously defining and ascribing specific emotions to "attachment," possibly to circumvent controversy. Trying to guess at the emotions that are going on inside an infant, when it is impossible to ask the child or to recall from our own infancy, can lead to controversy. The word "attachment" as used by Bowlby is open for interpretation and misinterpretation. People generally accept it without demanding a definition and think of it as love and bonding. The closest that Bowlby came to defining attachment was to suggest that it included safety, security, and joy, but primarily he thought of it as love.

The word "disorder" refers to an abnormal functioning of the mind or body.

Attachment disorder is caused when the attachment mechanism described above does not occur as it should. The attachment cycles break down when the primary caregiver does not respond to the baby's cry for attention. Unlike the baby who forms healthy attachment, this baby learns that the world is not quite such an accommodating place.

Since the baby has no preconceived notions of what the world should be like, he builds a model from scratch, a model which will be his basis for all future interpersonal interactions. He has no way of knowing anything other than what he learns from interactions with his caregivers. If the interaction lacks trust, love, joy, and so forth, then the child will grow up thinking that this is the way the whole world functions. Changing these feelings later when the child is older appears to be very difficult. This is exactly why we now know how important it is to make sure infants are not placed in institutions at birth; they must be placed with a single primary caregiver who will be attentive to the infant's needs almost twenty-four hours a day, seven days a week. This is also why we place the designation "reactive" on attachment disorder, because the infant reacts to his environment and bases his own personal model on his experiences. It is not an organic disorder; it is a learned disorder.

There are many ways that the process of forming attachments can go wrong. The mother or primary caregiver may not have the required skills or instincts, or may have problems of her own that interfere with taking care of the infant. Perhaps due to certain circumstances, the primary caregiver may be changed too many times, as might happen to a child in foster care. The child may be placed in an institution that does not have the resources or the ability to provide consistent childcare, and where the child may experience multiple caregivers even over a twenty-four hour period. The infant may have colic or some other physical conditions that make him feel as if his needs are not being met, even if the care he is receiving is excellent.

The diagnoses of reactive attachment disorder of infancy or early childhood (RAD) is rare, as it appears to be reserved for only the worst cases.[9] Appendix C lists the requirements for the RAD diagnosis. One of the requirements is that documented proof of abuse exists. A suspicion or opinion is not sufficient. This is proof that is often difficult to produce. Parents do not usually voluntarily admit to their ineptness.

I personally do not find the theory of attachment and attachment disorder difficult to understand or accept. In fact, I find it interesting that it took the world so long to embrace it. Bowlby struggled for almost thirty years from the time he first proposed attachment theory in the early nineteen-fifties until the late nineteen-seventies when his attachment theory was generally accepted. A preponderance of evidence now supports his theory, which today can be considered a non-controversial theory, that is well supported by documented scientific studies, and that has gained universal acceptance among those professional psychologists and psychiatrists who routinely deal with children.

Notes

[1] Cited in Karen, Robert Ph.D., *Becoming Attached*, 1994, p. 5.
[2] Watson, John B., *Psychological Care of Infant and Child*, 1928, pp. 81–82.

were choking you by blocking off your airway, your need for air would dominate everything else in your life. You would not care that your wife is leaving you or that your boss thinks you are a geek. More pre-potent needs take precedence over less pre-potent needs.

After Physiological Needs, he placed (in order of descending pre-potency) Safety and Security Needs, Belonging and Love Needs, Esteem Needs, and last, something he called Self-Actualization Needs, all of which is discussed below in greater detail. He called the more pre-potent Needs "lower level Needs," the lowest being Physiological, and the less pre-potent Needs "higher level Needs," the highest being Self-Actualization.

The ranking in terms of pre-potency means that until a lower level Need is somewhat fulfilled, the higher level Needs are essentially meaningless and irrelevant to the individual. We could say that they do not emerge or become important until the lower level Need is fulfilled. He also postulated that needs generally must be fulfilled from the lower level to the higher level in order without skipping a level. For example, if an individual were starving to death, he would not be aware of or concern himself with any need from a level above. When he finally satisfies his hunger by eating (and any other unfulfilled Physiological Needs), his next emerging concerns would be from the next higher need level of Safety and Security, not Belonging and Love (assuming, of course, that he is deficient in both). Only when all lower level Needs are somewhat satisfied would he be aware of any deficiency in the next unfulfilled higher Need level. Maslow felt that moving up the hierarchy clearly was a desirable goal and represented emotional growth, which is why he called those Needs toward the top of the pyramid "higher level Needs," and the Needs on the bottom of the pyramid, the more pre-potent Needs, "lower level Needs."

Usually his Hierarchy of Needs is represented as a pyramid with the lower level Needs at the bottom and higher level Needs at the top.

The pyramid is meant to graphically display his emphasis on fulfilling lower level Needs first, in a sense, to support or act like a foundation for the higher level Needs. It gives the impression that each higher Need level rests upon the ones below it. Note that Need levels that are higher in pre-potency are actually lower on the pyramid just as Maslow defines them as "lower" Needs and Needs that are lower in prepotency are actually higher on the pyramid.

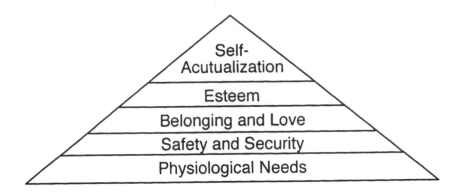

I do not know who first turned Maslow's Hierarchy into a pyramid. I do not think it was he, though he was a prolific writer and there is much of his work that I have not read. To date, I have never seen this pyramid in any of his books. Maslow never intended for us to think of higher level Needs being dependent upon lower level Needs. He only intended for us to think of lower level Needs being more powerful stimulators, more pre-potent with stronger urges, that when unsatisfied would overshadow higher level Needs and urges. The pyramid is somewhat misleading.

A better analogy than the pyramid would be the sun and the stars. The stars are present in the sky twenty-four hours a day, but they are not as pre-potent (strong) as the sun. During the day, when the sun is up, we cannot see the stars. The stars are there—just as the higher level Needs are there—all the time, but when the sun is out the stars seem to disappear, just as higher level Needs seem to disappear in the presences of lower level Needs. We would never draw a pyramid and say that the stars are higher on the pyramid than the sun and are somehow dependent on the sun to go down for them to come into existence. That analogy would be ridiculous.

There are two reasons why Maslow's Hierarchy of Needs is going to be important to us. When considering the child who did not consistently have his Needs met, as we did when discussing attachment disorder in the last chapter, it is going to be important that we all know what a need is, and that we be able to distinguish a need from a want. Secondly, we are going to want at some point to learn to observe the child and to determine where he is developmentally in the hierarchy. This will help us to understand and know how to react to his behavior.

Maslow states "the basic needs stand in a special psychological and biological status. There is something different about them. They *must* be satisfied or else we get sick."[2] In the previous chapter, we spoke about the observations in orphanages that babies that were not given emotional stimulation had significantly higher death rates. This observation is in total agreement with Maslow's theories.

In the 1960s, Maslow refined his hierarchy by grouping the four lowest level Needs together and labeling them "deficiency needs." He then added three more levels at the top of the hierarchy that, along with the already existing Self Actualization level, became a second group of Needs which collectively he labeled "growth needs." More often than not when you encounter in the literature the hierarchy represented as a graphic pyramid, it will be shown with just Self-Actualization at the top and no grouping by Deficiency and Growth level, exactly as in the graphical representation I presented earlier.

Following is a list of the Need levels with descriptions quoted directly from Maslow. Note that they are arranged in two groups. Going downward, my list would be the same as going upward on the hierarchy or the pyramid. The most pre-potent Needs, also called the lowest level Needs are presented first proceeding to the least pre-potent or the highest level Needs at the bottom of the list:

Deficiency Level Needs

- Physiological Needs—necessary for the existence of life, such as oxygen, food, water, warmth, and so on. Sex is considered to bc a Physiological Need.
- Safety and Security Needs—things such as a place to sleep, shelter, also knowing that your Physiological Needs will be met, at least in the near future.

"If the physiological needs are relatively well gratified, there then emerges a new set of needs, which we may categorize roughly as the safety needs (security; stability; dependency; protection; freedom from fear, anxiety, and chaos; need for structure, order, law, and limits; strength in the protector; and so on).[3]

- Belonging and Love Needs—the feeling of being part of a group, being accepted and being loved. Maslow envisioned love as being reciprocal.[4]

"If both the physiological and the safety needs are fairly well gratified, there will emerge the love and affection and belongingness needs, and the whole cycle already described will repeat itself with this new center. The love needs involve giving and receiving affection. When they are unsatisfied, a person will feel keenly the absence of friends, mate, or children. Such a person will hunger for relations with people in general—for a place in the group or family—and will strive with great intensity to achieve this goal. Attaining such a place will matter more than anything else in the world and he or she may even forget that once, when hunger was foremost, love seemed unreal, unnecessary, and unimportant. Now the pangs of loneliness, ostracism, rejection, friendlessness, and rootlessness are preeminent."[5]

- Esteem Needs—with two sub-categories, self-esteem and the esteem of others.

"All people in our society (with a few pathological exceptions) have a need or a desire for a stable, firmly based, usually high evaluation of themselves, for self-respect or self-esteem, and for the esteem of others. These needs may therefore be classified into two subsidiary sets. These are, *first,* the desire for strength, achievement, adequacy, mastery and competence, confidence in the face of the world, and independence and freedom. *Second,* we have what we may call the desire for reputation or prestige (defining it as respect or esteem from other people), status, fame and glory, dominance, recognition, attention, importance, dignity, or appreciation."[6]

"Satisfaction of the self-esteem need leads to feelings of self-confidence, worth, strength, capability, and adequacy, of being useful and necessary in the world. But thwarting of these needs produces feelings of inferiority, of weakness, and of helplessness."[7]

"The most stable and therefore most healthy self-esteem

is based on *deserved* respect from others rather than on external fame or celebrity and unwarranted adulation."[8]

Growth Level Needs (Originally all lumped together as Self-Actualization Needs)

- Cognitive—to know, to understand, and to explore.
- Aesthetic—symmetry, order, and beauty.
- Self-Actualization Needs—to find self-fulfillment and realize one's potential.
- Self-Transcendence—to connect to something beyond the ego, or to help others find self-fulfillment and realize their own potential.

Because Maslow was greatly interested in those individuals who had achieved psychological excellence, he spent a great deal of time writing and concentrating on the Growth level Needs. For example, Maslow felt that the reward for being in the top two levels, Self-Actualization and Self-Transcendence, was to have attained wisdom. While this is an interesting topic, the children we are considering (actually almost all children for that matter) are not even going to come close to reaching this stage at their young ages. I am simply including it for the sake of completeness.

Children in general, and reactive attachment disorder (RAD) children in particular, have issues that are rooted in the lowest four deficiency level Needs. I present all of Maslow's Need levels to give a complete representation of his paradigm, but I will only go into any detail on the lower levels because an understanding of them is important to understanding RAD.

Throughout this book when I refer to Psychological Needs, Safety and Security Needs, Belonging and Love Needs, Esteem Needs, and Self Actualization and have them in capitals, I will always be referring to them in the context of Maslow's Hierarchy of Needs paradigm.

Basic Needs

One popular author on child raising claims that children have a basic need to have some say over their own lives. He claims that "being in control" is a basic need. I question how he came to such a conclusion. He is not alone when he commits the error of wantonly purporting to ascribe basic Needs to human beings. You cannot do that. Maslow and others worked very hard to develop a comprehensive group of basic human Needs. Being responsible to the existing body of knowledge of psychology requires that we either stick with the commonly accepted list of basic Needs or we deviate from it only by presenting carefully constructed arguments.

Each and every so-called "basic need" must have a phylogenically evolved genetically programmed basis. The evolutionary process is at best, slow and plodding, and is unlikely to select for "basic needs" that do not have an obvious advantage for the organism. The odds for a random mutation that programs for a beneficial adaptive change becoming incorporated into an organism's genome are extremely low. It is nearly impossible to imagine that a characteristic that offers no adaptive benefit will somehow make it into the genome. The genome is the common set of chromosomes that a species passes on to its children.

Maslow's Deficiency Needs all meet the requirement that they can be shown to have a clear phylogenic advantage to the human organism and thus their natural selection in the evolutionary process is quite understandable. (I might question Maslow's designation as "basic" some of his Growth Needs that do not have any obvious argument for their conferring on humans some type of survival advantage, but that is a topic for another book with a different purpose from this book.) It is most unlikely that a random mutational event that does not program for an improvement in the survival characteristics of the organism will ever become incorporated into the genome for that organism's progeny. The genetic trait that causes sickle cell anemia, for example, has a survival basis. The sickle cell trait confers protection against malaria, and, not surprisingly, is found mostly in people who come from areas where malaria is prevalent.

Writers of psychological material cannot just create new "basic needs" at will. There must be discipline. The intellectual creation of a new "basic need" is going to require significant argument and significant research before it should be embraced by the psychological community at large. However, writers of psychologically based books do it all the time. They throw out statements that speak to the basis of our psychological fabric without regard to existing models, a need for common agreement, and without any supporting argument.

The psychological community needs improved self-policing. It needs to rail against writers that make unsubstantiated claims about the basic fabric of human makeup. Moreover, it needs to establish a mutually agreed upon model driving human behavior. It is the lack of such a model that not only allows but encourages individual writers to throw out unsubstantiated claims of "basic needs" without being taken to task by their colleagues.

Notes

[1] Maslow, *Motivation and Personality*, 1970, p. 48.
[2] Ibid, p. 53.
[3] Maslow, *Motivation and Personality*, Third Edition, 1987, p. 18.
[4] Ibid, p. 58.
[5] Ibid, p. 20.
[6] Ibid, p. 21.
[7] Ibid, p. 21.
[8] Ibid, p. 22, original emphasis.

3

What Is Trust?

Without even being aware of it, you have an automatic built-in trust meter that is always working, even when you sleep. Every time you enter a room, sit in a chair, meet a person, walk down a street, there is a part of your brain that is evaluating the situation for trust. Do you trust this situation, do you trust this person? If you do not trust the situation you will feel unsafe and insecure. If your feeling is strong enough you will take some type of action—turn back, run, prepare for a fight, or some other defensive measure. If a frightening looking person approaches you with a knife, a signal goes off in your brain. You know that the situation has danger in it. You cannot feel mistrust as an emotion. Rather, the emotion you experience is fear, but your trust level for that dangerous looking threatening person would be low as would your trust level for the situation.

You might be in your home. It is evening. The doors are locked. There is no history of danger in your home. Your family is there, and you know from experience that they will protect you if need be. You feel safe and secure. You trust the home environment, the locks on your doors, the neighborhood you live in, and you trust your family. Because you trust the people around you and the situation you are in, you feel calm and relaxed.

Trust is not an emotion. You cannot say, "I feel very trust," as you can say, "I feel very anxious." On the other hand, trust is quantifiable in that you can say, "I trust him a lot," or, "I trust him very little." Trust is usually outwardly directed, that is to say you would usually apply the word "trust" to somebody else or some situation, not to yourself.

It is assumed that you have control over yourself so you implicitly trust yourself. When you do not trust yourself it is usually as if you were a separate person evaluating yourself, such as when you might say, "I don't trust myself not to eat that candy so take it away." You know yourself well enough to know your own weaknesses to temptation, but generally trust is reserved for evaluating other people or situations (situations such as walking down a dark alley at night).

Like many words, trust can have multiple meanings. In the context of this book, there is one particular type of trust in which we are interested, the trust we have toward others and toward situations. We could say that trust is our internal measurement of the level of safety and security we feel with respect to situations and to other people.

The key phrase here is "measurement of safety and security level." Trust is the word that we would use to compare two different situations or two different people with respect to safety and security. When we say we trust a situation or we trust a person, what we are saying is that we feel safe and secure with that situation or person. When we say we do not trust a person or situation we are saying that we do not feel safe and secure.

For example we might say, "I trust your driving, but I don't trust Tom's." What we are really saying is, "You are a safer driver than Tom, and his level of skill is below my minimum acceptable standard for safety while yours is above." Clearly, in this example, trust is a Safety and Security issue.

Other examples, "I trust you with my keys," "I trust you with my life," and "I don't trust that doctor," are all Safety and Security issues. The most common usage of the word trust is to describe a relative measurement of the Safety or Security of a situation or person.

I say relative only because, even though trust is a measurement, it is not quantifiable. What I mean by not quantifiable is that we cannot place a number on it. It is relative only in the sense that when we use the word "trust" to communicate our level of belief in someone or something, if we want to be explicit, we are forced to use comparisons, as in, "I trust you more than I trust Mary," which is more meaningful than, "I trust you a lot," depending, of course, on what we know about Mary.

But different levels of trust do engender different levels of emotion, and there is nothing relative about that. A situation or person that you do not trust will evoke fear or anxiety. People or situations that we highly trust will evoke a sense of safety and security.

In general, we need a way to look at Maslow's levels and determine how well a level is satisfied. We know that when a level is satisfied, Needs from the next higher level will emerge. But exactly what do we look at to determine if a level is satisfied. Each level is going to be different, of course, and we might need to subdivide each level into components.

For example, if we subdivided the Physiological level into its components, and evaluated one of its components, food, the feeling for needing food would be hunger and the measurement of satisfaction would be fullness.

Our primary concerns for foster and adoptive children originate in the Safety and Security level. That is where most of these children are operating emotionally. Many are emotionally stuck in that level and our job as nurturing caregivers is to help them satisfy that level so that they can grow emotionally through Safety and Security into the higher levels toward Self-Actualization and Maslow's other Growth level Needs. We are going to be talking extensively about Safety and Security, therefore, we need to agree upon a measurement of satisfaction for Safety and Security.

Trust, then, is going to be our unit of measurement for evaluating fulfillment of Maslow's Safety and Security Needs. When a person is trusting, we can say that that person has satisfied his Safety and Security issues. When he is not trusting, we will say that he has not satisfied his Safety and Security issues, and that the bulk of his motivated behavior will be toward satisfying those Safety and Security Needs.

Maslow states that Safety and Security is a deficiency Need. What he means is that the individual will not ignore the Need if it is unsatisfied, but will strive to fulfill it. Maslow also states that the individual will strive to fulfill the lowest level deficiency Need first, so even though the individual might also be lacking esteem (the highest level of the deficiency Needs), he will not concern himself with Esteem Needs until his Safety and Security Needs are essentially satisfied.

Now, we have a single word about which we all share, most likely, a common intuitive understanding, a word by which we can measure fulfillment of Safety and Security Needs. I am not redefining the word trust. I am not changing its usage. I am just pointing out that trust is a measurement of Safety and Security.

Transferal and Situational Trust

When I used the word trust in the previous section, I repeatedly referred to trusting either a person or a situation. That was because there are basically two types of Safety and Security level trusts—the trust that you have with respect to a situation, and the trust you have with respect to another person or even institutions.

You can trust or mistrust situations. I will call this situational trust. A situation encompasses a specific place, at a specific time, with specific people present. For example a situation might be a classroom, in the morning, with three students absent, a substitute teacher, and a lesson on fractions. I could go on and on getting progressively more detailed, but still, it is a specific situation that I am describing and the situation may or may not engender trust.

You can trust one situation and not another. I might trust walking in the downtown of a city during the day but not at night. I might trust you with the keys to my Chevy but not my Ferrari. This second example has only one person in it, but there were two different situations with that one person.

I want to contrast situational trust to transferal trust. Independent of the situation you can have trust or mistrust in individuals, institutions, officials, governments, God, and so forth. I will call this transferal trust. It is where the trust of an individual or institution supersedes the trust of a situation. Though our trust is sometimes misplaced, we are taught as children to automatically trust teachers and police officers.

With transferal trust we feel safe, even in strange situations, assuming we are with someone who makes us feel safe, with someone who we have confidence will watch over us and look out for us. It is that person, or that institution, or that public official, or God who makes us feel safe. "Yea, though I walk through the valley of the shadow of death, I will fear no evil: For thou [God] art with me; . . . "[1] From this passage of *The Bible* clearly, regardless of the apparent danger of a situation, we are meant to feel safe and secure with God at our side.

Why is it important to make a distinction between the two types of trust? Because both types must be satisfied to truly fulfill an individual's Safety and Security Needs and allow him or her to move on without Need level conflicts.

Consider the difference between wild animals and domesticated animals. The wild animal, such as the lion, can never be tamed in the same sense that a cat or a dog can be tamed. The lion can learn that he is safe around humans and can learn to relax and not attack *in certain situations*, but he will never develop what I call transferal trust, where the human can do almost anything he wants and the lion will cooperate.

21

The dog on the other hand will follow his master into most any situation totally trusting his owner to look out for his safety and security.

Transferal trust has a different quality to it than situational trust, situational trust must be reevaluated constantly as situations change, transferal trust does not require constant reevaluation.

Transferal trust implies that you are giving over to another person some of the responsibility (or even all of the responsibility, in the case of the child toward his caregiver) of watching out for your safety and security. You resolve your safety and security needs by transferring responsibility for them to another individual.

You do not need to have a gun in your house because your police will protect you from bad guys. Your army will protect you from other war-like countries. Your courts will protect you from cheats and frauds. Your parents will protect you. These are all examples of transferal trust.

Prepotency of Situational and Transferal Trust

In Jack London's book, *Call of the Wild*, the main character, Buck, a sled dog in Alaska, gets into a situation where he is owned by an incompetent driver. The driver is about to drive his sled and dog team across a river where the ice is too thin. It is late spring and everything is thawing out from the winter. Our canine protagonist takes a stand, refuses to go on any farther, and refuses to go out on the thin ice. After attempting to beat Buck into submission, the driver hands Buck over to an experienced miner who is watching the unfolding drama. The driver then proceeds to drive his sled and remaining dog team across the river when, of course, the ice breaks. They all die in the freezing cold water—dogs, driver, and passengers.

A very strong bond develops between Buck and his new owner. At one point the new owner, who senses Buck's deep level of devotion and obedience but who wants to test just how strong it is, orders Buck to literally jump off a cliff. Without hesitation Buck leaps to what is certainly going to end up in the dog's death. His owner, however, grabs Buck as he is starting to jump and pulls him to safety, thereby averting disaster.

The point of this is that, with situational trust and no transferal trust, the dog was wary and always on guard. However, when strong interpersonal bonds developed between the dog and his new owner, the dog completely ignored the obvious situational danger involved in jumping off a cliff and relied solely on transferal trust. He placed responsibility for his safety and security completely in the hands of his new owner.

We might infer that given a contradictory situation, transferal trust always takes precedence over situational trust. I do not know if this would be a valid conclusion, but it would not be wrong to conclude that transferal trust can be very strong.

If I were to rank the two within the Safety and Security level, I would place transferal trust above situational trust, making situational trust more pre–potent. Using Maslow's argument on satisfying lower level Needs first, we see that people need to satisfy situational trust first before they become aware of, and need to satisfy transferal trust.

From Inward to Outward

As one moves up Maslow's Hierarchy, transferal trust (or what I might add to Maslow's Hierarchy as the Transferal Safety and Security level) mark the transitional point on the Hierarchy from the Need being inwardly oriented to its being outwardly oriented. An inwardly oriented Need does not require anybody else for its satisfaction. Outwardly oriented Needs do require other individuals for satisfaction.

The two highest levels of the Deficiency Needs (Belonging And Love, and Esteem) both have the individual concerned with another person or persons and thus I would designate them as being outwardly oriented. Physiological and Situational Safety and Security are both self-centered and thus inwardly oriented.

As an aside, defining love in terms that are consistent with the model we are creating, I would say that love is where one places the various Needs of another person on an equal footing or higher than one's own Needs. Which Needs? All of them that are important to the person doing the loving, for they are the only Needs of which the person doing the loving will truly be aware. Also, one could argue that self-esteem is inwardly oriented, but then I would argue that is how one feels about himself with respect to others leaving it still outwardly oriented.

While transferal trust may be self-centered, it requires the awareness of some entity outside oneself for it to exist.

I only make this observation to show that Maslow's hierarchy is also a progression from being concerned only about yourself to being concerned about others and then on to being concerned about humanity as a whole. This is especially so when we get into Maslow's self-actualization Needs, an area that I have purposely skimmed because of its little relevance to my subject matter.

Notes

[1] The 23rd Psalm from *The Holy Bible*, King James Version.

4

Trust Mechanism and Trust Disorder Paradigms

During my foster-parent training classes, required for all foster parents prior to receiving a foster child placement, I was presented with a model meant to help me prepare for and understand common misbehavior in older foster children. I was told that being abandoned or rejected in the past hurt these children so much that they are now afraid to make new attachments for fear of being hurt, abandoned, and rejected again.[1] I was told that these children would assume that I, as their new foster parent, would eventually reject them too, just as all the other adults had done previously in their lives, and that to protect themselves they would remain emotionally distant. I was told not to expect much affection, that foster children are simply not affectionate.

This is the behavioral model as presented in the classes, and when I received my foster child placements it was the model I was using to try to understand their behavior. Quite frankly, it was not working; it did not help me at all in shaping my treatment for the children. The only thing that I learned from such a model was just to hang in there and wait for the child to get over his fear. The implication was that only after having lived with you, the foster parent, for a long time would he be able to finally realize that you are not going to send him back, and only then can attachment form.

"Hanging in there" with these children for a long time, waiting for change, is not easy. Again, traditional wisdom suggests that they are testing me to see if I will really stay in their lives. Traditional wisdom has them being bad (and they can be bad) in spite of my being nice to them in order to test me to see if I really will keep them, and to give themselves a rationalization for why they will eventually be rejected from my house, which, I was told, they know in their hearts I most certainly will do in the future. They anticipate a bad outcome and in turn create it as a self-fulfilling prophecy. So they build a defensive wall in advance to guard against anticipated emotional pain.

This simple model seems to be universally accepted, though there are few if any scientific studies to support it. From where did this model come? We have as human beings a natural tendency to use ourselves as models to explain the workings of others. We ask ourselves the question: how would I feel if I were in that situation? There is nothing wrong with using yourself as a model; it is a good place to start when trying to understand the behavior of others. Models can be helpful to the understanding process; in this case, the model did not work.

Little things started popping up that led me to believe that the foster children I had were not suffering from any kind of attachment problem, at least, not as attachment had originally been presented to me. For example, they would start talking about long term plans, trips, or presents for their next birthdays—for things that were almost a year away. The way they were talking led me to believe that they had no expectation of being rejected or having to leave my house. They would often do this immediately after pushing my buttons. I would have thought that right after an angry encounter would be the time when they would be most expecting rejection. Furthermore, though always on their own terms, they would allow and even seek out affection. It just did not add up to what I was told were the characteristics of attachment disorder.

I started searching for another model, since I had rejected the attachment disorder model as I understood it at the time. I investigated the possibility of narcissistic personality disorder, and it seemed to work. My foster children were control freaks, argumentative, self-centered, manipulative, and could be extremely charming to strangers—all characteristics of this disorder. Then, I considered oppositionally defiant disorder, which also has a list of behaviors that closely matched those of my foster children. I became discouraged because the literature claimed that some of these disorders were basically uncorrectable. I could foresee either having to send the foster children away (which I knew would be a very painful event for both the children and me), or I would have to live with monsters. Neither option was very encouraging.

I felt I was being used by the children. With no relief in sight it seemed the only alternative would be just to give up. My persistence in searching for a diagnosis led one therapist to become impatient with me. With obvious annoyance in her voice she questioned, "Why it was so important to put a diagnostic label on a child?" This left me confused, because in every other branch of medicine, diagnosis always precedes treatment.

Then, almost overnight, in what seemed like an epiphany, a new model emerged; a model that did not seem to be too revolutionary requiring major changes in thinking, and that did appear to encompass everything that was already in the literature. The new model just placed a little different emphasis on the source of the children's problems. With the new model I could explain not only the children's difficulty to attach, but also their other behavioral characteristics.

In this new model, the children's apparent difficulty attaching is not based on having lost attachments in the past or being afraid to get close again for fear of being hurt. In fact it is not based on fear at all. There is no fear of losing attachment in these children, because they have never really been attached. They really do not know what they are missing. This new model is more closely aligned to Bowlby's attachment model, although it is not based on the children not experiencing love in the first years of life (I will explain).

The model as I see it, is different from the traditional model as described to me. It fits the observed behavior of these children more accurately. It is really more helpful in predicting their behavior and knowing how to manage them. Even more importantly, this model is far better in helping the children's caregivers create a therapeutic environment in which the children can heal and grow.

My foster children purely and simply just did not trust me. Not only did they not trust me, but they did not trust anybody else, either. They did not trust their mothers or fathers, aunts, uncles, siblings, caseworkers, therapists, teachers, anybody in their lives. The children were not suffering from a fear of being hurt by subsequent loss and rejection, the children were suffering from a fear of being hurt by losing control and being manipulated, and that is why they built an emotional walls around themselves.

It is interesting to note that the traditional model I had been taught, the one in which the children are afraid to attach because they have been hurt by attaching and being rejected in the past, is not a model supported by any reliable authority or expert. The psychological community ascribes attachment disorder to improper nurturing in the first year of life, not fear of rejection. This is the only scientifically documented model that I could find. It is also interesting to note that the model I came up with is not far from the existing attachment mechanism model in that trust is considered to be a component of attachment.

Some Background History

Bowlby's attachment cycle states that the infant signals to the caregiver through behaviors like crying or fussing that he has some sort of need, and the caregiver then satisfies the need. Bowlby did not go into great detail on what the specific needs were. Instead, he depended upon us, the readers, to intuitively interpret the meaning behind the cries of the baby and know what his needs were. Needs and emotions are internal to the child, therefore, they are impossible to observe. However, needs and emotions trigger behaviors which are easily observed. Concurrently, as Bowlby was developing his attachment theory, Abraham Harold Maslow (1908–1970) born just one year after Bowlby, was developing his theory on needs.

Both Bowlby and Maslow were trained in a world dominated by two famous psychologists representing two distinct and somewhat opposite psychological theories: Sigmund Freud (1856–1939) the father of psychoanalysis, and John Broadus Watson (1878–1959), the father of behaviorism. Behaviorism was later championed by Frederic Burrhus Skinner (1904–1990). Behaviorism, founded after Freudian psychoanalysis, possibly as a backlash by some who perceived the interpretations of the Freudians as far-fetched, denied the existence of motivation or needs. This was the environment that faced both Bowlby and Maslow when developing their paradigms.

Initially, Maslow was attracted to the behaviorist viewpoint. By the nineteen-fifties, he had abandoned behaviorist theories in favor of his own. It is interesting to note that his theories are totally based on needs and motivations. This is antithetical to the behaviorism he initially embraced. On the other hand, Bowlby, who came from a Freudian background rich in emotions and needs, avoided needs and emotions as part of his theory.

Bowlby's views were initially controversial; it took years for them to become accepted. Maslow's views seemed to be more enthusiastically embraced by a business community that was attempting to turn the art of management into a science than his own psychological community. Even if Bowlby and Maslow knew of each other (which is probable because they were contemporaries) it would be unlikely for either of them to incorporate the other's works into his own. Each of them was busy enough just promoting their own work. However, each of their paradigms does fit together nicely with the other. Now that the two paradigms are both presently accepted, it is time to merge them into one paradigm.

Some Modifications to Bowlby and Maslow

In his work on attachment, Bowlby avoided making a motivational definition of attachment itself. He never formally identified the emotions that the attached baby felt. He relied instead on a behavioral definition. In other words he described what attachment looked like on the outside, not what it felt like on the inside.

Yet, in the 1950s, his attachment theory was quite controversial. His avoidance of an emotionally based definition, a definition that could be challenged since nobody can really say with certainty what emotions are going on inside another individual, was probably smart. By choosing to define attachment based on observing the presence or absence of specific behaviors, like the baby turning or not turning toward the mother when she enters the room, the scientific part of his work would be unchallengeable, and people could conclude for themselves the significance of the behaviors. When I was initially presented with attachment theory, I personally concluded, as I think most people conclude, that attachment and love were the same.

The fact remains (even though the behavioral psychologist might disagree) that there are emotions that motivate the behaviors that Bowlby studied and defined as attachment. Furthermore, understanding these emotions is essential for understanding attachment. Perhaps Maslow can offer us some insight into the emotional side of attachment.

It is easy to jump to the conclusion that attachment is love. But how do we really know what is going on in a baby's head? We speculate using our adult self as the model. None of us can remember what it was like to be a baby, because our cognitive skills did not develop until later. Enter Maslow and his Hierarchy of Needs. Maslow provides us with an emotional model that almost begs to be projected back to the time of birth. It could be a developmental model just as it is a prepotency model, in that it could also describe the order in which emotions manifest themselves or show up in the maturing infant.

Without hesitation I can make the statement that not all emotions are fully developed at birth. Furthermore, it is reasonable to hypothesize that not all emotions develop simultaneously. In the absence of any other theories, studies, or information it is as good a guess as any that the order of appearance of the developing emotions in the newborn is the same as their order of pre-potency, that is to say, they develop in the same order as Maslow has them ranked in his hierarchy.

I am going to make this assumption because, not only is it the most logical starting place to build the model, but because it seems to work. Future studies and research can fine-tune it, but for now it works.

Assuming Maslow's hierarchy also describes the order in which emotions develop and emerge in the maturing infant we can say the following:

- Of immediate concern to the newborn are Physiological Needs, taking its first breath, eating, comfort, and so on.
- Next would be Safety and Security Needs. In Chapter 3 (What Is Trust?), I suggested that Safety and Security and trust are related, and that trust can be divided into situational trust and transferal trust. I am going to include that division in this model, both because I think that it is accurate, and because it is important. So the next thing on the baby's agenda is to develop Situational Safety and Security, which we measure as situational trust.
- Next to evolve after the Situational Safety and Security Need is satisfied, would be Transferal Safety and Security as measured by transferal trust.
- After the above three are satisfied the baby would move into the Belonging and Love level.

Now here is the rub: I do not think that the infant ever makes it into the Belonging and Love level. I do not mean to say that this is because we routinely fail to satisfy his lower level Needs, blocking him from moving up the Hierarchy. It is instead because the higher-level motivators on the Hierarchy, just like cognitive skills, may not be active at birth. The ability for them to manifest themselves develops or emerges, probably in the same order as they are presented in the Hierarchy. So the limit on how far up the Hierarchy the infant can potentially progress is age-dependent, just as motor skills and cognitive skills are age dependent.

Just as it is unrealistic for us to expect the newborn to perform even simple mathematics, it is also unrealistic for us to expect the newborn to love. Just as with intellectual skills, motor skills, and physical size, emotions are going to start out at a very rudimentary level and grow with age. So when an emotion kicks in (so to speak) it has not simply appeared overnight. It is instead a gradual process that progressively gets stronger until it reaches its natural limit, just as growing taller is a gradual process that stops when we reach the limits of our natural height.

Modified Attachment Cycle

The following is a sequence of events in the developmental life of the newborn. It is a hierarchy, just like Maslow's, except that it is a little more refined in that it suggests ages at which events might occur. As Maslow predicts, if any step is unfulfilled, the baby will not move on to the next one:

- The baby is born and its immediate Physiological Needs are quickly resolved by its caregiver.
- The baby's situational Safety and Security Needs start to activate within days or weeks of birth.
- Assuming Bowlby's attachment cycle occurs, the baby develops situational trust.
- The baby's transferal Safety and Security level Needs start to activate at about one month of age.
- Assuming Bowlby's attachment cycle continues to occur the baby develops transferal trust.
- The baby's Belonging and Love Needs activate at say a year of age. (Could be two years, could be nine months, it is hard to say.)

How Needs Develop

When I say that we have a Hierarchy of Needs, which is to say that the Needs are ordered in terms of their respective need for fulfillment from most pressing or pre-potent to least pressing, and that the least pressing are higher level Needs, and that these higher level Needs do not manifest themselves until lower level Needs are essentially satisfied, I am really saying the following:

The trigger for the activation of a higher level Need is the satisfaction of all lower level Needs.

Maslow never addressed the situation with the infant and the development of Needs. Looking at the emergence of Needs from more of a developmental viewpoint I have suggested that not all Needs mature at the same time, that some may mature earlier than others, and that the order of emergence might be the same as the order in Maslow's Hierarchy.

Taking this a little farther, there are two possible models for the emergence of Needs:

- Needs develop based on some genetically determined timetable and order (pre-programmed theory). In this model the child's ability to feel a lack of Belonging and Love happens at a certain time in the child's life. It might happen sooner for some children and later for others, but for any one child it is pre-programmed to happen at a specific time and will happen at that age no matter what.
- Needs do not develop until after more pressing Needs have both developed and have been satisfied (developmental theory). In this model, the satisfaction of a Need level would act as a trigger for the next Need in line to start developing. If a level is not satisfied, we do not even develop the ability to feel the emotion of the next higher levels.

At first glance it would seem like the differences between the pre-programmed theory and the developmental theory are academic. But there are some important though subtle differences implied by the two theories.

- With the developmental theory it would probably take longer for the next level to emerge when a lower level is fulfilled.
- Growth and development generally stops when the individual reaches maturity. If this is true for emotional growth (if emotional growth stops when the individual reaches the end of his

32

growth and development stage, that is to say when he becomes an adult), then, with a limited amount of time available, short-changing the child with improper nurturing would permanently stunt the child's emotional potential, just like shortchanging the child with improper nourishment will stunt the child's physical growth. This can be true both in the range of available emotions that the child can experience (how far up Maslow's Hierarchy the individual can progress) and the depth of each emotion.

A third possibility is a combination developmental theory with a pre-programmed sequence and timetable for the emergence of Needs and emotions; the level of intensity of each Need or emotion would be based on stimulating that Need as it emerges but the timing of emergence of each Need would be pre-programmed to a specific age in the child's life. This would be equivalent to intellectual skills not emerging until the child is a year or two old, and then we know that we must still stimulate those intellectual skills if we want the child to grow to his full potential. Throw a child with the makings of a genius into an environment with virtually no stimulation and he or she will never attain anything near his or her potential.

Even under ideal nurturing conditions, the Needs are still going to evolve in some kind of sequence and timetable; and when they first manifest themselves they will be weak. They will get progressively stronger as the child matures until they reach their final adult limit, a limit which will undoubtedly vary from individual to individual just like height, or anything else we can measure, generally does. Just as we can say that, from a development standpoint for the typical child, walking does not usually occur until the fourteenth month of age, future psychological research may someday give us new insight into love so that we will be able to say that the ability to feel love does not usually occur until say the Xth month, where the Xth month might be anywhere from birth to eighteen years of age (I am purposely making the range ridiculously large to avoid any possible controversy on something that would be a total guess on my part). My younger biological son walked at eight and a half months and I was so proud of him for being able to do that. How much prouder would I have been if I could have bragged that he loved at eight and a half months?

Unlike walking, measuring the emergence of Needs in the infant is not going to be easy. A Need is not going to go from nonexistence

33

to full strength all at once. The Need undoubtedly starts out at zero and increases until it reaches the threshold of significance for shaping the baby's emotional makeup. It slowly grows from there until it reaches its final adult level. Defining the threshold level and then finding a meaningful and accurate method to measure the threshold will not be an easy task.

It seems reasonable to tie the growth and development of Needs to the growth and development of the individual as a whole, starting from infancy and lasting until adulthood. If you accept my hypothesis of a connection between physical growth and development, intellectual growth and development, and emotional growth and development, then it is important the child be repaired as quickly as possible, because delayed repair will lead to an emotionally stunted child, and though the child himself may not appreciate what he is missing in life, we do.

Trust Mechanism

Take a little bit of Bowlby's Attachment Mechanism, mix in some of Maslow's Needs, stir in a few modifications, think about it for a while, and, voilà, you have Trust Mechanism. The only change required to Attachment Mechanism is to ascribe emotions to the definition of attachment. The only changes required to Maslow's Hierarchy are to break trust into two types; situational and transferal trust, and to project the Hierarchy back to the developing infant.

I have presented Maslow and Bowlby, and I have discussed and attempted to support by argument my assumptions and modifications to create a new paradigm of what I will call the trust mechanism. Without making reference to Maslow's or Bowlby's models, I will give a summary definition of trust mechanism:

The trust mechanism is the emotional developmental learning process by which human beings remove safety and security protective barriers that inhibit further emotional growth and intimacy.

A more detailed definition of trust mechanism also without any reference to Maslow and Bowlby would be:

The trust mechanism is the learning process that starts soon after birth through the repetitive successful completion of fulfillment cycles, the fulfillment cycle being the infant signaling to the primary caregiver that it has a need and the primary caregiver responding by fulfilling that need. By virtue of the fulfillment cycle rarely failing the infant never learns to distrust its primary caregiver, or, alternately, by virtue of the fulfillment cycle usually succeeding the infant learns to trust its primary caregiver.

I believe that the infant never learns to distrust versus the alternative, that he learns to trust, and I feel that the difference between the two speaks to the level of intensity that safety and security issues attain later in the child's life. Let me explain.

Using a form follows function analogy, whenever we use, exercise, or stimulate a system in our bodies, that system tends to become stronger, more robust, or increase in capacity. For example, it we exercise our muscles they become stronger. If we stimulate our intellect it too will increase in capacity. These things we know for a fact. It follows that if we stimulate a child's need for Safety and Security (as we would in a breakdown of the attachment cycles) it too may become stronger, possibly leaving the child more Safety and Security conscious for life. Perhaps if you stimulate the child while he is in his growth and development stage, it makes a greater difference than if you stimulate him later. Now I appreciate that there is somewhat of a logical stretch here in what I am saying, but evidence does show that children who have a breakdown in the attachment cycles are emotionally damaged, and nobody else has put forward a reason why merely supplying later what they missed as an infant is not enough to fully repair the emotional damage.

Based on what we know, the trust mechanism attachment cycles must start early and I would suggest that they must begin concurrently with the start of the infant's growing Need for Safety and Security so that the infant never learns *not* to trust his primary caregiver, a Need which may emerge within weeks of birth. While the child's Safety and Security Need is maturing we should go out of our way to be sure that it gets minimal stimulation with the intent of keeping it (the child's Safety and Security Needs) underdeveloped.

The need for Safety and Security may never end but the need to successfully complete the attachment cycles ends at a age when the child can intellectually understand and rationalize why his caregiver might not be fulfilling his Need or Needs. This ending age has traditionally been considered to be two years of age but may be much later. By satisfying the child's Safety and Security Needs early and continuously, the child never develops the intensity of Safety and Security Needs neither as an infant or at any later time in his life—as he would if they were left unsatisfied at an early age.

Trust Disorder

If the attachment cycles go unfulfilled too many times (that is, too often the baby cries and nobody comes) the baby learns to mistrust his caregivers. His Safety and Security levels, as measured by lack of trust, go up. He learns that the world is not a place where you can expect to have his Needs met by others. This is all happening at a time when the baby's intellectual capacity to understand and rationalize his situation is yet non-existent, but his Safety and Security Needs are rapidly developing, and due to the unmet attachment cycles are possibly being overstimulated. This is a failure of the trust mechanism, and it leads to something I call "trust disorder."

I would propose that the name trust disorder is a more appropriate name for what is generally labeled attachment disorder. What is the difference between trust disorder and attachment disorder? First, attachment is defined as a set of behaviors while trust is a measurement of Safety and Security. I am using an emotionally based definition instead of a behaviorally based definition. While it may be more difficult to prove an emotionally based definition, an emotionally based definition is going to be far more helpful in understanding the nature of the disorder and in formulating treatment for the child. Secondly, I would not limit trust disorder to the extreme cases but, unlike attachment disorder, would include a large range of severity; nor would I require documented proof of mistreatment in the first year of life, I think that we can make the diagnosis based on symptoms alone.

Love does not play a large part in my model because love does not emerge until later. To me, Bowlby's attachment is the forming of transferal trust. Transferal trust, as I have stated in Chapter 3 (What Is Trust?), is when we feel comfortable placing (transferring) the responsibility for our safety and security into the hands of another person or entity.

Just as children that are fed a diet deficient in proper nutrients never reach their potential maximum adult height, children who are not properly nurtured probably do not reach their full emotional potential. But if you intervene early enough with a good diet the child can make significant progress in catching up on his physical growth and, though maybe he does not reach the height he would have attained had his diet been good from day one, he does generally become tall enough to be considered at least an average height adult. It should be the same for emotional growth. The key, though, is to intervene while the child is still in his growth and development process, while he is still a child.

A Few Words on Models

Throughout history, empirical techniques generally preceded scientific understanding. For example, mankind has been making leavened bread long before there was any understanding or concept of microbial yeast activity. Trial and error, and even lucky accidents, have occasionally led to important discoveries. Sometimes it is only after the discovery is made, perhaps even centuries later, that somebody sits down and tries to figure out the theory behind why it worked or happened. To put it another way, this is the process of turning an art into a science. But even without understanding, there can be progress and a refinement of empirical processes.

So it is with reactive attachment disorder. In reading through much of the available literature, there are common treatment techniques that surface time and again. They keep coming up because they work. Since they work I have an obligation to respect them and incorporate them into my model.

A good model can really help us understand why the empirical techniques work. Admittedly, not all models are good, and some have led to disastrous results. For instance, in the early part of the twentieth century, the death rate of infants in orphan homes was found to be much higher than in the general population.[2] Louis Pasteur (1822–1895) and Joseph Lister (1827–1912) had developed a theory of disease, which was based on germs serving as the causative agent. With germs implicated as the culprit in the higher death rate of the institutionalized infants, there came a new model for their care. The new model suggested that the children's exposure to germs should be reduced. The attendants were then required to wash their hands and to don sterile gloves and gowns before approaching the babies. Also, they were limited in the time they were allowed to spend holding and touching the babies so that they only spent the duration required to fulfill the infants' basic physiological needs. However, with the advent of this new emphasis on sterility, mortality rates soared to as high as seventy percent.[3]

There was a major flaw in the new model. It did not take into consideration the child's lowered resistance to disease due to lack of emotional stimulation that the reduced touching and holding was causing. We now know that a child needs emotional stimulation to be physically healthy. This is a prime example of a treatment modality based on a model that was flawed or incomplete.

But as disastrous as the model was to the poor children who suffered from its implementation, some good was actually gained. From it we learned the importance of emotional stimulation and the necessity of attachment. Sometimes models may lead us astray, but throughout scientific history there are many more examples of models that give us new insight into the problem.

Empirical treatment modalities, those that are based on practical experience rather than theory and scientific proof, are great, but to truly understand a disease process, you need a model. There is a tremendous benefit from having an accurate model. An accurate model might suggest new or alternate treatments, but it should never contradict empirical modalities that work. An accurate model allows us to fine-tune the remedies and to balance out the various treatments so that there is an optimal use of resources. By knowing the relative importance of the various independent elements, and redirecting our attention to the more critical ones, we maximize the efficiency of the child's repair. For example, when you are baking a cake, you need to know not only what ingredients are necessary, but also how much of each is needed. A cup of salt and a teaspoonful of sugar would not taste right.

My TD model is going to help us to understand the rationale behind the empirically sound treatments and to see the relative importance of the ones that already exist. It is also going to help us optimize those treatments. Plus, it should help us to understand when and why empirically sound treatments might not always work.

Empirical treatments that seem to work include holding therapy, behavior management, and structure. Empirically, traditional psychotherapy, including play therapy, does not seem to be very effective for TD children. Traditional psychotherapy is based on the therapist developing a trusting relationship with the patient, and after gaining trust, working through the patient's problems and attempting a resolution. The problem here is that TD children have a tendency to manipulate the therapist which negates the benefits of treatment rather than to develop a trusting relationship with the therapist.[4] My TD model explains why the child would do this.

Notes

[1] Keck & Kupecky, *Adopting the Hurt Child*, 1995, pp. 64 and 70.
[2] Karen, Robert, Ph.D., *Becoming Attached*, 1994, p. 19.
[3] Ibid, p. 19.
[4] Keck, Gregory et al, *Parenting the Hurt Child*, 2002, p. 31.

5

Evaluating Behavioral Motivation

When Maslow developed his Hierarchy of Needs, he postulated that Needs are both innate and universal to all human beings. They are innate because they are genetically programmed into us from the time we are conceived. They are universal because all cultures, all races, all people on this planet have the same Needs.

He considered these Needs to be motivators. What this means is that the Need—or more specifically, the unfulfilled Need—triggers a specific emotional response. Exactly which emotional response is triggered depends upon which Need is unfulfilled. The emotional response, in turn, will motivate us to take some type of action; action intended to correct the deficiency in that Need.

The action that the motivating emotion evokes is called a behavior. Behavior, in this sense, becomes a very broad term; it includes everything we do, even extending to both thinking and what we think about. Not all behaviors, though, are motivated by emotions. Behaviors fall into two categories, motivated and unmotivated. Unmotivated behaviors are not intended to fulfill a Need. Walking down the street and randomly kicking at pebbles is a behavior that would have no apparent underlying motivation from a Need. What we are most interested in here are motivated behaviors, those behaviors designed to help the individual satisfy or fulfill a specific Need. When I refer to a child's behavior in this book it can be assumed that I am considering it to be a motivated behavior.

Behaviorism

A schism in psychology at the beginning of the twentieth century led to the creation of a group of psychologists called behaviorists. Behaviorists place little emphasis on internally programmed motivators, considering behavior to be a conditioned response to external stimuli. John Watson and later B. F. Skinner were the main proponents of this theory. While the behaviorists did not deny the existence of emotions, they felt that emotions, in and of themselves, are just another category of behaviors. They claimed that emotions are not innate to the organism but are conditioned responses externally programmed or taught. They deny the existence of internal emotional motivators.

I agree with Maslow and disagree with the behaviorists. There are internal motivators or needs that are basic and common to all mankind. These Needs cannot be "programmed away" through conditioning, nor can they be denied in developing a psychological model. What can be programmed away through conditioning, though, is specific behavior. But if you did program away a specific motivated behavior through conditioning, our model would predict that the individual would then attempt to find an alternative behavior to satisfy the underlying Need or urge. If you did succeed in convincing an individual on an intellectual basis that a Need or urge is bad, and did convince them to leave it unfulfilled, they most likely would experience frustration.

Transcending

People can deny themselves Needs without seeming to be frustrated and move on to higher levels; this is called transcending. Transcending allows us to move on to higher level Needs (to be working at satisfying higher level Needs) while skipping or leaving unfulfilled a lower level Need.

It is very difficult for human beings to transcend a Deficiency Need (Maslow's four lowest level Needs as a group) during their childhood. Transcending requires a level of maturity not found in children. Typically, you must fulfill the Needs sequentially just as Maslow says in order to move up to the higher levels. Usually transcendency occurs when a person has matured into the Growth Needs (Self-actualized) with all his or her Deficiency Needs fully satisfied, and subsequently loses one of his Deficiency Needs. A self-actualized person who loses a Deficiency Need may choose to transcend the loss in order to remain self-actualized, not attempting any radical new behaviors, rather than drop back down to lower levels on Maslow's scale and attempt new behaviors designed to replace the lost Need (regressive behaviors designed to re-satisfy the re-emerged urge). This is particularly true in situations where re-fulfilling the Deficiency Need may be logistically difficult or impossible.

Sometimes the reasons for the loss of fulfillment of a Need level come from outside the individual. For example an individual might be caught up in armed conflict, be imprisoned, be placed against his or her will into a chronically unsafe situation, lose a spouse or loved one, or divorce. Other times the loss may come from inside the individual, from disease, an accident that leaves the individual paralyzed, cancer, and so forth. While many individuals faced with hardships regress, others do not. They do not lose their composure, their wisdom, or their appreciation for life. Faced with starvation, parents may transcend their Physiological Need for food, giving their portion to their children or to others they deem more in need than they. Individuals thrown by fate into an unsafe situation may transcend their Safety and Security level loss and remain essentially the same persons that they were before the loss.

The question remains, then, if we all have the same innate Needs, why do we all act differently? Why is there such a wide range of observable behavior in the world? The answers are that there are a myriad of behaviors available to satisfy a single emotional Need, different cultures dictate acceptable behaviors, and lastly not all behavior is oriented toward satisfying emotional Needs (unmotivated behavior).

The purpose of this chapter is to develop a method and a skill for looking at a child's behavior and determining his underlying emotional motivation. Determining the underlying motivation will tell us where the child is on Maslow's Hierarchy. For example we see a child who is afraid to sleep in the dark (the behavior) and we might conclude that the child has unmet Safety and Security level Needs (the underlying motivation for the behavior).

We can consider this from two different viewpoints and both are important.

First, we can consider it from the viewpoint of where the child is emotionally right now at a specific point in time—say, 3:30 P.M. on Friday afternoon. This is going to be important because, whenever we interact with a child it is always at a point in time. It is very helpful in shaping the nature of our interaction for us to understand the emotional motivation of the child right at the point in time when we need to interact with the child.

We are going to use Maslow's Hierarchy to help us understand the unfulfilled Need driving specific behavior. We are going to assume that moving higher up his Hierarchy is a desirable thing, that the child being able to emotionally function at progressively higher and higher levels on the Hierarchy is the same thing as emotional growth and maturity. We want the therapeutic environment that we attempt to build to repair the child to be designed to help the child move up the Hierarchy.

The second viewpoint from which we can consider evaluating the child's emotional level is as an aggregate of the child's overall emotional level that gives us a picture of where the child stands not so much at a specific point in time on a specific day, but as a general overall measurement of his emotional growth. This helps us to track the child's emotional growth as the years pass to insure that we are making progress. Tracking the emotional growth of the child is a task often done by professionals such as psychologists and psychiatrists. Unlike knowing the child's emotional motivation from hour to hour—which is necessary for the caregiver in order to properly react to the child's behavior—we may choose to let the professionals track the child's overall emotional growth. At the end of this chapter I have a section on determining the overall developmental progress of the child using Maslow's Hierarchy. I have separated it from the main text of this book because it is secondary to the message of this book and can appropriately be skipped for those who are not interested.

Maslow's Pyramid Rotated

In Chapter 2 (Maslow's Hierarchy of Needs Paradigm), I showed Maslow's Hierarchy as often being depicted as a pyramid. I suggested there that the pyramid representation might not be a good way for presenting this paradigm graphically, because it implies that higher level Needs require the underpinning or the lower level Needs to exist. I stated that according to Maslow, higher level Needs exist all the time, even when lower level Needs are unsatisfied, but that the pre-potency or strength of the lower unfulfilled Need overshadows the higher unfulfilled Need so that we are just not aware of the higher level Needs.

A horizontal axis might be a better way to represent Maslow's Paradigm. It is essentially the same thing as the pyramid except its being aligned horizontally versus vertically (take the pyramid and rotate it ninety degrees).

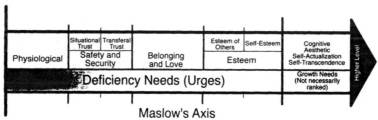

Maslow's Axis

I have taken the Safety and Security level and broken it into two parts, situational and transferal trust. Safety and Security is still just one level, just as Maslow first envisioned it. The two parts that I have created, situational trust and transferal trust only represent two different ways that Safety and Security may be satisfied with the caveat that the child must first learn and use situational trust before he can learn and use transferal trust.

Though the above diagram looks a little like the axis we use in Cartesian mathematics (remember the old x and y axis?), it has some very non-Cartesian characteristics. We are saying that the various needs, physiological, safety and security, and so on, that we plot along the axis are separate and unique from each other, but at the same time they are related in that we can place them in order on an axis. But in fact they are separate and unique (like apples and oranges), and in Cartesian mathematics only one variable can be placed on one axis, not separate and distinct variables as we are doing. Yet the diagram works fine if the child is at only one place on the axis at a time, which is usually the case when evaluating behavior observed at a specific point in time.

If we consider just a single point in time, then placing the child on the scale becomes simple. For example the child might be acting defiant at 3:30 P.M. and want to be picked up and held at 7:45 P.M. The defiant child at 3:30 P.M. is being motivated by a lack of situational trust and is trying to be in control. The same child at 7:45 P.M. is being motivated by his Belonging and Love Needs. Some might say that the child finds your lap as a safe and secure place to be, so we are still just looking at one Need level, just two different behaviors to satisfy the one Need. Even so, looking for you as the source to satisfy his Safety and Security Need has an element of Belonging and Love or, at minimum, transferal trust so there definitely is movement on the scale. One child, two different points of time separated only by hours, and we have two different places on the scale. Graphically we would represent it as follows:

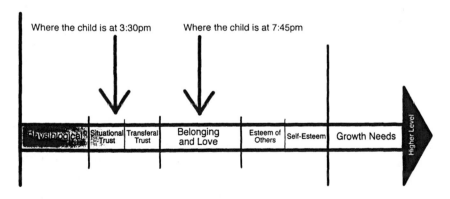

As the child's primary caregiver, being able to evaluate the child's behavior and determine his underlying motivation is going to be a very useful skill. When interacting with the child, hour-by-hour, minute-by-minute, we continuously evaluate the child's behavior for emotional motivation and use our evaluation to guide the way we interact to best help the child grow. Without too much effort this evaluation process will become intuitive.

The Tools of Evaluation

The chain of events that cause a behavior looks something like this:

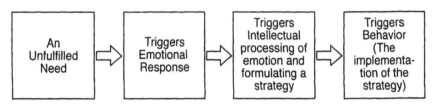

How unfulfilled Needs trigger behaviors

Needs are innate and universal to all humans. We are told by our body when a Need is unmet by an emotion. Not all emotions cause us to feel bad, but the ones that do generally act as a motivator for change. The intellectual process in the third box leaves a lot of room for a range of possible behaviors to alleviate an unfulfilled Need.

In the animal kingdom there are a myriad of strategies for handling the same unmet Needs. Consider all the different ways that animals behave when threatened. Some run while others attack. Some play possum, some freeze, and some seem oblivious. However, within a species, variation is limited and behavior is usually predictable. Not so with humans. Whereas the emotions are preprogrammed into us, the intellectual process and the strategy resulting in a behavior is not preprogrammed. Different people respond differently to the same emotion.

It is our job to identify a child's unfulfilled Need by observing his behavior. We have only his behavior to go on because we cannot see or know for sure any of the parts of this chain other than behavior. Below are descriptions of the four Need levels that are of primary interest to us in evaluating TD children. I leave out Physiological Needs because, hopefully, they are all well satisfied for the child, and I leave out Self-Esteem and Growth Needs because, unfortunately, at this stage of the child's emotional growth and development they are still too overpowered by the more pre-potent lower level Needs to be significant motivators.

Interestingly enough, we as human beings do not have as great a range of positive emotions to experience upon satisfying a Need, as we have for telling us that we have a deficiency in a Need. Furthermore, the good emotion experienced when a Need is satisfied is often short lived. The good feelings associated with having satisfied a Need evaporate when the next higher level unsatisfied Need's motivating emotion emerges.

I list emotions for when a Need is deficient, that is, unfulfilled. Typically, at any one point in time, the child will have one dominant emotion from one Need level, even though over a period of time he will experience emotions from more than one Need level. As previously discussed, unfulfilled Needs lead to an emotional response, and that emotional response shapes our behavior in such a way as to cause us to try to fulfill that Need. In this sense, emotional responses can be thought of as "agents for change."

Using the information below, you should be able to evaluate the child based on his behavior to determine where he is functioning at a point in time on Maslow's emotional axis.

Safety and Security Level

Safety and Security can be thought of as planning for maintaining future Needs. The keyword for Safety and Security is planning. From a survival standpoint, there is the here and now. I am starving right now, and I need food now. After the here and now is fulfilled then there is the future. I am fed now, but I need to make preparations for my next meal, for tomorrow, for next week, and for next winter when food might be scarce. The most important here and now Needs (and most pre-potent) are Physiological Needs.

The future can be seconds away or decades away. If there is an armed gunman with a weapon in your face, Safety and Security is planning your immediate response. Alternatively, it can be saving for your retirement forty years in the future.

Survival can be both providing for current and future Physiological Needs, so we need to specify that we are concerned primarily with survival in the future when we discuss Safety and Security. In addition, we include in the concept of Safety and Security something called quality. We not only want to survive, but we want to survive well. We hold back on overextending ourselves now so that the future will be just as good as the present. We may want things to get better with time. This is all part of Safety and Security.

Everybody alive has Safety and Security concerns. The intensity of these concerns, how they are directed, how long term they are, each individual's method of satisfying or attempting to satisfy them, and how valid they are—all these factors vary significantly between each individual.

It is not hard to understand why, after we have satisfied our Physiological Needs, Safety and Security is next in line on the Needs axis. Clearly, if we do not make some kind of plan for the future, build a house to sleep in, find a tree to hide in, harvest our crops and store them for the winter, there is a good chance that we will die. Consequently, this Need has a high level of pre-potency. It is second in line right after the "right now" Physiological Needs.

The only problem is that for many of us, Safety and Security is not really as important an issue as our psyches make it out to be. Most of us—at least the people who are reading this book—live in a relatively safe and secure environment. Furthermore, the children who are the focus of this book hopefully have been removed from any bad situations that they might have been in and also are now in a safe and secure environment. In spite of the fact that most people today have neither lions nor tigers nor bears lurking outside their doors, the Safety and Security Need is deeply programmed into our being and we can not ignore it. It might seem that we, as human beings, are being emotionally held back by being genetically pre-programmed with a too pre-potent Safety and Security level Need. A need that in many cases inappropriately blocks our emotional growth and development. Our strong need for Safety and Security becomes an emotional hurdle that too many people never negotiate. It is locking too many people who do not receive the appropriate childhood nurturing into a life of struggle, a struggle that really in many cases is unnecessary and pointless.

I have divided Maslow's Safety and Security level into two parts. I do not break Safety and Security into situational trust and transferal trust because they are so different that they must be separate groups. They are both of Safety and Security—they both share the same underlying survival motivation and the same emotions. My rationale in separating them is that the way we approach satisfying each of them in the

48

child is different, and the child's caregiver needs to be aware of this. We satisfy Situational Safety and Security by creating a familiar predictable routine for the child. Structure and boundaries are the common buzz-words for creating an environment for the child where he can relax and feel safe because he knows what is going to happen around each corner and he knows what is expected of him. He finds comfort in the routine. I am sure that you have encountered expert opinion hyping the virtues of structure and boundaries for raising children, not just TD children but all children. It is a common mantra in the child rearing press.

I may be one of the few authors to relegate structure and boundaries to a lesser role in the repair of the TD child. I use only as much of it as I have to, because it is transferal trust that I really want in the child, not situational trust. I want the child to place his trust directly in me, not in my predictability. If I say, "Hey, we're not eating at five today, we're eating at six," I want him to "go with the flow." We achieve satisfaction of Transferal Safety and Security by removing that familiar routine, possibly just a little at a time, eventually forcing the child to trust us for his Safety and Security and not structure, boundaries, and the comfort of routine. We want the child to be comfortable with change and to trust his caregivers sufficiently such that any change in his routine does not evoke anxiety and require super-vigilance.

Situational Safety and Security Level

We would not be normal human beings if there were not situations that made us feel uncomfortable, where we felt vulnerable and defenseless. Fear of heights is a good example of a Situational Safety and Security level emotion.

Measurement:	Situational Trust
Deficiency Emotion:	General
	Distrustfulness, Insecurity
	Non-acute
	Anxiety, Worry
	Acute
	Fear,
Behaviors:	Avoidance, On-guard, Hyper-
	Active, Restless

49

Associated Terms: Positive
                      Trusting, At-Ease
                      Negative
                      Wary, Furtive, Worry

Transferal Safety and Security Level

Though this is a step up from Situational Safety and Security, it is still at the Safety and Security level and shares with Situational Safety and Security the same emotions and behaviors, when unfulfilled.

Transferal Trust, or transferring the responsibility for our Safety and Security to another person is just another way to satisfy our basic need for Safety and Security.

Measurement: Transferal Trust
Deficiency Emotion: General
                      Distrustfulness, Insecurity,
                      Wariness
                      Non-acute
                      Anxiety, Worry
                      Acute
                      Fear, Anger, Jealousy
Behaviors: Aggressive—(Characterized by
                          being Controlling)
                      Defiant, Manipulating, Controlling,
                      Lying, Stealing (unless the child is so
                      hungry that he is stealing for food),
                      Hoarding, Aggressive behavior, Use of
                      profanities boasting (about power),
                      Denigrating, Ruthlessness, Self-
                      centered, Suspicious, Bullying,
                      Intimidating
                      Passive/Aggressive—(Characterized
                          by being Defensive)
                      Argumentative, Cannot Be
                          Wrong
                      Passive
                      Subservient, Shy, Non-confrontational,
                      Avoid Eye Contact, Clingy, Stand-
                      offish, Suspicious, Cautious

Previously I discussed the possibility of multiple behaviors to fulfill the same deficient emotional Need. I also differentiated between motivated and non-motivated behavior (motivated behavior is designed to fulfill a Need, that is to say it is motivated by a basic Need). Here is a perfect example of one Need level with multiple possible motivated behaviors all designed to satisfy that one Need. Some individuals will exhibit aggressive behavior as their approach to satisfying their interpersonal Safety and Security Need deficit. Others will take a more passive approach. Most individuals will mix some aggressive behavior and some passive behaviors depending on both the situation and with whom they are interacting.

Passive children with TD, because they are not major discipline problems for their caregivers, often do not get diagnosed or receive any special treatment. This book focuses on the TD child with aggressive behavior. The following list of associated terms applies mainly to the aggressive child though some would apply to both.

Associated Terms: Positive
Trusting, Sharing, Open
Negative
Cold, Callous, Insensitive, Unfriendly,
Self-absorbed, Insolent, Rebellious,
Insubordinate, Oppositional, Cagey,
Distrustful, Mistrustful, Guarded, On-
guard, Circumspect, Careful,
Apprehensive, Skeptical, Doubting
Narcissistic, Stuck-up Hostility, Hate,
Resentment, Walls, Money, Greed,
Stingy, Hoarding

Achieving transferal trust gives the child the ability to be resilient to change. If the child is fine until you put him into a new or different situation, then he has not developed transferal trust. If the child is fine in new situations as long as he is with you, then he has transferal trust. If you heartily endorse some new experience, food, situation, etc., and the child adamantly refuses to try it, he does not have transferal trust, at least for that particular type of situation.

Belonging and Love Level

Inwardly the loss of this Need level is felt as sadness, a sense of emptiness, grief, loneliness, friendlessness, and rootlessness.

Measurement:	Caring
Deficiency Emotion:	Loneliness, Sadness, Sense of emptiness, Grief, Friendlessness, Rootlessness, Depression
Behaviors:	Clinging, Joining, Participating, Being a pest, or other behaviors designed to get attention
Associated Terms:	Positive Kind, Gentle, Helpful, Considerate, Compassionate, Concerned, Sensitive, Warm, Friendly Negative Cold, Callous, Insensitive, Unfriendly, Self-absorbed, Narcissistic, Stuck-up

Esteem of Others

Esteem is a sense of being different from everybody else. It is a sense of self as a unique individual. It can be either negative or positive.

Measurement:	Pride
Deficiency Emotion:	Embarrassment, Shame, Inferiority, and Weakness
Behaviors:	Attention seeking behavior (look at me, mommy), Boasting to impress (most boasting is to intimidate, a Safety and Security level behavior)
Associated Terms:	Positive Feeling honored, Negative Humiliation, Blame, Resentment, Guilt, Propitiation

Self-Esteem Level

Measurement: Self-confidence
Deficiency Emotion: Embarrassment, Shame, Inferiority,
                      and Weakness
Behaviors: Shyness, Lack of Self-Confidence
Associated Terms: Positive
                      Self-Esteem, Self-worth,
                      Strength, Capability, Adequacy,
                      Thoughtful, Being Useful and
                      Necessary in the world
                  Negative
                      Apathy, Disengagement,
                      Despair, Aversion, Rejection

Paradoxical Behavior

Often an individual's behavior will be motivated by a Need level that does not seem to be the appropriate Need level for the situation. The most common examples of this are an angry response to a loss or an angry response to criticism.

You may see somebody react angrily to criticism. Criticism is an attack on a person's skills, abilities, personality, and so on and should lower a person's feeling of self worth or value. However, it is more common for a person to respond to criticism with anger rather than feelings of diminished esteem. This anger is not coming from the Esteem Needs. The individual has discounted the content of the message and is interpreting the criticism as a personal attack, thus it becomes a Safety and Security level issue. If they regarded the criticism as valid, their response would be a loss of confidence, and they would feel weaker. Actually individuals often feel both weaker and angry at the same time.

For example, when you call somebody an idiot, he or she will often become angry. According to Maslow this should not be the case. Maslow would predict that calling somebody an idiot should speak directly to the Esteem level, and should result in feelings of inferiority and weakness. But this is not usually what happens. Instead, the result is anger and defensiveness. Why? Because an insult like this is generally not a sincere comment on intelligence, but is instead an expression of hostility or callousness, and thus the recipient responds at the Safety and Security level, resulting in anger. He or she ignores the meaning of the message and responds instead to the hurtful intent behind it. Here we can see how an attack on one level elicits a response on another.

The key word is *attack*. Anytime you attack you can anticipate a Safety and Security level response of anger. In this example it is obvious that, even though the words spoken are directed toward esteem, the intent was to hurt and the anger response is appropriate. The following example is not so obvious.

When someone loses a loved one to death they go through a grieving process. The stages of grieving or bereavement are well studied and well documented. They are generally described as first denial, then anger, followed by sadness, and finally acceptance and moving on. Why do they experience anger before sadness? Death is a loss of companionship so after all, should it not be just sadness?

Death is certainly a loss of companionship, which clearly translates into a loss at the Love and Belonging level, which clearly should elicit a response of sadness. However, it is also a loss of stability and all the support that the lost person supplied. Furthermore, having to go out and establish new relationships can be scary. So there is an element of Safety and Security to the loss. We know that Safety and Security is more pre-potent than Love and Belonging and thus, the anger supersedes the sadness in terms of demanding that it be dealt with first in the bereavement process.

Generally speaking any incident that can be interpreted as having impact on two different levels will get an emotional response from the lower, more pre-potent level first. What appears to be a paradox is really not.

Measuring Emotional Development

The other way we can consider time is as a measurement of a child's stage of emotional development. For example we might evaluate the child and determine where he might be placed on the axis at age ten, and then six months later reevaluate the child and see if he has moved to another location on the axis, hopefully up. Used this way the graph becomes a valuable tool for tracking overall emotional development progress.

Unfortunately, the graphical representation that worked quite well for measuring a child's emotional state at an instant in time as we earlier discussed, does not work so well when trying to profile a child's emotional development. The previous example on page 45 shows the problem. The child at any particular time during a day usually is functioning in only one level. However it would be most unusual if over the course of a day or week, he did not cycle through several levels. If we try to use a graph that shows the child functioning at many different levels over the course of a day to figure out the emotional growth and maturation of a child, it is not obvious at which level we would place him.

For a simple method to measure overall emotional development we could observe the child over an entire day constantly plotting his position on the graph. After collecting data for a day we could just place him for purposes of measuring emotional growth and development in the level where he spends most of his time. However this method would not show subtle movement along the scale. The child would remain in one level until all of a sudden he jumped to the next level. We need a method that is more refined because we know that the TD child is going to spend a long time in the Safety and Security level and we want to measure progress within each level, not just between the levels.

Even though each level on the axis is discrete we could consider the axis itself to be continuous. Then the position of the arrow could represent an average for the child. For example, let's say the child's overall emotional development is halfway between situational trust and transferal trust. We could show the child's position on the axis as follows:

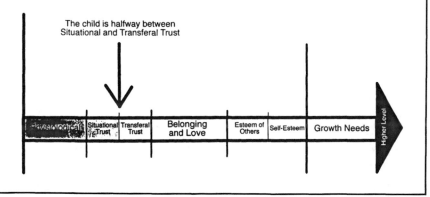

While this method does indicate the position of an average emotional level for the child, it still leaves us a little in the dark when it comes to understanding how that average is derived. The different items on the axis are discrete and uniquely different entities. To average them is like comparing apples and oranges. Though the items are related to each other by being ranked in terms of pre-potency, which is our rationale for putting them on one axis, after that they are not the same thing at all. Furthermore, the axis assumes that all individuals share the same pre-potency ranking for all their different Needs, which also may not be true, something Maslow himself admitted.

Another method of showing the child's emotional development would be to indicate what percentage of the child's time is spent in behaviors motivated by each need. A bar graph with bar heights representing the percentage of time over the course of the observation period (which could be a day, a week, or whatever) the child spends at each level. All the bars would add up to one or one-hundred percent. Using this approach the graph for a typical TD child might look as follows:

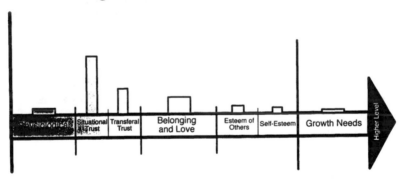

Some Definitions

When discussing TD children there are two terms that I use that will occur again and again. One is the word "functioning" or "functioning at" and the other is "highest significant Need level." When I say, "The child is functioning at the Situational Trust level," what I mean is that the Situational Trust level is where the child spends a preponderance of his time, as shown in the last diagram above. The bar graph for situational trust is higher than any other bar on the axis. When I say, "The child's highest significant Need level is Belonging and Love," what I am referring to is the highest Need level that has a significant impact upon the child's behavior being Belonging and Love, again as shown in the last diagram above. The bar graph for Belonging and Love is high enough to indicate that the child is significantly influenced by his Belonging and Love Needs, though he is not routinely functioning at that level. The level of the bar graphs for Esteem and the Growth Needs are not high enough for us to worry about his having significant Needs in those areas.

Awareness

The best and most accurate way to look at it would be to introduce the concept of awareness. We would say that the child has both an awareness level and an awareness potential for each Need.

The awareness level is a relative level of how aware the child is of each Need. It is relative in that it is a comparison between the Needs. Take any two Needs, the child will be more aware of a deficiency in the need that has the higher awareness level. An example of awareness would be hunger or loneliness.

The Awareness Potential is the maximum awareness level that a child will have for each Need if it is left unfulfilled. It is obvious that the awareness potential for Physiological Needs is very high. Panic will set in very quickly if you are choking whereas you probably will overlook the fact that a stranger does not hold you in high esteem and probably will not go out of your way to impress everybody you meet.

The awareness level can never exceed the awareness potential. As a child fulfills a Need his awareness level for that Need goes down. This makes sense. He has eaten. He is full. His awareness of hunger goes down. When a Need is totally fulfilled his awareness of that Need becomes zero.

The following graph introduces the concept of placing on the vertical axis a measurement of awareness. The curved line labeled

Awareness Potential is a good guess at what the typical relative strengths of the importance of the different Needs would be when left unfulfilled. Note that the lower level (more pre-potent) Needs have greater awareness potential. Remember we said that a more pre-potent Need overshadows or dominates over a less pre-potent higher level Need. For example if you are dying of thirst you do not care if anybody loves you.

If all Needs are left unfulfilled they will all shoot up to their respective awareness potentials. Physiological Needs, the ones with the highest awareness potential, will dominate the behavior of the child because their awareness level will be higher than all the other awareness levels of the other Needs even though they are also maxed out at the highest levels they can reach.

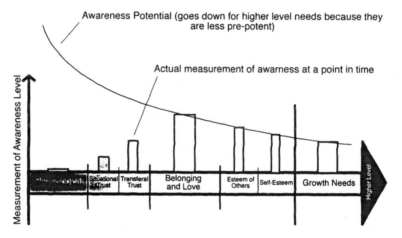

The Need at any particular point in time that has the highest awareness level is going to be the Need the child is "functioning at." For example, in the above graph the Belonging and Love level is the Need that the child is "functioning at." It is the Need that dominates the child's behavior. This can either be considered to be at a particular point in time, such as little Billy is hiding behind his mother and we can confidently say that at this point in time little Billy is functioning at the Safety and Security level; or it can be considered to be an average for little Billy and we can say, little Billy usually behaves in a manner motivated to increase his Belonging and Love fulfillment even though right now he is hiding behind his mother, a behavior which is unusual for him.

The graph above would represent a fairly emotionally healthy young child. The child has all of his Physiological Needs met so that his awareness of Needs at this level is relatively low. Perhaps it is dinnertime and he is hungry which explains why his awareness level of Physiological Needs is not zero on the graph. The child has learned to trust and as such his Safety and Security as measured by Situational Trust and Transferal Trust are low. However he is a child. He still feels and is aware of a need for his being protected, so these levels are not zero either. He stays near his mother because he feels safer there. His behavior is motivated by a need for Belonging and Love. He also has maximized his awareness for fulfillment of Needs for Esteem and Growth. Their relative awareness potential is lower than Belonging and Love. They do not motivate his behavior, at least not to the degree that we see Belonging and Love motivate his behavior. He is not as sensitive to criticism as he is to being separated from his mother. Should his mother insult him he shows little reaction, but if she moves away from him or ignores him he reacts.

In Summary

We want to measure emotional progress by observing and evaluating the motivated behavior of the child. I have differentiated between a measurement at a point in time and an average or conglomerate that would represent the child's overall state of emotional development. When we look at a child we are always looking at him at a point in time. Then, after looking at him numerous times over the course of, say, a week or so, we then can create the composite evaluation that gives a true picture of the child's overall emotional development. This will help us to track the child's emotional progress.

6

Behavioral Characteristics of Transferal Trust Disorder

If you are raising a TD child, and that is why you are reading this book, this probably is not the first book you are reading. You are reading books with titles that include the words "adoption," "difficult child," "problem child," "attachment disorder," "foster child," "challenging," "parenting," and so on. You have probably gone to the Internet to look for information on RAD. Each of these sources often has a list of behavioral characteristics of the children. Most likely all the characteristics you will encounter are included in the list compiled below. None of the lists I encountered are as long as the combined one that follows. I have taken a number of lists from different sources and merged them together to create the following list:

Cannot give/receive love
Oppositional
Argumentative
Defiant
Emotionally insincere
Manipulative
Controlling
Frequent or intense tantrums
Angry
Sad things do not make him cry
Resists closeness and touch
Not trustworthy
No conscience or empathy
Superficially charming to strangers
Avoids eye contact
Indiscriminately affectionate (strangers)

Not affectionate
Destructive
More disobedient for mom than dad
Animal cruelty
Steals
Lies, even about obvious
Impulsive
Hyperactive
No cause and effect logic
Gorges or hoards food
Few friends, loner
Macabre preoccupation
Chatterbox
Demanding and clingy
Sexual acting out
Puerile
Bossy
Affectionate with strangers
Accident prone
Delayed learning (developmentally delayed)
Abnormal eating patterns
Preoccupation with fire
Abnormal speech patterns
Triangulation of adults
False allegations of abuse
Hyper vigilant
Attitude of self-importance
Control problems
Act out negatively
Like power struggles
Negative self-concept
Cannot regulate their affect
Avoid shared fun and laughter
Will not ask for help
Enveloped by shame at the origin of the self[1]
Have trust issues[2]
Hostility to caregiver
Mood swings
Intense fear or sadness
Inappropriate bathroom habits[3]

The list is quite long. It includes characteristics that are common to many other disorders as well. I really do not expect this list to be very helpful to you. Frankly, lists like these leave me just as confused after reading them as I was before I read them. I come away with more questions than answers. Which are the important characteristics, which are not? Are some of the characteristics related to each other, which ones are common to all RAD children and which are not, and so on?

I claim that TD children, of which I consider RAD to be a subset, all have trust issues which cause them to always want to be in control. They want to be in control because they feel less safe and less secure when other people are in control of them. While three of the lists that I consulted to create the above merged list did rank controlling behavior first,[4] another list had controlling behavior as the third item, another had it third from the last,[5] and yet one list altogether omitted controlling behavior as a characteristic of RAD.[6] Interestingly, only one source mentioned trust issues.

I am going to make some sense out of all these lists. All of the symptoms of TD can be directly traced back to one of two significant differences between the normal child and the TD child.

- Because of pathogenic care in infancy Safety and Security level issues take on exaggerated importance for the TD child. The child's need for Safety and Security may be heightened for life. He may always have difficulty trusting others; be hyper vigilant, even when there is no reason not to trust. Simply stated the TD child has a deep-seated mistrust of others so he will *behave in a controlling manner*.
- Because the Safety and Security level issues were not satisfied, the child did not go on to develop higher level Needs such as Belonging and Love and Esteem. His emotional development was blocked by unfulfilled Needs in the Safety and Security level. This is right from Maslow's paradigm: one needs to satisfy lower level Needs before higher level Needs manifest themselves. Simply stated, because the child's development was blocked at the Safety and Security level, the child will *be emotionally immature*.

Go back and look again at the list of behavioral characteristics presented at the beginning of this chapter. See if I am not right. Every entry on the list stems from either lack of trust, which causes the child to be controlling, or lack of emotional maturity.

I do not want to be guilty of generating yet another list of behavioral characteristics because I do not think that that is a good way to understand TD, but there are a few characteristics that are so common to TD children that they should be mentioned, and, unfortunately, it is going to be a list.

Clearly not every behavioral characteristic on the above list manifests itself in every child, but there is one characteristic that is invariably common to all the children that fit into the category of TD:

They are all control freaks.

I very strongly claim that children with TD are control freaks. Because they do not trust others they do not want others to be making decisions on their behalf. To protect themselves from others they have a great need to be in control. If they are not in control they will go to almost any length to gain or regain control. I have suggested that upon examination, much of their motivated behavior is directed toward gaining or maintaining control.

Who Should Be Included in Trust Disorder

In Chapter 5 (Evaluating Behavioral Motivation) we discussed motivated versus non-motivated behavior, and the idea that motivated behavior is a learned or conditioned strategy to fulfill unmet Needs. I briefly discussed the concept that for all the various Needs that we have as humans, for each and every one of them, there invariably exist more than one behavioral strategy available to satisfy those Needs. In other words, when it comes to satisfying Needs there is more than one way to skin a cat.

Being in control is a common behavioral strategy used by children who lack trust in others (transferal trust). But there are other strategies to accomplish the same thing. Should we include all possible behavioral strategies in the TD description? If we do then my statement that all TD children are control freaks becomes inaccurate. Before we answer this question let us examine the other strategies, then after that we can consider if we want to expand our description of TD to include them.

We talked about three different behavioral approaches to satisfying unfulfilled Safety and Security Needs in Chapter 5 (Evaluating Behavioral Motivation): aggressive (controlling) behavior,

---

passive/aggressive (defensive) behavior, and passive (non-confrontational) behavior. The aggressive controlling children go immediately on the offensive trying to control every situation (the best defense is a good offense), the passive/aggressive defensive children will wait to be attached, then defend themselves, and the passive children will run from the battle putting distance between them and their apparent enemies. For the most part we have painted our picture of the TD child as a child who relies primarily on the aggressive, controlling behavioral strategy to protect himself as we have already discussed.

Surely there must be some children somewhere who use either a passive/aggressive defensive behavioral approach, or a passive non-confrontational behavioral approach to achieve the same or similar resulting protection.

There are probably far more children who do not use the aggressive approach than who do use the aggressive approach. The reason that we do not write so many books about these less aggressive children, do not include them in our target population of children who we have labeled as having a "disorder," do not make such a fuss over these children, is because these children are not so difficult to raise. The passive/aggressive defensive child's behavior would be considered to be within normal limits and the passive non-confrontational child's behavior is hardly a management problem for the parent.

What does the passive/aggressive (defensive) behavior look like in the child? That's easy to answer; he looks like most every other child on the playground. If somebody comes up and attacks him either verbally or physically he defends himself; if the person who is attacking him is bigger (a bully) or has more authority (a teacher), he will opt for a passive approach, he will run from a bully and acquiesce to a teacher. For the most part the child who uses the middle approach, the passive/aggressive approach, is a normal child. His feeling that other people cannot be trusted is usually rational, in that it is not universally á priori applied to all other people but only those he has learned through experience not to trust. The children who seem to polarize to the all aggressive or all passive approach are the ones with the emotional problems, they are the ones with the deep seated trust issues, the ones who learned in early childhood that the people supposed to tend to your needs do not always follow through (ala Bowlby's attachment disorder paradigm). This is not to say that there cannot be children with trust issues who use a passive/aggressive defense mechanism, but if there are, it will be difficult to differentiate them from normal children.

What about passive non-confrontational behavior. What does it look like? This child is shy, he withdraws from others in order to protect himself. He too feels that others may not have his best interest at heart, may want to use or hurt him if they are in control, he too has trust issues, but he uses a different mechanism to protect himself. He hides himself, withdraws, tries to blend into the background, does little to attract attention to himself. He becomes a chameleon, not drawing the attention (and ire) of those who may hurt him.

The passive non-confrontational child needs healing just as much as the aggressive controlling child, but he generally does not get it. This child is very easy to raise, he does not demand his parent's attention. There are far fewer books written on raising the shy child than are written on raising the difficult child. Furthermore, almost all the books that are written on shyness are self-help books, whereas there are few self-help books on aggressive behavior. Apparently shy children are doomed to receiving little or no help as children and having to figure it out for themselves, perhaps using self-help books when they get older. This state of affairs makes me feel both sad and angry, their childhoods are not filled with the joy that most children experience and they struggle and they certainly are not getting the attention they deserve (though for the most part they are quite content to not get the attention), but the good news is that most of these children do in fact work through their shyness on their own and overcome it as adults.

Why might the child with trust issues favor the passive approach versus the aggressive approach? I admit that I am speculating here, but being accused of speculating has not stopped me before. I would suggest that the basic difference between the two approaches is that the shy child, in addition to having significant unmet Safety and Security Needs as indicated by poor transferal trust (does not trust others), also has significant unmet Esteem Needs as indicated by being easily embarrassed, shamed, or feeling inferior. The aggressive controlling child really does not care about the effect his behavior has on other people, the passive shy child cares a great deal.

This book is not about shyness, so I will stop here, other than to answer the question I posed above: should we include all possible behavioral strategies in the TD description?

No, we should not. For the most part, children who use the middle passive/aggressive behavioral approach cannot be considered to have a disorder, so they should not be included. Children who use a passive behavioral approach, while they definitely have emotional problems, have a different profile of unmet Needs and require a totally different approach to creating their therapeutic environment. Though they share a common trust-issues root to their emotional problems, they share almost nothing in the way of treatment techniques.

The children who use an aggressive controlling behavioral approach need their own unique category and giving that category the name "trust disorder" works for me.

Selecting the Name Trust Disorder

A little aside on how I settled on the name trust disorder. I wanted a name that was not too long or tedious; TD is that abbreviated name. The disorder is really a reactive disorder (reactive meaning coming about as a reaction to the environment versus an internal or somatic disorder) so the name should be reactive trust disorder. Furthermore, the type of trust referred to in TD is transferal trust so it should be named reactive transferal trust disorder. Now, in this section, I am suggesting that people with reactive transferal trust disorder can be either aggressive or passive, if we add that to the name we get: reactive transferal trust disorder with aggressive behavior. It becomes ridiculously long, TD works fine as a name.

Just by virtue of the way we define TD we can say that all TD children are control freaks, if they are not then we will place them in a different category.

I am going to present you with my list below of characteristics of the TD child, a list that comes directly from my personal experience. The list is not complete, because I only include characteristics that are commonly found in TD. Most of the characteristics on the list are either related to or are behavioral variants of the TD child's being a control freak, and the fact that other TD children may have found different ways to behave that are not on my list to satisfy their need for control does not change the underlying reasons for their behavior—nor does it significantly change our treatment techniques.

Being a control freak is very common behavior for children who do not trust others to fulfill their Safety and Security Needs. If you cannot trust anybody else to do a job then you'll just have to do it yourself. This is the child's mindset with respect to his own rearing. People who feel they cannot trust others end up doing everything for themselves. The problem for the child is that we as parents sometimes interfere with the child's self management agenda by making unreasonable demands like: come to dinner, take a bath, or go to bed.

Seriously, though, the child's need for control stems directly out of not being able to trust others to look out for his needs (transferal trust). There are two ways that his need for control manifests itself. First, he needs to be in control of his life because historically others in control have botched the job. Secondly, he needs to be in control of you because that is the only way he can get his Needs met. If he leaves control up to you, he anticipates that his Needs will be overlooked.

As he grows older, his need for control extends to wants as well as Needs (which is reasonable since he never learned to differentiate between the two) and often seem irrational and unreasonable. You give him something he wants and you think, there, that ought to satisfy him for a while, but it does not. He just immediately starts in on the next thing. There is no sense of, "I've got enough, I do not want to be a pig about it."

The following characteristics are manifestations of the TD child's need to be in control:

Not Being Wrong

When you get into some kind of discussion on his behavior he often will deny wrongdoing, or come up with a myriad of excuses for his not being in the wrong. Admitting that he is wrong is very difficult for him. Often his arguments will become so obtuse that any thread of logic is completely lost. Your reasoning, your impeccable logic, has no obvious effect on him. It can be exasperating. If he senses that he is losing the argument he will change his tactics to denigration.

Defiance

Defiance is a very direct statement from him to you that you will not control him.

Lying

One reason that people do not lie is because, if discovered, it can destroy trust. Trust is a Safety and Security issue. Another reason that people do not lie is because of the associated feelings of guilt. Guilt can be a Love and Belonging issue. The last reason that people do not lie is because of esteem. They see themselves as being honest individuals and lying would spoil their self image. It would also spoil their public image or reputation if others found out that they lied. Lying is a method of manipulation.

Lying seems like an appropriate behavior for somebody who has been lied to all of his life. Worrying about destroying trust is beyond the scope of the TD child's ability.

Manipulation

Manipulation, like lying, is a technique used to get needs fulfilled. Manipulation is an overt way of exercising control over others and to them is a basic survival skill.

Master Negotiator

They will negotiate the pants off the devil. This is another method of control.

Bad Language

Bad language serves two purposes: they use it as part of their denigration routines; and they also use it to try to trigger your hot buttons. If they can trigger your hot buttons then they have controlled your emotions, which is a way that they can affirm that no one controls them. Adults use bad language, children do not. Adults are in control of their own lives, children are not.

You will hear more bad language when they are with their peers. Boys, particularly, feel more powerful when they can pepper their speech with curse words. Doing it to you in front of peers is a way of demonstrating who is the boss.

Trying to Make You Angry

Anger is one of the big issues, and I am not talking about the child's anger which is a given, but yours as the child's caregiver and the anger of other authority figures in his life such as his teacher. All of the classes on behavior management, all the books (and I assume all the experts) all say that you cannot effectively manage a child's behavior if you are angry; that consequences delivered in anger become a punishment. What they do not say is what you should be feeling. If you are not feeling something positive toward the child it is probably still punishment.

There are a couple of reasons why the child wants to make you angry. First, being able to make you angry is an obvious way that the child can manipulate your behavior which gives the child a degree of control over you. Secondly, the child probably has had much experience living in an angry environment, understands it, finds it possibly more predictable and familiar than a warm loving environment (situational trust), and perversely, feels safer when you are exhibiting an emotion that he understands rather than one that he does not.

Charming to Strangers

For a while I questioned whether or not there really was such a thing as a "honeymoon period" with these children (or with any children, for that matter). I speculated that what really happens is that after

69

what we deem to be an appropriate period of time we change our attitude toward the child, we increase our expectations and decrease our support because we figure it is time for the child to give and do more for us, while getting emotionally less from us. I figured the end of the honeymoon period occurs only because we get impatient and rush the child. If we did not rush the child then the honeymoon could go on forever. Wouldn't that be nice! Though I do not think that this is necessarily wrong, I do think that a similar, if somewhat different process, is also occurring in the child that can also cause the end of the honeymoon period.

Any child placed in a strange home is going to be stressed. The TD child who has little trust in individuals and derives his safety and security from familiar situations (situational trust) is going to be really stressed. On top of this, the child may act charming (which is a learned manipulative skill he has found to work well on new acquaintances); but all this takes energy. After a short period of time the child is going to emotionally crash and his true colors will emerge.

The "charming to strangers" observation is a manifestation of the child's skills at manipulating people coupled with the honeymoon period accorded each new acquaintance. Strangers and new acquaintances are easy to manipulate because they do not know the child and are generally willing to accept what he says and does at face value. They respond with apparent interest whether feigned or real.

In response to the child's charming act he will receive much attention and praise. If he is good at it he will improve his performance through practice, but it does require a tremendous amount of energy so that the performance is usually short lived. The charming act is not unique to TD children, it is only mentioned because it seems out of character for these children.

Denigration

Denigration is name calling, typically abusive and derogatory and unpleasant names such as "bitch" or "asshole." Furthermore, they are not used in a subtle way but more of an in-your-face way. Denigration is their last defense mechanism that they use when all the others fail. They sense that they have lost the battle; they resort to denigration. They will just sit there and throw invectives at you.

They have lost the battle, they know it, and the only thing left is to reduce you in size so that your apparent control over them is reduced in size. By blowing you off and demeaning you, your threats and criticisms become trivial. If they cannot control you then at least they can make you as small as possible.

Diabolical Laugh

This is a laugh that they copy from watching cartoon TV villains who laugh, as they are about to take over all of humanity with some diabolical scheme. It has an evil quality to it. It is really annoying. It is the laugh of somebody who thinks they are in control.

Difficulty Accepting and Asking for Help

This is going to be one of the more difficult characteristics to spot because it is something that they do not do rather than something they do, but it is very important. The child does not trust other people, does not want to relinquish control of his life to other people, along with his having no expectation for other people to want to help him; consequently, asking for help when he needs it is just not part of his culture. He wants to be independent and self-sufficient, he does not feel comfortable when he must rely on somebody else for anything.

Raising independent self-sufficient children is not necessarily a bad thing, so why do I include it in this list? First off, this list is not necessarily a list of bad things, just a list of characteristics of TD. Being independent and self-sufficient is good; acting independent and self-sufficient is not necessarily good, especially if you are in trouble and need help, then is it a problem. Then it is probably better to ask for and allow others to help you rather than allowing yourself to fail.

This characteristic of TD, not asking for help, often first surfaces when his school calls you and tells you that he is failing three subjects. All along you have been asking him if he needs help and if everything is going well at school and he says everything is fine. When you find out how bad things have gotten and how far behind he is you are shocked. You thought you were doing your part in showing concern, asking about his progress, offering help. What went wrong?

71

He was hiding the truth from you. He did not want you to know because he expects that you will increase the levels of control on his life: enforce study time, restrict outside activities, institute limits on his freedom; no TV, no seeing his friends; all to manipulate him into putting more time into his school work.

He does not avoid asking for help because he feels in order to do so would require that he swallow his pride. He is not embarrassed about asking, nor is he concerned about being seen as weak because he needs or asks for help. These are not the emotions that will prevent him from asking for help. All these emotions derive from the Esteem Needs. He is not working at the Esteem level. If his motivation were coming from the Esteem level, he would probably seek help early on to avoid the embarrassment and shame of failing.

It is more of a case of him not giving up control because he does not trust you nor does he really expect help anyway. These are Safety and Security level issues. He is not concerned about the potential embarrassment he will experience when deficiencies are eventually exposed. Whereas nobody likes to be embarrassed, it is not the major motivator in his life.

The following characteristics are not directly related to control, but are related to the same thing that causes control to be so important to these children:

Their Anger

It comes as no surprise that a child who has gone through what these children go through is angry. I will present an anger paradigm (Chapter 7, Anger) where anger is an indication that some Safety and Security level issue needs addressing because anger is a secondary response to a problem.

Since we know the child has problems we accept his anger as a necessary part of the healing process and we are glad that he is not complacent about his situation.

Misinterpret Intentions of Others

A friend of mine received a call a few days ago from her mother telling her that there were flood warnings on the radio and that she should be careful driving home. She was annoyed with her mother's interference, and felt like she was being treated like a child. She knew she was perfectly capable of handling herself without the unsolicited advice, after all, she's a big girl now. She felt that her mother was being meddlesome and controlling.

As an outsider it occurred to me that it is also possible that the mother just really loves her daughter, is genuinely worried about her safety and security without any ulterior motive, or maybe she misses talking to her daughter and is only guilty of using the weather as an excuse to call and talk to her.

Good intentions are often misinterpreted. This may be a perfect example of what goes on in the TD child's mind. Based on past experiences he assumes that anybody giving him direction or trying to do anything for or with him does so with an ulterior motive. He just assumes that they are trying to manipulate him. He cannot see that they may truly love or care for him. So his apparent fear of attachment is more a fear of being conned, losing control, because he assumes that everybody is out to manipulate him to their advantage. So even if you try to do something nice for him he assumes that you are somehow trying to trick him in some way to benefit yourself. Concomitantly, he feels justified in manipulating others.

Affection is perceived the same way. Because love and affection can be given in a manipulative fashion, the TD child may discount your overtures. It is possible that the love given during his first year was based more on the mother's needs, not the child's. She used her emotional schedule rather than the child's and then more to satisfy her need to be loved than the child's need for love. I am sure that she was frustrated because typically babies are not good at satisfying the emotional needs of their parents. With this improper attachment cycle the baby learns that he cannot trust his emotional and physical needs to others, that he has to be constantly vigilant.

Do Not Like Change

It is ironic that attachment disorder children will sometimes choose to remain in bad situations rather than move to good ones. It is something that you read and hear over and over again and at times it seems to defy logic—why do people stay in bad or abusive relationships, in bad situations, especially if there are obvious alternatives. Instead of an "any port in a storm" mentality, one would think that they would move even if there was a chance of improvement.

I think the answer is based on expectations or the lack thereof. I have seen a child in a class where there was an obvious mismatch between the teacher's personality and the child's personality and yet watched the child cry hysterically when told that he was going to be moved to a new classroom and a new teacher. I am sitting on the sidelines wondering why the child is not relieved to be moved. I have had a child cry hysterically on the bus home from the last day of school before summer vacation, a bus ride that I recall was one of the happiest events of the school year.

In both cases the child was going from a known situation to an unknown situation. It was change in their lives and they did not know what to expect from the new situation. The old situation was familiar and from experience they had grown to know that it was safe, or at least safer than some imagined unknown. Change in their lives has almost always been for the worse, has almost always been emotionally traumatic, and has almost always been associated with upheaval.

Transferal trust is feeling that the other person will look out for and not willingly abuse our needs and welfare. Trust, for the child with TD, is less based on transferal trust and more based on situational trust. Trust for him is knowing that historically, in certain situations, he is relatively safe; and knowing when and where he can relax his defense mechanisms. Being on guard, being on the defensive takes much energy; even people in abusive relationships have times when they can get some rest from being on guard; every new situation for these children represents the need to be on guard all the time.

A healthy child gets moved to a new classroom and he has preconceived expectations of what is going to happen, that the teacher will be fair, caring, trustworthy, etc. The TD child goes into the new classroom with no expectations; because life's situations in the past have not been consistently safe so he has no reason to believe or expect that this new situation will be safe. Simple change is going to be far more traumatic for this child than for the healthy child. They will opt to stay in a bad situation rather than move to a better one.

When we see the child in what we consider to be a bad situation it becomes a real dilemma to decide whether to move him or leave him. I am not going to pretend that I have a good answer to this.

We can say that for the TD child, his trust comes from situations, not people (it is situational trust, not transferal trust).

This ends my list of characteristics of TD children that are motivated by the child's need to be in control.

Immaturity

The TD child is emotionally immature. His emotions are so strongly entrenched in and focusing on the Safety and Security level that he will be blatantly missing emotions from the higher level Belonging and Love Needs and Esteem Needs. We are going to see him as appearing not to need the warmth, cuddling, or approval of his caregivers that most children crave. The following characteristics stem from this emotional immaturity. Please appreciate that emotional immaturity can manifest itself in a myriad of ways so the list is far from complete and none of these ways are unique to TD.

The TD child has a diminished capacity to appreciate the emotional state of those around him. Awareness of others is clearly part of the maturation process. The baby cries when it wants to be fed, it does not stop to think if the time is convenient for mom to come. Maybe mom is tired; the baby cries anyway. At the other end of the spectrum the mother comes when the baby cries, she does not stop to think if she is too tired or too busy to take care of the baby's needs. The baby puts its own needs first, the mother puts the baby's needs first (or should).

The process of moving from being self-centered to being outwardly centered is a major part of the maturation process. When the child does not get proper nurturing in the early years its maturational development stops. Emotionally the child is stuck in those early years hopefully still waiting and receptive for the nurturing that has not occurred.

The maturational process involves moving from lower to higher levels on Maslow's Hierarchy. By the time the child reaches ten he should care what others think about him; he should be able to feel embarrassment; he should be functioning at least some of the time in Maslow's fourth level (Esteem Needs).

The child is emotionally stuck. His Needs have not been met consistently and he has learned not to trust others. He is in a struggle for survival; too much of his energy is going into worrying about himself, with little left over for others. Trust is a Safety and Security Need issue and if the child is stuck in the Safety and Security Need level, he will not manifest his higher level Needs—especially Esteem—since it is as far away as you can get within the deficiency level Needs. Searching for the esteem of others requires an awareness of what other people are thinking.

Moving up Maslow's Hierarchy pushes the child from being self-centered to being outwardly-centered. He may behave in public in an immature and embarrassing way, behavior that is totally age inappropriate. He faces losing friends and social ostracism with this behavior. All this is manifested in a child who is rapidly moving into the age group where normally the fear of social ostracism is more pervasive than it will be at any other time in his life. He should be afraid to make social faux pas. You will find yourself embarrassed in his place. He does not get embarrassed and that is because he does not care what others think. He does not care what others think because he has no need for esteem from others. He has no Esteem Needs, he is not yet working at the Esteem level, he is immature. Having no Esteem Needs is different and not to be confused with low self esteem. You must be mature enough to have Esteem Needs to have low self esteem.

The child's apparent lack of conscience is based on his belief that everybody in the world is out to get him and it is his duty to himself to take advantage of others first. He sees that as the way the world works and has no qualms about manipulating people, using people, lying, cheating—whatever it takes to remain on top. He justifies this as necessary for survival. He sees the underdog as just a necessary role that other people will have to take so that he can be the top dog. He does not worry about what other people think or feel and is pretty certain that they do not worry about him either.

Fear of attachment

I included this only because it is supposed to be one of the characteristics of children with attachment disorder. I have never seen any kind of fear associated with attachment per se, only mistrust.

Sub-Types

Emotions are absolutely invisible; they cannot be seen. What can only be seen is behavior. Emotions, though, motivate much behavior. Not all behavior is motivated, there is unmotivated behavior, such as kicking at a stone while walking, which would have no apparent emotional motivation as discussed in Chapter 5 (Evaluating Behavioral Motivation). Everybody is different, cultures differ, families differ, parental attitudes differ, genetic makeups differ, all these differences allow for a broad range of possible behavioral types even when they are all motivated by the same underlying emotional needs. Simply stated, different people find different ways to behaviorally express similar emotions.

Dr. Becker-Weidman identifies four sub-types of RAD children based on behavioral characteristics. They are as follows using his descriptions copied almost verbatim from one of his Internet postings:[7]

- Ambivalent—an "in-your-face" child. This is the child who is angry, oppositional, and who can be violent.
- Anxious—is clingy, anxious, shows separation anxieties, among other symptoms.
- Avoidant—is often overlooked. Very compliant, agreeable, and superficially engaging. This child often has a lack of depth to his emotions and functions as an "as-if" child; meaning that he tries to do and say what you want, but is not genuine, authentic, or real in emotional engagement.
- Disorganized—often presents with bizarre symptoms.

The bulk of this book focuses on Dr. Becker-Weidman's ambivalent sub-type. I feel a little guilty about this, as the other sub-types are just as in need of help as the ambivalent sub-type, but they do not make the demands on the caregiver as the ambivalent so they do not get the attention. They still do not trust, therefore should rightly be included in the umbrella diagnosis of TD, but they have not adopted controlling behavior as a means of allaying their anxiety over having other people run their lives.

Notes

[1] http://www.danielahughes.homestead.com/fdaintro.html
[2] http://www.reactiveattachmentdisordertreatment.com/ssi/article2.html

[3] http://www.abcofpa.net/Symptoms.htm
[4] http://www.attachmentdisorder.net/Symptoms_Causes_Research.htm, http://danielahughes.homestead.com/fdaintro.html, http://www.abcofpa.net/Symptoms.htm
[5] http://reactiveattachment.com
[6] http://www.attachment.org/rad.htm
[7] Becker-Weidman, Arthur, CSW-R, PhD., DABPS, http://www.center4familydevelop.com, September 2004.

7

Anger

Anger is a major topic as far as children with TD are concerned, and it just would not be right if I overlooked it. I had originally written more about this topic than is present here, but after having discussions with a friend of mine who is a psychologist[1] I later went back to the subject and decided that most of what I had written either missed the mark or was not viable from a practical point of view. I rewrote this section focusing on key points that are important to know when one is dealing with angry children.

Anger is an emotional response, and undoubtedly a familiar feeling to anybody reading this. We all know what causes anger, we all know what it feels like, and we all know what anger makes us do when we are overcome by it. Rather than explain what we already know, I am going to try to intellectualize the anger process so that we can understand what it means and what its significance is for us in working with the child.

Here is where a distinction must be made between anger and angry behavior: They are not the same thing. Anger, as already stated, is an emotional response. Though we can often spot anger in others by observing their behaviors (ones that we know from past experiences are anger-driven), we should also realize that anger in and of itself does not imply any specific behavioral pattern because it is instead *an emotion*, while rage, for example, though triggered by anger, is *a behavior*. It is a consuming, impulsive, irrational, and emotionally-driven behavior pattern characterized by lack of self-control and often destructive or harmful actions. Rage is possibly beneficial in some situations, like scaring off an enemy, but has little benefit or application in the area of child rearing. In short, anger is an emotion, rage is a behavior. In the context of what follows, when I mention anger I am never talking about rage or wrath, or any other specific anger-driven pattern of behavior. I am talking about the underlying emotion of anger itself.

To appreciate the value (yes, the value) of anger we need to explore the situations that trigger it. Think about it: every time you became angry, something had been done to you or someone you care about, or you became aware of something that seemed wrong to you, and so you then wanted the situation fixed. For example: someone cuts in line in front of you; someone whom you trust abuses that trust; someone says something hurtful to you, your spouse, your child; or you witness a social injustice.

What did you do? Quite possibly you took some kind of action to right the wrong. You spoke your mind. You wrote a letter. You probably also became angry. In fact, if you had not become angry, it is very likely that you would have done nothing, ignored the wrong, and complacently left things the way they were. So your anger served a very important function, it propelled you into action to right a wrong.

Anger actually triggers the body's release of various hormones associated with energy, epinephrine, norepinephrine, etc. These hormones improve performance, both physically and mentally. Consequently, anger has an immediate benefit in providing us with the "juice" needed when we enter mental or physical combat. That's a good thing, because it improves our chances of obtaining the desired outcome from our combat.

The point I am trying to make is that anger generally motivates us to tackle problems, and conveniently at the same time gives us additional mental and physical resources to do so. The phrase used by my friend the psychologist was, "Anger is an agent for change."

The emotion of anger is only initiated by events that threaten the individual at the Safety and Security Needs level. A perpetually angry child would be stuck in the Safety and Security Needs level because you really cannot get out of this level while you are angry.

We unwittingly use anger all the time in the process of raising children (not necessarily our anger but theirs). As they get older we routinely stop doing things for them that we feel they are old enough to do them for themselves. Their first reaction is often anger, but then they change for the better (we hope). Would they have changed without the anger as a motivator? Possibly. We tell people things that we know they will not like, but we feel they need to know. At first their anger is directed at us, but often they see that what we are saying is valid on an intellectual level. They can then redirect their anger internally to change what they find to be wrong with themselves.

I could make an argument that one facet of the maturational process is the gradual transfer of the fulfillment of Physiological Needs and Safety and Security Needs from the parent to the child. I could also argue that the strategic removal of our satisfying these Needs creates some anger, anger which is useful and helpful to the child in the process of becoming self-sufficient. I could argue that the anger seen in the teenager is a necessary part of the maturational process, that with a quickly maturing intellect and body, the anger prods him to complete his emotional maturity, at least the part associated with providing for his own Safety and Security. His life is changing rapidly and he does not necessarily want to leave all the comforts of his past. He is torn between the past and the future and the internal clash generates anger (directed at the caregiver, of course), which helps him to move on.

I can also tell you that I have seen situations where I wanted to see people get angry, where I felt that a person was in a situation that warranted anger, and I was upset with his or her complacency and acceptance. If he would only get angry, then maybe he would do something about the situation.

It was anger that initially motivated me to write this book, and it is anger that is going to motivate you to send me an email letting me know how little you think of it. Now you can see how anger is a good thing!

Anger can be directed outwardly at whomever the individual sees as the source of the insult. However it may also be directed inward, undirected, or altogether misdirected. The concept of anger, though, begs for direction. It is common for the primary caregiver to be the recipient of the child's anger, even when it is obvious that the primary caregiver is not responsible for the underlying situation causing the anger. The child feels that the primary caregiver should be aware of all the things that conspire to make his life difficult, and thus should intervene on his behalf.

Anger is an emotion of which we want to rid ourselves. We do not much like being angry. Addressing and fixing the situation that caused the anger is the best cure for it, and anger is meant to propel us to do that. Anger is an agent for change.

Foster children typically appear angry (exhibit behavior commonly associated with anger) and probably often are, certainly when they are first placed in a new home. If nobody addresses their anger and takes corrective action then they may always be angry. Unlike adults, children are less able to resolve their own anger. Before taking corrective action, it would be helpful to understand the source of their anger. Do you think that a foster child who has just been moved for the fifth time (or first or second) into your home is angry because of the way he was raised in the first year of his life? Or is it because he was just moved from a known situation to a completely unknown situation where he feels powerless to control what is happening, and is lost and overwhelmed? Obviously the latter is why foster children are angry, though the former probably is the reason they do not form attachments and are subsequently rejected by parents, relatives, and foster families.

My point here is that the anger the child is feeling today is not a manifestation of wrongs committed in the past as might be suggested in some of the literature. I do not buy into statements that the child is angry because he was poorly parented during his first year of age, and he has thus been seething slowly all the following years. The child is angry over something that it is missing or bothering him *right now*, at the time of the anger.

I am saying that if the child is angry right now, then there is something bothering him right now. This may be hopeful thinking, but I think it holds true. It is hopeful because I cannot change anything that happened in the past, but I can change the present and the future. If I can discover the source of the child's current anger, there is a chance that I can remedy the problem. And so can you.

I am also suggesting that anger is a *symptom* of a problem, not the problem itself. Many underlying factors can trigger it, and dealing only with the anger without trying to discover its source is a superficial, short-term approach to solving the child's problems. Do not punish a child for being angry, though you can consequence him for unacceptable anger-induced behavior.

Furthermore, I am saying that the anger in the child can be viewed as a positive indication that the child is not complacent about the problem and is open and ready to change, but will probably need your guidance or professional help to bring about the change.

Is it normal for a child to expect to be cared for? Whether he learned to expect others to take care of him, or whether it is instinct, I do not know, but it does not matter anyway for what we are doing here. The point is that the child expects for his caregiver to take care of his needs, and will likely respond with anger if his needs are not met. One thing is for sure: the child does know what its basic needs are, and he knows when they are unfulfilled. You would not argue whether or not a child knows when he is hungry, and you would probably not argue whether or not he knows if he is feeling insecure, unsafe, or anxious. I also hope you would not argue that the child knows, at least at some level, when he is unloved.

As much as we might not like anger, especially in others such as children with whom we share the same house, think of it this way: The child has identified that something is wrong and he is preparing to do battle to right that wrong. Now of course he thinks that the wrong is external, something that somebody else did to him, or more likely in the child's case something that somebody else did *not* do for him in terms of unmet Needs. Unfortunately, as the primary caregiver, you are often the target of his anger, even though you may not be responsible for creating his TD. In a sense it is correct that he should be angry with you. Regardless of who created the problem, you are the current caregiver, and you are now supposed to be fixing his problems. The problems triggering the anger he is feeling are in the present and you are the one who is supposed to be fixing his problems right now.

Among individuals there is a broad range of different levels of stimulation required to trigger anger, just as are there a variety of ways individuals express anger. These differences are partly extrinsic, such as a family's or society's cultural differences, and partly intrinsic, such as one's personality. But it does not matter in developing our paradigm because anger is not the problem anyway. We just want to manage it as necessary and if needed, and also see it as an indication that there are current underlying problems that need immediate attention. In the process of addressing those problems, we can use anger as an agent for change.

Anecdote

A distant relative of my foster child wanted to spend some time with him but was reluctant because of all the anger she saw in the child. As she was talking to me on the telephone about all the child's anger I became more and more confused. I was not aware that the child was burdened by so much anger. After our

---

conversation was over her words kept coming back to me until it finally occurred to me what was happening.

The TD child's defense mechanism, being oppositional and defiant and untrusting, could easily be interpreted as anger. Ask him if he wants to do something and he says no. Short cryptic answers with no eye contact and little enthusiasm, these behaviors too can easily be misinterpreted as anger.

I am repeating myself when I say we cannot see emotions such as anger, we can only see the behavior motivated by these emotions. There is such a vast difference between the emotional fabric of the TD child and the emotional fabric of the typical (hopefully normal and well adjusted) adult observer it is understandable that there are going to be mistakes made by most adult observers in interpreting which emotions are driving specific behaviors in the child. That is exactly what happened when she interpreted the child's behavior as being driven by anger.

The child's behavior was being driven by anxiety over losing control and being in an uncomfortable new situation. I helped her to reinterpret the child's true emotions based on observed behavior. Knowing this, the relative was in a much better frame of mind to help the child. First, she had been avoiding the child because she thought that she was contributing to his anger. With new understanding she quit feeling guilty and started to initiate contact. Secondly, with a better understanding of the real emotions in the child she then knew what she had to do; she already knew all the skills necessary to deal with a frightened child, all she had to do was use them.

TD children are not as angry as people think, more likely than not, when they are acting as if they are angry, they are really scared or anxious.

Notes

[1] Discussion with Robert Rabinowitz, Ph.D. in clinical psychology.

8

Addictive Personality Paradigm

In his book *Psychological Care of Infant and Child,*[1] John Watson warns against excessive coddling. He says, "The adult effect of too much coddling in infancy is invalidism. As adults we have too many aches and pains." Though an absurd statement there is value in projecting early childhood psychological difficulties into adulthood.

Following Watson's lead, I make the same kind of projection. I take my TD model and use it to predict the outcome of what happens to the TD child as an adult. Undoubtedly I can present a more valid causal relationship between the condition of TD in the child and its ensuing adult effect than Watson made in his projection. I realize that I must also work far harder at establishing my case than did Watson. I have a more critically demanding, better educated, and more deeply aware audience than he had. Furthermore, I am touching a topic where most people have at least indirect experience, and usually have their own ideas on what causes these problems.

The whole subject of addiction is a hot topic with many people in the general population. Current studies lean toward a combined genetic-environmental basis for addiction, even though a specific gene or set of genes has yet to be found as the culprit to support a molecular biologically based genetic theory. Studies abound, yet there is still no concrete scientific conclusion that can definitively answer how much of addiction is caused by nurturing (the way one is brought up) or nature (one's genetic composition).

There do seem to be people who, once they start drinking or using drugs, are just not capable of stopping, and the abused substance occupies a pervasive part of their lives. On the other hand, there are many individuals who seem totally immune to addiction.

My definition of an addictive personality is one in which there is a propensity for the individual to become addicted to a mind-altering drug, usually one that induces some sort of state of euphoria, such as alcohol, cocaine, crack, heroin, LSD, and so on.

Here I will present a model or paradigm for addiction. Let me make it clear that though I do not claim that my model will apply for all addictive tendencies or behaviors, I do think that my model will apply to a majority of the addictive personalities in mainstream American culture. I also do not claim that it is the only valid model for addiction. However before I present my model, we need to do a little ground work.

Do TD Children Become TD Adults?

It is my opinion that TD is a significant factor in addiction. Since addiction is primarily an adult problem, I need to identify the source of TD in adults. A common source, perhaps the most common source, is TD children who carry it over and develop into adults who have TD. Since the designation TD is my own, it follows that, at the time of this writing, no studies regarding TD have been conducted. Therefore, I cannot say with scientific certainty that, left untreated, the child with TD progresses on to become an adult with TD. No one has as of yet even looked at the prevalence of TD in children. The closest group identified to TD for which we can find any studies or information is reactive attachment disorder (RAD). My definition of TD encompasses many more children than does RAD. RAD, depending on which expert you ask, often only includes the most severely affected children. I include a whole spectrum from mild to extreme affliction in TD. Thus, by my definition, all children with RAD suffer from TD. Not all children with TD have RAD. RAD is a subset of TD.

Even without the benefit of scientific proof, I do not think it a stretch to assume that TD children often go on to become TD adults. If I pessimistically thought that all TD children became TD adults (that is to say once a child has TD he is stuck with it for life), I would not have bothered to write this book. One of the beautiful things about humans is that we can change. The process of change in adults often involves intellectualizing our emotional responses and gaining mastery over undesirable emotional responses through that understanding. This is the basis of psychotherapy. The process of changing a child is difficult to put into words, but it would generally be considered to be the same as nurturing. Through nurturing and good parenting, we shepherd our children to adulthood. The TD child has missed out on some necessary nurturing and has some catching up to do, as I have discussed earlier. He has not learned to trust.

Although there are not any current studies to back me up, I still feel comfortable saying that without intervention, TD children often become TD adults. We know that children with RAD have difficulties that do not disappear with only the passage of time, and that they often cannot form good relationships as adults. In fact, this is the basis for this book, as well as many others written on the subject of facilitating attachment: that we need to intervene in the life of the TD child and heal the child now, because time itself will not repair the child. Time (waiting around and doing nothing) is the worst treatment for TD children.[2] It logically follows that if children with TD require treatment of some sort to heal, that without treatment they will stagnate and not mend.

I did find a study that showed attention-deficit/hyperactivity disorder (ADHD) to be a predictor of later substance use.[3] The study compared a group of 142 children with ADHD against a control group of 100 children, following them up to adolescence (13–18 years old). The study found the risk of substance use disorder (SUD) to be significantly higher in the ADHD group than in the control group. Interestingly, it also found a high co-morbidity between ADHD and oppositional defiant disorder/conduct disorder (ODD/CD), a finding that I would expect since I believe there is a significant relationship between ADHD, ODD/CD, and my TD.

My foster children were previously diagnosed with ADHD, and were placed on a drug regimen, primarily to make them more tractable at school. This was all prior to any involvement on my part. While under my care, the ADHD diagnoses were proven incorrect. The children had the ability to control themselves almost instantly if they wanted to, whereas a true ADHD child does not have that ability. My argument is anecdotal and consequently does not constitute scientific proof, but it is quite possible that many of the children labeled ADHD, just like the children with whom I have had direct experience, really have TD, and if you accept this, then the evidence would support my hypothesis.

My Hypothesis

To state this as simply as I can, I believe that there is a direct causal relationship between a person having TD as a child, and being an addictive personality as an adult. I am not claiming that all TD children become TD adults, nor am I claiming that all TD adults become alcoholics or other drug abusers. I am also not claiming that the only cause of alcoholism or other drug abuse is TD.

I am saying that many TD children, probably a majority of those who never receive any kind of healing treatment for their disorder, become TD adults. Furthermore, I am predicting that if studies are done regarding this, they will show the incidence of addiction in a population of TD adults will be significantly higher than in a similar demographic group of non-TD adults. I also predict that there will be such a strong correlation found between TD and addiction, that TD in children will become the primary indicator for predicting future drug dependency.

Just the possibility that I am right should underline the importance of diagnosing and treating TD as early as possible. Addiction is so devastating to the life of any individual, to his or her family and friends, and so costly to society as a whole, that even the likelihood that TD is a major cause should at the very least make it a priority on our part to carry out some scientific studies. Without the studies this is only speculation. Allow me to present the model for addictive personality since I feel so strongly that it is fundamentally accurate, and that time will prove it so.

What Benefit Does One Get from Alcohol or Drugs?

First, let us consider what drugs do for us. A quick answer would be, "They make us feel good."

Someone might respond, "But I already feel good."

"Yeah, but you will feel even better if you get high."

"But I *don't* feel better when I am high!" Now here is the dilemma: not everyone feels better when they get drunk or use drugs. If everyone felt better when they used drugs, then we would all be potential drug abusers. Only self-discipline, ignorance (never having the experience of knowing how good if feels), excessive expense, or lack of availability would keep us from going that route. But this is not the case. Many people do not like the feeling they get when they are on drugs; they derive no apparent benefit from getting high. So then, why do some people abuse drugs, others use them occasionally, and still others abstain? The answer lies in a deeper understanding of the question: what do drugs do for us?

Drugs blunt all our mental processes, but they effect our inhibitions and other emotional centers faster than they impair mental acuity, which gives us a relative sense of euphoria before we get inebriated or high to the point where we pass out or are unable to walk or think. All emotions, which are functions of the brain, are dulled. Of course with enough drugs in our system, all areas of brain function would be impaired beyond consciousness.

Do we feel better when our emotions are dulled? That depends on the individual. Does the person who has just fallen head-over-heels in love feel better when his or her feelings of passionate love are dulled? Absolutely not! Does the person who is feeling some kind of emotional pain feel better when his or her emotional pain is dulled? Absolutely yes! So who is going to benefit the most from the use of drugs? Obviously the person who is experiencing some type of emotional pain will feel better. The person experiencing chronic emotional pain will be the one most likely to become addicted to drugs. The person who finds joy in life may drink alcohol (because it is legal, socially accepted, and culturally expected at certain times), but will most likely never become addicted.

One way of viewing drugs or alcohol is to consider the blunting or dulling of emotions to be the desired therapeutic effect, while considering the impaired intellectual and motor functions as undesirable side effects. People use drugs when the benefits from the therapeutic effects outweigh the negatives of the side effects. More specifically, people with chronic emotional pain use drugs or alcohol to self-medicate, and chronic use leads to addiction.

Another possibility is that people have a gene that predisposes them to alcoholism or other drug abuse by causing their body to have some sort of physical craving or need for the drug even prior to becoming addicted. Perhaps such a gene pushes individuals to drug and alcohol abuse. I do not think this is the case, but I will discuss this later.

How My Model Evolved

About fifteen years ago, I had a patient in my practice who was a Ph.D. psychologist at the Horsham Clinic, a clinic that hosts a major drug and alcohol treatment program. One time, I jokingly suggested that he and his colleagues make people happier through their program. The psychologist stopped me short and emphatically said, "No we don't, we just make them function!"

He proposed an interesting model for alcoholism and other drug abuse that went something like this: most everybody has the ability to care and love, some more, some less than others. Just as no two snowflakes are alike, and just as no two people have exactly the same intellectual or athletic capabilities, it makes perfect sense that no two people have exactly the same caring and loving capabilities.

In his model he differentiated between the *ability* for an individual to care and love and the *need* for the individual to care and love. He stated that in spite of an individual's diminished capacity to care and love, the individual still has the *need* to care and love. This inability to fulfill a basic need for caring and love creates a pain within the person who has an addictive personality, a pain he or she feels as loneliness. The person then uses alcohol to self-medicate to ease away this pain, and through chronic use becomes addicted.

What my friend meant by "We just make them function," was that their treatment program cannot help the addicts to resolve any emotionally based caring issues. Psychologists and psychiatrists today do not have the ability to teach people to care more. What they can do is help individuals lead normal lives by teaching them to use their intellect to supplant many of the little things emotionally healthy people do automatically, such as giving hugs and kisses, bringing home flowers, remembering birthdays, and so on.

He did not stress or give reason for the individual's inability to care and love, other than to mention the natural variations that would occur between different people. My friend did not grapple with the dilemma of people who wanted love so badly that it would create enough pain that they would need to self medicate to ease that pain, and at the same time, would not want or need love badly enough to go out and get it. I accepted his model because it fit my experience in terms of describing the personality and behaviors of addictive people I knew, but the dilemmas regarding caring and love did leave me some-what perplexed.

Everything I have mentioned thus far is a paraphrase of his words. In converting to the language I have been using, we can identify what he referred to as "caring and loving" as originating in the Belonging and Love Needs. Basically, he created a model of a major conflict within one Need level. The individuals desperately want love, but at the same time they are unable to get it due to some kind of inherent disability. I no longer agree with this part of his model. I do not think that the conflict is all within the Belonging and Love level. Instead, I think that it is *between* two Maslow levels, and I will go on to explain this later. I partly agree with the result of the conflict, which is that the individuals are left with unsatisfied Belonging and Love Needs that they are incapable of filling. Unsatisfied Belonging and Love Needs translates into the individuals being lonely. They have an inability to satisfy their Belonging and Love Need in a meaningful way.

I now see it as a little more complicated. I see the conflict as arising out of two levels and their emotional pain will also arise out of the same two levels. This makes sense because it is easier to imagine two separate emotional centers of the brain sending out competing messages than for one emotional center to be sending out two competing messages.

For the moment, though, please accept my statement that the addicts are individuals with some sort of emotional pain. I will develop the source and nature of that emotional pain later. First, let us consider what drugs or alcohol can do for people with emotional pain and why they might become addicted.

How Does the Addiction Help the Individual?

Individuals suffering from chronic emotional pain will find self-medicating with drugs or alcohol beneficial: It rids them of their emotional pain.

The emotional pain of abused-drug users is just as real as the somatic (body) pain of arthritics who use over-the-counter painkillers for the rest of their lives. Who wants to live in pain? Would we say that the arthritics who chronically use aspirin are addicted? Would we say that the arthritics are abusing aspirin? Maybe some purists who abhor the use of any medication might, but most of us are happy to see arthritics receive relief from their chronic pain, and feel the long-term use of painkillers for somatic pain to be quite justified. We even regard as acceptable the chronic use of morphine or other physically addictive pain killers when the somatic pain is too strong to be controlled by weaker, non-addictive pain killers. It is a dual standard to accept as acceptable the chronic use of medication for somatic pain, while condemning as unacceptable the chronic use of medication for emotional pain. It trivializes emotional and mental health issues.

What about individuals who do not suffer from emotional pain? What will the drugs or alcohol do for them? Basically nothing other than give them a novel and interesting experience, maybe relax them. If their lives are filled with joy and love, it will blunt those emotions as well. They will lose those good feelings, and as a result will most likely not want to use drugs or alcohol often or to excess.

Most abused drugs interfere with the individuals' ability to perform routine daily duties as a responsible adults. Chemical dependence makes quitting, even for short periods of time, nearly impossible. Losing their jobs, their families, their self-esteem, and control of their lives—these are all negative side effects of addiction.

The therapeutic benefits from the drug must be strong enough in the individuals to outweigh all the negative side effects. This is only true for a percentage of our population with severe emotional pain. Consequently not everyone is going to become an addict.

The Addictive Personality Emotional Model

While building my model for TD and incorporating both Maslow's and Bowlby's paradigms, another piece to the addiction model puzzle fell into place. People who were lonely always perplexed me: why did not they just go out and make some friends? I thought that the explanation was that they have a diminished capacity to care, and they cannot make the deep emotional connections required to satisfy their love need. Yes, they can have relationships, get married, father or mother children, and often function reasonably well within society, but the depth of the relationships just is not there. Consequently their lives often have a history of poor or broken relationships and divorces.

I thought about this model for years, applying it to my personal experiences with people who I considered drug abusers, and it worked.

It did accurately predict behavior. But the part about diminished capacity to care and to love kept haunting me. I agreed that they did have a diminished capacity to care or love but it seemed to me that if they really wanted to care and love, then what was to stop them? Or if they were simply unable to care and love, then why would it be so important to them? And if it was not important to them, then why would it cause emotional pain? But the model seemed to work so I dismissed my doubts.

Then along came my recent experiences with TD children, and another piece fell into place. In building my TD model, I realized that TD children also have a diminished capacity to care and love, and my TD model explains exactly why this is the case. I got really excited when I first developed my TD model and compared it to the addictive personality model as presented by my friend from the Horsham Clinic.

The TD child is stuck in the Safety and Security level, and as such cannot function well on the Love and Belonging level. Since trust is a necessary part of the foundation for any strong loving relationship, the person just cannot form these strong relationships that require a high level of commitment. They want to, and they have the *need* to. Then their Safety and Security level deficit of trust gets in the way of their Belonging and Love level affection Needs.

The problem is not a diminished capacity to care and love as my friend stated: it is a diminished capacity to *trust* that interferes with their capacity to care and love. By changing this part of the model as it was presented to me, it makes sense that they want love but cannot achieve it. Now we can see why they have such pain: they *want* to have love, and they *need* to have love as much as anybody else, but they just cannot make the emotional connections required because they do not trust. As such, they are perpetually conflicted.

But many addicts do enter into relationships, probably the majority of them. Are they all feeling lonely? Yes, I think they are. I believe this is so because they have not, nor are they capable of, making the strong emotional commitment to their partner that our Belonging and Love level demands in order to feel satisfied. Thus they cannot truly love. I define love as putting another person's emotional needs on an equal or higher priority to your own. The TD adult with trust issues of an addictive personality stemming from the Safety and Security level cannot do this.

But is loneliness all they are feeling? No. Their problem is one of a conflict between two levels. If they are in a relationship, they are going to have negative emotions from both levels. Any relationship is going to require a certain amount of cooperation, and when we cooperate with another person we give up control. Relationships automatically have a certain amount of loss of control built into them, at least any healthy relationship. Loss of control is implicit in putting another person's needs before your own. People who do not have TD cannot easily understand this because they do not sense any loss of control when they perform unselfish loving acts for their partners and friends.

TD adults do not want to lose control. They do not trust other people, and they feel very vulnerable when not in control. When they enter into a relationship, their level of anxiety will increase. When their relationships end in divorce, they might say things like, "I was smothered in that relationship," or, "She/he made too many demands on me." A husband might describe his wife as his "ball and chain."

So TD adults are forced to choose between the anxiety of a relationship, and the loneliness of no relationship. Even in a relationship they are lonely, though not as lonely as they would be if they were out of a relationship. Even out of a relationship they are anxious about losing control, though not as anxious as they would be if they were in a relationship.

When in a relationship there is pressure to get out. When out of a relationship there is pressure to get in. Their lives oscillate between satisfying their Safety and Security Needs and their Belonging and Love Needs. You might see a ping-pong effect where they have multiple romances in their lives, and possibly even multiple marriages and divorces.

My TD model definitely does not predict that all TD adults will become addictive personalities. It does, though, predict that a certain sub-group of TD adults will become addictive personalities. It predicts that the TD children can evolve into one of three sub-groups as adults, depending on how much progress they make moving up Maslow's Hierarchy. Note that my model never predicts that individuals will move *down* the Hierarchy: if they are going to move at all, it will be upwards, at least in the model.

When following the emotional progress of a group of TD children to adulthood, a certain percentage will remain so entrenched in the Safety and Security level that they will never develop any Belonging and Love Needs. These are the individuals with severe trust issues, issues so strong that they block all emotional progress.

My TD model predicts that individuals with severe trust issues will not necessarily become drug users. Because of their severe trust issues, these individuals are so preoccupied with Safety and Security Needs that Belonging and Love is not important. These individuals are so involved with becoming safe and secure that they have little emotional energy left to feel lonely. While these people are chronically stuck in the Safety and Security level, they do not have the emotional dilemma of the individuals who move on, because their Belonging and Love Needs are not strong enough to create the internal conflict between the two levels. They will not experience the ping-pong effect of relationships.

For these individuals, control and vigilance will be paramount. Being under the influence of alcohol or drugs increases their feelings of being vulnerable, defenseless, and out of control, actually increasing their level of anxiety. This would seem like a contradiction because the therapeutic effect of alcohol and drugs is to blunt emotions, not to increase them.

People can and do fight the effect of drugs all the time, a situation seen routinely in clinical situations. For example, dentists often administer nitrous oxide to their patients. Nitrous oxide is an inhaled gas that has the therapeutic effect of calming the patient during treatment. The feeling of being under the effects of nitrous oxide is best described as the equivalent of having a few drinks. Many patients find the calming effect of nitrous oxide to be very helpful in overcoming the anxiety of sitting through dental procedures.

With the nitrous oxide, as with any mind-altering drug, comes a certain feeling of disorientation, and with this disorientation comes a sense of loss of control. While many people enjoy this feeling, in some it serves only to increase their level of anxiety, not to reduce it. For these individuals the therapeutic effect of the drug is not strong enough to overcome the side effects of anxiety.

There are two reasons that individuals with severe trust issues will not become addicts. First, they have not developed the conflict between trust and love that creates the emotional conflict which requires medication. Second, they are very Safety and Security conscious. The disorientation of the drug will increase their feelings of being out of control, feelings that they do not like. They will not become addicts.

Referring back to our theoretical group of TD children that we are following to adulthood, there will also be some who adequately resolve their Safety and Security Needs issues and healthily move on to the higher Need levels. These children become normal healthy adults without TD. They will not become addicts.

There is however a middle group, a group sitting somewhere in-between the TD children who make little emotional progress and evolve into severe TD adults, and the TD children who make significant emotional progress and overcome their TD as adults. This group of individuals who move partly toward health but do not make it all the way, are the candidates for drug abuse and addiction. They are the ones with unresolved issues from the Safety and Security Needs that block their moving up and being able to fully enjoy the potential pleasure and satisfaction that can derive from their Belonging and Love Needs being fulfilled. They do evolve some Belonging and Love Needs that emotionally nag at them throughout life for fulfillment.

The Emotional Loneliness of the Addictive Personality

Because trust is such an issue for TD adults, the relationships they enter into often dissolve with time: They develop no true deep long-term emotional bonds with others.

Feeling alone for extended periods of time, being aware that other people are making emotional connections left and right, watching movies that depict the ease with which people appear to form loving relationships: these are all reminders that serve to make the individuals with an addictive personality very much aware that there is something missing in them emotionally, that they are left out, and that they are thus somehow defective. Since they do not experience the joy that "normal" people experience, they feel like they have a hole in themselves, and what was supposed to be in that hole is missing. They feel empty and they want that emptiness filled.

The loneliness is real, and it is consuming because it will not go away. These individuals have an emotional disability that makes forming strong emotional bonds nearly impossible. To make matters worse, we live in a culture that has many reminders built into it that will not let them forget their loneliness. Just like the torment of the starving man who is allowed to see and smell food but is not allowed to partake, consider the torment of the lonely man who witnesses all the cultural signals that serve to remind him of his situation.

We are all being barraged with the myriad of movies, books, television shows, and commercials that all tout the pleasures of romance and true love. They are pervasive in our culture, and if we are lonely they do not let us ignore our loneliness. Most of our secular holidays have a family, belonging, and love theme to them. Then there is Valentine's Day, which is dedicated solely to lovers. Consider how the holidays often bring on depression and sadness, a time when people should be rejoicing and happy. Why do the holidays bring on the opposite effect of what they are supposed to bring? Because for some people they only serve to remind them of what is missing in their lives, namely belonging and love. They do not fill the hole, and they force these individuals to examine their emptiness.

Individuals without TD issues should be able to appreciate this part of TD people's pain. Most everyone has at some point in his or her life felt really alone and knows the same feeling of loneliness that the individual with TD feels most of the time. Even with other people all around, they are still very lonely.

The individuals are functioning somewhere between their Safety and Security Needs and their Belonging and Love Needs. They have unmet and unresolved Safety and Security Needs that directly interfere with being able to meet their Belonging and Love Needs. These individuals are chronically dealing with two Need levels that demand satisfaction while the nature of their demands are directly at odds with each other. One Need level dictates not to trust others because people cannot be trusted, while the other Need level dictates that they should trust others, fall in love, and be close to them. These individuals are truly stuck on the horns of a dilemma.

A further twist to the model that I have not previously considered is the conflict between the intellectual part of our brain and the emotional part. If our intellect is telling us that our emotional inability to trust is irrational, and that we should ignore our emotions and enter into a transferal relationship for which we are really not emotionally ready, then we have yet another source of conflict and pain.

Variations on Addiction

The individuals who suffer from this internal emotional conflict that I have been talking about clearly want relief. So far I have concentrated on the use of alcohol or drugs as the source of their possible relief. Are there other ways to get relief? The answer of course is yes: the individuals can get relief by just engaging in activities that do not allow them to think about their problems. They can forget their worries by distracting themselves.

A common way they can distract themselves from their emotional pain is to become a workaholic. Submerging themselves into a job or any other activity can be a way of occupying themselves to the point of not having time to think about their negative emotions. Plus—work and other activities can lead to all kinds of interactive situations that can marginally satisfy a need for connection.

Other individuals may throw themselves into hobbies, physical exercise, running, charity work, etc. These are all things that are very nice, but they usually throw themselves into these activities with such intensity that their lives seem out of balance. These people are probably using the activity to distract themselves from their emotional pain.

Sometimes you will see a mixture of drug or alcohol abuse in addition to such distracting activities. Consider the intense businessmen who come home late from work then get sloshed every night. Weekends, like clockwork, they might head straight for the golf course, followed by a drinking session with their buddies in the clubhouse. With their intense business drive, these individuals are often financially quite successful, make big salaries, and have big houses; but because of their emotional dilemma from which they are running, they find little true happiness.

The problem with using drugs instead of work to soothe their pain, is that drugs, though they do alleviate the pain, also limit these individuals' ability to fit into society, frequently interfere with their ability to support themselves, limit their ability to drive automobiles, or to maintain their relationships they do have. These people become a burden and a danger to the rest of us. Workaholics, on the other hand, help our economic system to produce more goods and services and end up indirectly benefiting the rest of us (except for the people who have to live with them).

Nature Versus Nurture, Is There a Genetic Component?

It is not always clear to lay people what researchers mean when they suggest there is a genetic component of addiction or alcoholism. There are two different possibilities. First, it could suggest a direct relationship: that there exists a gene or genes that would cause an individual's body to crave or need alcohol. Once the body experiences alcohol, this gene causes a strong signal to be sent to the brain that it wants more. Or perhaps it suggests the converse, that individuals *lack* a gene that allows for self-regulation, and that it is the lack of this self-regulating gene that explains their inability to drink alcohol in moderation.

Second, it is possible that the research suggests an indirect relationship between our genetic make-up and addiction. Perhaps there can exist a gene or genes that predispose an individual to the type of personality characteristics that are commonly seen in addictive personalities, and that those personality characteristics would then predispose the individual to addiction.

Much research has been done in this area and we can say without equivocation, based on epidemiological studies, that there is a genetic component to alcoholism.[4] Epidemiological studies can only indicate the presence of a genetic component, they can not differentiate between a direct cause or an indirect cause.

It seems apparent that there is a genetic component to personality, and what I mean by this is that the relative importance of the different Need levels (or the amount of satisfaction required to satisfy each Need level) can genetically vary from individual to individual. Maslow never said everyone needs the exact same level of satisfaction of Safety and Security to achieve trust. He never claimed that we all have the same innate capacities for Love and Belonging or Esteem. He simply described a systematic method in which Needs manifest themselves. Still, we are all different, and some of those differences most certainly are a result of our having diverse and unique genes. It follows that if we receive our genes from our parents, then we will probably inherit some personality characteristics from them. In this way, there is likely an indirect genetic component for addiction.

Even when present this indirect genetic component is not strong enough, however, to sentence children to a life of alcohol or drug abuse. It may make them more difficult to raise requiring more and better nurturing, but it will not condemn them to a life of addiction.

What many researchers are looking for today is a direct casual relationship between a gene or a specific set of genes and addiction. As of yet no gene or conversely no lack of a gene (lack of a gene meaning a person missing a gene that prevents alcoholism versus having a gene that causes alcoholism) has been found that would predispose an individual to drug addiction or alcohol.

If such a gene or the converse lack of a gene is ever found, expect it to be headline news; you will most definitely hear about it. Drug and alcohol addiction is a major problem in the world today, and many people suffer from it, including famous and very powerful people. The pressure to turn it into a "good" disease rather than a "bad" disease is intense. Of course there is no such thing as a "good" disease, but if you must have a disease, at least let it be one that you can battle honorably and discuss at any cocktail party. You can talk about your hernia operation or your horrible experiences with your latest root canal at a cocktail party, but you would not bring up your latest bout of depression or schizophrenia. Mental illness in this country is still a disease to be hidden and denied.

If it were found to be true that addictive personality resulted from the presence of a bad gene or from the lack of a good gene, the outcome would be the same: alcoholism would become a genetically based disease, and future research would target correcting that genetic deficiency. Furthermore, all social stigma associated with alcoholism would be removed since the disease would be taken out of the mental illness category. This would make many people very happy.

A gene that predisposes us to addiction has not been found. The evidence that such a gene may exist is wholly based on studies that purport a statistically significant correlation between individuals with similar genes and the incidence of addiction.

The first studies to show such a correlation were conducted using the offspring of alcoholics. There is no doubt that the children of alcoholics are at four times the risk of becoming alcoholics than children of non-alcoholics.[5] While this finding was interesting, it did not support the gene theory because, even though the children share their parents' genes, they are also raised by their parents, so they also share their parents' culture and environment, so it is far from obvious which caused their higher risk for addictive behavior, nature or nurture.

Then came the idea of studying children separated from their addictive parents at birth and raised in a "normal" environment. The problem with this approach is that we do not raise those children in a so-called "normal" environment. They are put into foster care or adoption, which, while it can be very good, is not "normal."

Then came the numerous twin studies but there again the children were not always separated immediately at birth but later. Finding a population of identical twins separated immediately at birth is very difficult. Not all researchers have considered this significant but Bowlby has shown that it is. Environment, even in the first weeks of life, can influence an individual's later personality. Unless the twins are separated immediately at birth they do share some of the same environment.

It has been far easier to prove and is considered conclusive that environment is a major factor in risk of alcoholism.[6]

Studies abound but they still have not shown addictive personality from a molecular biological standpoint to be directly genetic. The model that I present is robust. It makes such sense that I do not see any need to dwell on a genetic component to addiction.

I am saying that addiction is primarily a mental illness or mental disability caused mostly by environment, and not primarily a genetic disorder. That is a pretty powerful and controversial statement. Addiction is so common in our society and touches so many people's lives either directly or indirectly, and the idea of having mental illness is so painful, that it does not surprise me that we as a society have decided to blame it on genes. The gene theory takes away all the social stigmas of having a mental disorder, and instead it becomes a condition, like diabetes. Either way, of course, whether or not it is genetic disorder or a mental disorder, the person has a problem. But we as a society hold people who battle genetic flaws in high regard. We treat their conquering or controlling their condition as a true sign of strength, and we hold them up as examples of heroes for our young.

I think that the genetic theory of addiction and alcoholism is just a culture in denial. Of all the current studies none purport genes to be the primary cause of alcoholism. If down the road addiction turns out to be primarily genetic (and I mean more than the genetic factors that influence personality) then I will be humbled, but unless that happens (and I doubt that it will), we as a society need to work with the best model we have to date, and that model is not a genetic one. The sooner we acknowledge a non-genetic model, the sooner we can quit pretending that alcoholism is something that it is not, and get on with the process of finding true healing solutions.

That begs the question: are there any true healing solutions for drug addiction? That really depends on how you define a solution. Currently the thinking is that once you are an alcoholic, you are always an alcoholic. You can never touch the stuff again in your life. You must always abstain. If you do use it, even if it is just to have a little drink socially, you will invariably slide back into addiction. In other words, you do not become a non-alcoholic; you become a *recovering* alcoholic. A recovering alcoholic is an alcoholic who is no longer using alcohol. The current solution for recovery is to never drink or use drugs again.

Is it possible that we might be able to heal those people who are addicted so that they would no longer need alcohol or other drugs to ease the emotional pain as I have previously discussed? If we could do that, then they could become just like all the rest of us who drink alcohol socially without abusing it. They would also benefit in many other ways too, such as being able to enter into intimate relationships without becoming anxious over losing control, being more competent at the give and take involved in a marriage, developing their higher level Needs, and being free of the internal conflicts that I claim plague the person with an addictive personality. Why not go for a real cure, not just a Band-Aid?

I do think that it can be done. I believe that with a better understanding of the etiology of addiction (and I like to think that this book will contribute to that understanding), that programs can be tailored to address the addict's real issue, which I suggest is trust. The individual is going to have to admit to having a problem, and he is going to have to want to change. Given these conditions, I think it possible that a real cure can be had.

I do not have any kind of personal dislike of a genetic theory for addiction other than I think that it has become an emotional crutch for many addicts, friends, and family members of addicts. It allows them to deny responsibility for addiction and deflect any kind of stigma that would be attached to it if it is considered a mental disorder. The genetic theory is holding us back from really helping these individuals. I understand and sympathize with their need for denial. However the longer we hypothesize that genetics causes addiction, and the longer we pursue a search for that nasty elusive gene at the expense of real understanding, the longer we avoid making real progress toward a cure. We spend too much time, energy, and money looking for the lost ball in the wrong playground.

In thinking over this whole controversial issue, a thought occurred to me: a way that we might quickly dispense with this nagging questions about the genetic theory so that we can, as a society, redirect our research efforts to be more effective. I would like to propose yet another study: if one could find a population of individuals who were true addicts who later went on to become non-addicts, who could drink and stop just like anyone else, that would prove the viability of a non-genetic theory which, at minimum, could coexist alongside a genetic theory. If you have a gene for alcoholism or other drug addiction, then you could hardly argue that that gene would disappear with time. If it is genetic, then the gene is always in you, and you can never change its effects on your composition. Finding a population of individuals who have changed would not eliminate, but would severely undermine the genetic argument.

I know people who fit that category, people who have changed; but admittedly, my evidence is anecdotal, and my clinical observations are unscientific. It would be interesting, however.

Characteristics of the Addictive Personality

The addictive personality has the same personality traits as the trust disorder child. With age, they are able to soften some of the rough edges that are seen in the child, but essentially they are just adults with trust disorder. As such, we would expect them to have similar traits to the child with TD, which would include:

- Control Freak
- Never Admitting to Being Wrong
- Lying
- Manipulation
- Master Negotiator
- Denigration
- Reduced Empathy and Maturity
- Charming When You First Meet Them

See Chapter 6 (Behavioral Characteristics of Transferal Trust Disorder) for a complete discussion of these traits and their underlying causes.

I have always been confused by the situations where a person cheats on his or her spouse, and then goes on to profess true love and faithfulness, and then the spouse takes him or her back. If you cheat even once, the trust is gone. Even if you do not get caught you know the trust is gone. I can only assume that these relationships to begin with were never built on trust.

Conclusions

My definition of an addictive personality is an individual with some sort of long-term emotional pain, a deep-seated pain which gives a sense of hopelessness in terms of ever being resolved. As such, they can only see drugs or total immersion in some distracting activity as a solution. My model for addictive personality has TD as the most common source of that emotional pain. There are certainly other sources, such as poverty, chronic unemployment, long-term illness, any long-term situation that creates emotional distress, but in mainstream American culture, the most common source is TD.

My model can be summarized as follows:

- The infant learns to mistrust or does not learn to trust others due to a breakdown of Bowlby's attachment cycle.
- The infant evolves into an adult who mistrusts others.
- The adult progresses enough emotionally to develop some Belonging and Love Needs, which results in loneliness.
- Because of unresolved Safety and Security Needs (as indicated by lack of trust), the adult cannot form good interpersonal relationships.
- The adult ping-pongs between relationships and no relationships, feeling alternately anxious and lonely without either emotion ever going away entirely.
- The adult uses some form or combination of drugs and/or work to ease their emotional pain.

Before leaving this topic, I should emphasize the effect of alcohol on individuals who allow themselves to love deeply, who are involved in good relationships, and who truly enjoy the good emotions that come from being close to other people. Drugs blunt the emotions. The individuals in this situation are going to lose something when they drink too much. They will lose something from which they derive a great deal of enjoyment, and they are going to lose good feelings. There is not a chance in the world that they will routinely use drugs; it would totally degrade the quality of their lives (unless, of course their body contains a defective gene that will drive them to drink).

Sometimes parents will share a concern with me that their son or daughter is living in a society rampant with drugs and alcohol, and they worry that their child might become a drug or alcohol abuser. Occasionally they fear also that the child might be experimenting with drugs with peers. If I know their child, I will do an assessment of what I feel to be the child's ability to care, love, and to connect with others; and often I will see the parents' concerns as unfounded. Their child just is not a candidate for chronic drug or alcohol abuse; he or she would just lose too many good emotions.

I would consider changing the name of Alcohol Dependence[7] to Alcohol Dependence Secondary to Adult Trust Disorder. Why change the name? Because this new name emphasizes the underlying cause of the problem (trust disorder), which helps the patient, the patient's family, friends, and healthcare providers to better understand, deal with, and treat the patient's condition.

I Saw Her Again
(Denis Doherty & John Phillips)

I saw her again Last Night and you know that I shouldn't
Just string her along it's just not right If I couldn't I wouldn't

. . .

I'm in way over my head now she thinks that I love her
Because that's what I said though I never think of her

Notes

[1] Watson, *Psychological Care of Infant and Child*, 1928, pp. 75–76.
[2] Thomas, *When Love Is Not Enough*, 1997, p. 22.
[3] Molina & Pelham, "Childhood Predictors of Adolescent Substance Use in a Longitudinal Study of Children With ADHD," *Journal of Abnormal Psychology*, 2003, Vol. 112, No 3, PP. 497–507.

[4] Prescott, Carol A., Ph.D.; Kendler, Kenneth S. M.D. Genetic and Environmental Contributions to Alcohol Abuse and Dependence in a Population-Based Sample of Male Twins. American Journal of Psychiatry: 1999. Vol. 156. Pp. 34–40.
[5] http://www.aacap.org/publications/factsfam/alcoholc.htm.
[6] Theodore Jacob, Ph.D; Brian Waterman, MPH; Andrew Heath, Ph.D; William True, Ph.D, MPH; Kathleen K. Bucholz, Ph.D; Randy Haber, Ph.D; Jeff Scherrer, MA; Qiang Fu, MD, Ph.D. *Genetic and Environmental Effects on Offspring Alcoholism: New Insights Using an Offspring-of-Twins Design.* Archives of General Psychiatry. 2003, Vol. 60 pp. 1265–1272.
[7] Code 303.90 in the *Diagnostic and Statistical Manual of Mental Disorders*, Fourth Edition.

Section II
Practice

9

Introduction to Practice

Before moving forward with the specifics of how to repair the TD child, I want to recap what I have spoken about thus far because it is important to understand the theory behind the problem if one is to do something about it. The most important part of the theory can be summarized as follows:

- As an infant, the child learns to mistrust or does not learn to trust others per a breakdown of Bowlby's attachment cycle.
- With little trust in others, the child attempts to run his own life.
- Adults perceive the child's attempts to run his own life as defiance.
- The child and his caregivers become locked in a control battle.
- The child makes little or no emotional progress toward developing his Belonging and Love Needs and Esteem Needs according to Maslow's Hierarchy of Needs.

Repairing the child is simple: all you have to do is get him to trust you.[1] OK, in theory understanding what needs to be done is simple, but there is nothing simple or easy from a practical standpoint about what needs to be done to develop that trust. It is much work and requires time, persistence, and loads of compassion and love. And it does not stop with simply developing trust, because after you develop it (and the attachment that will more or less follow), you still have to help the child learn the other emotional lessons that all children must learn. There are many things that a child needs to learn to become a healthy adult, and even though your child might be ten years old, he is almost at day one emotionally. First you are going to have to undo the damage caused by an infancy wrought with bad emotional lessons, a daunting task in itself. In addition to this, you must re-teach him all the good emotional lessons he should have been receiving from infancy. The TD child has fallen behind, and has a way to go before catching up.

You are often going to be doing this repair work in the face of criticism from friends and families, because people just do not understand what you are up against, why the child acts the way he does, and why you do not just force him to behave and cooperate. There are rewards, though, and at times the child will surprise you with little displays of appreciation that will be totally unexpected and make it worthwhile.

Trust is the first thing that we need to address before we concern ourselves with any other issue. There are many books that suggest techniques for repairing the child, and I am also going to suggest some of my own that seem to work. Do not be surprised if some of the techniques that help to develop trust seem to be at odds with other seemingly age-appropriate lessons that you think the child should be learning. You have only one main lesson in the beginning, one that takes precedence over all other lessons: to teach the child that you are someone whom he can legitimately trust, and that if he trusts you then things will go better in his life. If other lessons are at odds with this one, they will just have to wait.

The first thing you need to consider before even starting to work with the child is enlisting as many allies as you can in the campaign to repair the TD child. If the child is a foster child, and a parent or other extended family members are still in the picture, perhaps with visitations, you should try to get them on your side. You are going to try to get them to trust you, and that will do a lot to help you to help the child. If they do not trust you they will certainly telegraph their mistrust to the child, reinforcing his natural tendency to mistrust. If getting the trust of parents and family is not possible, the task of repairing the child is going to be more difficult.

I hypothesize that TD adults often raise TD children (albeit a stereotypical un-researched and unproven hypothesis). It is not a stretch to assume that the natural parents of your TD child have trust concerns of their own. They might even wonder why in the world you would want to take their child into your home and raise him. It is likely that they will assume the worst, that you have some ulterior, selfish motive in raising their child, until you show them otherwise. Before you even start you are an adversary. Commonly natural parents will assume (often an accurate assessment on their part) that you, the foster parent, want to steal their baby from them and keep him as your own. Years ago, contact between the natural parents and the foster parents was limited. Today, that contact is encouraged when it is safe and appropriate. It is through this connection that you can diffuse one of the potential blocks to trust building.

The potential block that I am speaking of is the inability of the natural parent(s) to trust the foster parent(s). I have already said that the child's Needs were not adequately met during the early stages of life, and consequently he has learned to not trust his parent(s). But that does not mean that the child completely discards any credence in the verbal and non-verbal messages the natural parent(s) sends his way. He can still consciously pick up on subconscious clues, and will still listen to what the natural parent(s) tells him. If that is a message of "I don't trust your foster parent(s)," then the TD child will most likely have a problem placing his faith in you. This just adds another obstacle in your path toward repairing the child.

As much as possible, as much as appropriate, and as much as you can, it is important to develop the best relationship feasible with the natural parent(s). At every step of the way it is going to help you to help the child. Plus there is one huge added benefit to having a good relationship with the natural parent(s). If in the end the child becomes reunited with his natural parent(s), there is a good chance that they will allow you to continue being a part of their child's life—but only if they develop trust in you. They, just like any good parent, would never let their child go unsupervised with someone they did not trust. If you never gain the natural parents' trust, then it is unlikely you will be able to continue to be a part of their child's life once he returns to them. Of course, if the child has no contact with his natural parent(s), then you are not going to have contact with them either, and gaining parental trust will not be an issue.

As already stated, in theory fixing the child is easy: you must teach him to trust. You are not going to teach him to trust *everybody*, and you would not want to anyway. You are only going to teach him to trust *you*. That is all that is necessary. Once he learns to trust you, he can transfer that trust to others, just as the healthy baby or child learns to do. If over time you fulfill the four basic rules I am about to describe, the child will get the message that you are a reliable and truthful individual. Remember, even though his outward behavior may suggest that he is primarily concerned with Safety and Security Needs, he still can have Belonging and Love Needs (we hope), and as he matures those Needs will become even stronger. Simply stated, the TD child suffers from a conflict between Safety and Security Needs and Belonging and Love Needs in that he does not yet have the capacity to trust, yet he still needs to trust you both for his survival and to fulfill his Belonging and Love Needs. It is these higher level Needs that will drive him toward healing if you just provide the correct path.

The path that I am offering is a kind and gentle approach, an approach that pulls the child upward toward Maslow's higher levels by giving the child a taste of Belonging and Love while simultaneously in a firm and loving manner lets the child know that you are in control and that he is still safe and secure while you are in control. In a sense my approach pushes the child out of Safety and Security while at the same time pulls him into Belonging and Love.

There are other paths that you can follow to heal your child, paths that also work, and there may be times that they would be more appropriate than the path proposed in this book.

Later in this book I am going to suggest that holding plays a strong role in the treatment of the TD child and that it should be used liberally. I am going to suggest that the reason it is so effective is because if satisfies all of Maslow's Need levels. There is a major problem with holding the child who has passed through puberty and has a drastically increased sex drive. Holding this older child can have sexual overtones. Psychologists classify the sex drive as belonging to Maslow's lowest level Physiological Needs. My concept of pulling the child up Maslow's Hierarchy is to feed into his higher level Needs in order to stimulate and develop them. If holding the child is stimulating his sex drive, as it may in a child who has reached puberty, then holding may in fact pull the child down the Hierarchy rather than up the Hierarchy. Down, being the wrong direction, is counterproductive to our goal of growing the child emotionally.

Once the child has passed through puberty a major tool, holding the child, is effectively removed from your armamentarium, treatment becomes more difficult with fewer options. The "Push-Pull" approach that I am going to present might not work in the older, more severely afflicted TD child.

There are going to be times when the child is just too damaged for a full cure approach, or the caregivers just do not have the time, energy, skills, or commitment for a full cure approach. As mentioned, perhaps the child is too old for all of the techniques that I propose to be appropriate or valuable. There are times when we need to compromise, times when we accept success as just raising an individual who can meet his basic obligations and responsibilities as an adult without creating too much havoc in other peoples' lives (for example staying out of jail and/or not leaving a trail of fatherless babies).

I set a pretty high goal in this book. I strive for complete repair; a child who does not use drugs as an adult, who has the capacity to experience the full range of human emotions, who develops deep and lasting relationships with life-time commitments, and who in Maslow's terms may even become Self-Actualized.

There are two other approaches to repairing the child that need to be considered. Neither of these set the same high goal standard of my Push-Pull technique. For some children they will be more appropriate, or they may be the only options available.

The first is the boot-camp approach. The boot-camp approach severely challenges the child directly at the Safety and Security level. Drill-sergeant type individuals strip the child (or recruit) of all sense of self, remove all sense of control, and make it abundantly clear to the child that, fair or not, he has little or no control over his life. Life becomes unpredictable. Instructors may yell one time and not another. Punishment is often unfair, excessive, and arbitrary. Once the child is demoralized and depersonalized, then a sense of Safety and Security is offered to the child in the form of rigid structure in exchange for the child's relinquished control of his life. The child is in such need of Safety and Security that he will willingly agree to relinquish control to get it.

Many formalized programs employ this technique to shape individuals into "good soldiers." Place stress on the individual to the point where his internal defenses break, then offer him the Safety and Security of the group with the only requirement that he buys into the values and code of conduct of the group and is willing to follow the rules of the group.

It works. Extreme programs, such as the military, either get the outcome they want or kill the individual in the process. The less extreme programs still can point to high success rates.

Some programs, such as Tough Love, appreciate that they cannot legally and morally run a program that actively places stress on a child and subsequently breaks him. They achieve the same result, though, by getting the parents to stop enabling and supporting their child, letting him "hit rock bottom" on his own. The parents are told that if they love their child, then they must kick the child out of their home. They must inform the child that the only way he will ever be allowed back in their home is if he participates in the Tough Love program. The parents are told to quit bailing him out of jail, paying his fines, covering his debts, and providing resources for the child to follow his life style. When things get bad enough, the child is meant to follow his parents' orders and seek out the Tough Love program. He will then live with one of its counselors. His counselor will indoctrinate him with the values and morals of the group.

"Rock bottom" often occurs when all support has been removed from the child. Left completely on his own things often get bad. The parents' enabling behavior allowed the child's controlling behavior to work. The child thought he was in control—and in a sense he was, because he had learned to effectively manipulate his parents in a way such that the consequences of his poor decisions were always deflected away from the child by his parents.

With his parents' shield removed, the consequences of his bad decisions fall directly on the child's shoulders. Ultimately life becomes miserable. He experiences a complete sense of loss of Safety and Security. The child is so stressed out at the Safety and Security level that he is willing to do what was previously unthinkable to get back some Safety and Security into his life. The child appreciates that his being in control is no longer working. He is willing to give up control, if in fact he sees no other option other than giving up control in order to regain a sense of Safety and Security. He is literally forced to trust—most likely for the first times in his life.

No one will doubt that our military produces competent and compliant soldiers able to follow commands and execute complex and precision instructions even when they do not understand or question the intent or validity of their orders. They trust their superiors even if they have doubts. They are programmed and trained to trust.

The military boot-camp approach is a very cost effective, efficient, and predictable way of producing individuals who will obey orders even under threat of death or harm. So why not use this approach as our first choice in repairing the TD child? Because for all its successes in producing trusting like behavior, it does not encourage movement up Maslow's Hierarchy. In fact, in order to keep its fighting machine tough and strong, it really encourages locking its individuals in a Safety and Security mindset. We do not need lovers on the battlefield, we need soldiers. The entire role of the military in any society is totally based in Safety and Security.

If possible we want more for our TD child; we want him to grow emotionally. We will not use this approach as our first approach, but will also not rule it out if our first approach fails or just seems to stall.

Besides the Tough Love programs, Outward Bound employs a mild form of this technique. There are a variety of programs that seem to have come out of Colorado that employ variations on holding bordering on restraint which reportedly have had success. I have had no personal experience with these techniques or programs and consequently cannot either advocate or condemn them.

The second of the two approaches that I made reference to above depends on the intellectual capacity of the child. After puberty holding therapy perhaps becomes inappropriate. As the child grows older we lose that major and valuable tool but we hopefully gain another, the child's intellectual capacity grows and we can possible use that to our advantage.

With this technique we use the child's innate need to manipulate others along with his increased intellectual awareness, to show the child that there are more effective ways to manipulate others than outright confrontation. We teach him to say nice things, behave in socially appropriate ways, give presents at appropriate times, to do all the little things expected of adults, and on an intellectual basis he learns that by behaving in these ways he achieves greater success in social situations.

As devious and superficial as it may sound, every parent uses this technique to some extent in raising their children. Unless Johnny says the magic word (just in case you do not know the magic word, it is "please"), he cannot have what he is asking for. Is it not superficial to have the child say "please" with every request even if he is thinking, "Give it to me right now, darn it!" Would not it be better for the child to *feel* some consideration for others rather than to be just programmed to act considerate of others? This approach to child raising is extended to many other behaviors such as: writing thank-you notes, apologizing when you do not really mean it, saying hello to people you do not like, standing in lines, picking up his trash, cooperation in general.

115

Of course it would be better for the child to feel so truly grateful for receiving something that he would jump to the opportunity to genuinely and faithfully always show his gratitude by adding kind and thoughtful words such as "please" and "thank you" to each and every request, but we as adults accept that they will first be taught to add these words on an intellectual basis, through the repeated drill of being asked "what's the magic word," and we do this drill hoping that the underlying emotion will someday follow.

Many of the programs that treat addictive behaviors use an intellectual approach to repairing the adult. They do not truly repair the individuals emotional deficit, what they do is teach the individual appropriate behaviors to live in society. A small example would be teaching a husband to purposefully write a reminder of his wife's birthday on his calendar so that he will be sure to bring home a present and a card and not forget it. A seemingly small thing—but not to the spouse who's birthday is forgotten. The emotional cure, teaching the addict to care enough about his wife to never forget a birthday is too difficult to achieve. They are intellectually taught to behave in ways that make them appear to be caring.

On an intellectual basis you can teach a person to trust. You can point out controlling behavior and give the individual exercises to relinquish control. Over time a person can learn that he does not need to be in control to be Safe and Secure. A lot can be done to change an individual using an intellectual approach, it is a very powerful tool. With time and effort emotional basis can be changed. The intellectual approach is the basis for psychoanalysis. There is only one major problem with using an intellectual approach for changing somebody, and that is they have to *want to change*. The intellectual approach will not work if the individual does not want to change.

Many behavioral management techniques are based on an intellectual approach to change. The desired behavior is identified and points are awarded when the behavior is achieved. The child is rewarded when he reaches a certain point total goal. The child intellectually decides that the reward is valuable enough for him to work for it by cooperating with the desired behavior. Failure always occurs as a result of the child choosing not to cooperate, not to change.

The rest of this book if devoted to an approach that I will call the "Push-Pull" technique. You push the child out of the Safety and Security level by both satisfying all his Safety and Security Needs and forcing him to be aware of the fact he is trusting you to satisfy those Needs, that the satisfaction is not a result of his controlling behavior as he previously believes; and you pull him into the Love and Belonging level by stimulating his emotions in this area causing them to grow and ultimately pull him up the Hierarchy. You push from below and pull from above at the same time.

Any technique that you employ that does not foster trust will not be helping the child. Letting the child live on in your house and continue with his controlling behavior is ultimately not going to help him grow emotionally. Allowing a child or person to be controlling of you is enabling. Being enabling does not help the child to grow. You cannot depend on time itself to heal the child. It will not; you must not let the child manipulate or control you.

Good luck. I hope the Push-Pull technique works for your TD child, because it affords your child with the greatest chance for emotional growth. If your child is older I appreciate you might have to resort to one of the other mentioned techniques. But do use a thought out trust building technique, do not just shuffle along from day to day dealing only with behavioral issues without some plan for developing the child's ability to trust, and do not expect him to trust you just because you are trustworthy, it will not happen, it just is not enough.

Horse Breaking

I am not any kind of expert on horses, but from reading and watching movies I recall that there are two ways of taming a horse. I present this analogy because taming a horse is all about teaching the horse to give up control and trust having a rider on its back.

First, there is the quick way where a rider gets on the horse's back and breaks the horse by forcing the horse into submission. Then there is the slower, but far gentler way, where the horse is slowly introduced to the saddle and then to having a rider in the saddle.

I see the harsh breaking of the horse as analogous to the boot-camp technique and the slower gentler trust building technique as being analogous to my Push-Pull technique.

Notes

[1] Greenspan, Stanley I., M.D., *The Challenging Child*, 1995, p. 135.

10

The Four Rules of the Push-Pull Technique

I have spoken a great deal thus far about how important it is that you, the caregiver, gain the child's trust if you expect to help him; but have not said how you should go about doing so. These rules do exactly that, and as such are the most important part of this book. They are the elements you need in order to provide the proper environment for the child's emotional growth.

- **Rule number one: Supply all his needs.** This rule may seem obvious, but be sure that you include love as one of his basic needs. For the most part, it is likely that the child outwardly exhibits Safety and Security Need level behaviors (is functioning at the Safety and Security level: defiant, angry, and controlling). Even though he may not exhibit Belonging and Love Needs, you should assume that he would respond positively to affection and give it to him anyway (Belonging and Love is his highest significant Need level).

  Though I doubt anyone would disagree with this rule, people often do not think beyond the child's Physiological and Safety, and Security Needs. This is because the angry, defiant, controlling child just does not seem to want or need love. Most children with TD are going to be functioning at the Safety and Security Need level but with significant latent Belonging and Love Needs, so even though you do not see his need for love, it is still there.

  Whatever the case may be, whatever level the child is functioning on, it is your task to figure out how to help him fulfill all his needs. As you probably suspect, there is not going to be a "one size fits all" solution to the repair puzzle. The most critical aspect of supplying all of the child's needs is how you go about fulfilling the child's *highest* significant Need level. As I said, usually this will be the Belonging and Love level.

Maslow wrote about how lower level Needs must be satisfied before higher ones emerge in importance, however not everyone who fills lower levels moves up to higher level Needs. Part of the parenting process is to work a little ahead of the child in helping them to develop all of their latent Needs, to pull them up to higher levels. Giving them a taste of the next level will spur them on to move toward that level. In other words, in addition to fully providing for the Safety and Security of a child who is primarily seeking the Needs for that level, you should also provide that child with love to urge him upward to the next level.

Just as an aside: if you happen to have a child who is functioning primarily at the Belonging and Love level (probably not your TD child), for this child, in addition to giving him love, give him praise to urge him upward to the Esteem level. My point is, while you are always working to satisfy the child's functioning level, at the same time, make an effort to feed into his next higher level. This helps any child to grow emotionally.

It is not unusual for a person to spend his entire life trying (with mixed success) to master the Safety and Security Need level, or the Belonging and Love Need level. And unless the child is unusually intelligent, he probably will not surpass the highest Need level of his primary caregivers.

Avoid skipping a Need level: this will not be helpful to the child. For example, if a child is hungry, in addition to providing food, you would also want to address the next Need level, which is Safety and Security. Give him food, and assure him that there will be more when that is gone. His need for love is too remote at this point for him to respond to affection.

The TD child will usually be controlling, manipulative, combative, argumentative, and defiant, all behaviors that stem from a lack of trust. In addition to addressing the child's issues of trust directly, you also need to provide him with love and a feeling of belonging. This does not mean that he needs compliments to build his esteem. Do not skip a level; he will misinterpret compliments as an attempt to manipulate him. Evaluate his

119

behavior, address the Needs from the level that you determine is motivating his behavior, and also address the Needs that are one level higher than his current behavior.

- **Rule number two: Be trustworthy.** The value of this rule is obvious: Nobody is going to trust another who lies, or whom he feels is deceptive and manipulative. If you say you are going to do something, be sure you do it. Do not lure the TD child into the car with a promised trip to the mall, only to end up at the dentist. If the child learns through your example that you are trustworthy, then he will be spurred on to put his trust in you.

- **Rule number three: Be sure the child knows that he is trusting you (i.e. that you are in control).** I originally phrased this as "place the child in a situation where he must trust you," but that is wrong. Like it or not, the child must trust you, and even if he does not know it he is already in that position. Unless he lives on the streets and is hustling for existence, the child is by necessity trusting someone. However the child must be made aware of the fact that you are in control, that he is in a sense at your mercy. He must *know* that he is trusting you. If the child can get away with lots of little things, he may not realize that you ultimately control the big decisions. When he is both very much aware that 1) things are going well for him and 2) you—not he—are responsible for, and in control of, the good things that are happening in his life, only then will he realize that it is safe to give up control and trust you. He will not voluntarily give up control of his life, and you are going to have to wrestle it away from him. The TD child cannot learn to trust unless you do in fact wrestle control away from him so that he has some experiences where he has trusted somebody. Trusted somebody who did not take advantage of him, ignore him, or use him for their own purposes. He needs to see that all can turn out well even when he is not in control. In this sense, learning to trust is like learning to ride a bicycle, you have to do it to learn it. Unlike learning to ride a bicycle, he is not willingly going to want to learn to trust (some children do not willingly learn to ride a bicycle either).

Few human beings are readily going to give up control. The TD child can be very manipulative, and his awareness of who is really in control can be distorted. He sees the day-to-day control battles as defining who is in control, and he misses the big picture. If all is well in his life while at the same time he is winning the predominance of little battles for control, he will think that things are going nicely in his life because of his being in control. He sees it as if you are a puppet and he is pulling your strings which of course is the reason he thinks why things are going well, all the while still never learning to trust. Things that go well when he feels he is in control will only reinforce his need to have the advantage at all times.

Often people will give into the so-called "bratty child" on numerous small issues because it is easier than fighting with him. The child becomes used to being in control, and sees himself in charge. What I am describing here is defiant, manipulative, controlling behavior on the child's part. Sometimes when the parent does make a decision, he or she may act as if a third party is forcing that decision upon them. For example, if a child is running around a public swimming pool, you might tell him not to do so because the lifeguard says that it is dangerous since he could slip and hurt himself. In this example, the lifeguard would be the third party forcing the restriction upon him. This action, of using other people as authority figures instead of yourself, diminishes your control in a misguided attempt to avoid some of the child's anger. Obviously the parents do not let the child make every decision, but the child probably does not pick up on the quality of the decisions that he is making, never realizing that he is only winning the minor battles, so he sees himself as winning the majority of all battles and thus feels that he is in control.

There are some obvious reasons for not tolerating "bratty behavior." The child does not grow socially, and he retains the self-centeredness of the baby or infant. While this is true, there is another very important lesson that is lost on this child, one that he needs and is not getting: He never learns to trust his caregivers because he is never made to feel dependent upon them (despite the fact that he is). He will have situational trust, but will not develop transferal trust. In order to learn to trust,

121

he has to experience and practice it, just like any other skill. Only when he has experienced trusting on his own will he become comfortable being in a relationship where he is in a position of dependence on others.

In summary, somehow you have to force the child to be aware of the fact that you are in control, and that he is not. It is imperative that the child learns that he is dependent upon you.

- **Rule number four: Be emotionally strong.** No one would trust his welfare to somebody who is weaker.[1] Strength does not define a set of actions, but a state of being. For example, being physically strong means that you have large, well-developed muscles, but it has nothing to do with how you *use* those muscles. Being emotionally strong means that you have a well-developed and mature emotional base. You know your strengths, weaknesses, limitations, and your hot buttons. You also have control and understanding of your emotions. It does *not* mean that you are rigid or dogmatic, controlling, or judgmental. If anything, it means just the opposite of these things. Here again, your strength is a signal to the child that you are someone with whom he can trust his life.

    Dr. James Dobson in his book, *The Strong-Willed Child*, says of parents who do not "Respond with confident decisiveness," " . . . instead of being secure and confident leaders, they [the parents] become spineless jellyfish who are unworthy of respect or allegiance."

Ideally, the most effective person for repairing the child is the primary caregiver, but often this is the same person who created the problem. However, if the mother, who did not get parenting right in the first couple of years of the child's life when the required skills were simpler, more instinctual, and required less intellect, is she likely to do it later when the task is far more difficult? If she was addicted to drugs in the past, but is now clean and sober, then maybe she could do it. This is an extreme instance, but if I did not think people could change, I would not have written this book.

The primary goal of therapy should be to develop one good attachment in the child's life, one that the child will use to pattern all future good attachments.[2] This attachment is probably not going to be with a therapist, but with the primary caregiver. I do not want to belittle the role of the therapist or traditional therapy, which places emphasis on the relationship between therapist and patient.[3] However, I strongly agree with the notion that much of the therapy should be directed toward supporting the relationship between the primary caregiver and the child, not toward developing a relationship between the therapist and the child. After all, it is the primary caregiver who is going to be instrumental in facilitating the child's repair. Therein lies the source of the problem, and therein lies the best and quickest way to mend the child, even if the child has experienced multiple primary caregivers along the way. Professional therapy should be directed as much toward fixing any parenting deficiencies in the current primary caregiver as toward directly fixing the child.

These four rules present a real dilemma for the primary caregiver. Simply stated, how do you create an environment of peace and love while at the same time fighting (and winning) control battles? Books on attachment disorder discuss both of these elements in great detail, but generally fail to give strategies to balance the two. If either is ignored, treatment will fail. Putting the two together is not simple because you are dealing with two Need levels simultaneously: control battles stem from the child's Safety and Security Need level, while love is part of the Belonging and Love Need level.

Appreciate that the primary goal of this book is to create an understanding of all the elements that go into affecting a therapeutic environment for the TD child; that is to say, to provide the reader with the Four Rules, an understanding of the theory and paradigms that support the Four Rules, and to give the primary caregiver a feeling for the balancing act that is required to create this therapeutic environment. Do not be fooled into thinking that creating a purely rigid, "tough-love" kind of environment is going to solve the TD child's problems. Discipline is not a substitute for love, and it will not satisfy the child's Belonging and Love Needs. Do not be fooled into thinking that you are going to solve the TD child's problems with love alone; without discipline the child will just manipulate and use you. You are going to have to figure out a way to be in control without the household being a constant battleground. You are going to have to figure out how to show love without giving up control.

The typical TD child seems to enjoy argument and confrontation. He feels more comfortable and at home interacting with you if you respond to him on the Safety and Security Need level because that is where he has spent most of his life. He is going to push you, and try to lock you into interacting with him on issues that originate from that level. You are going to have to address his Safety and Security Need level issues, defuse them, and take control in such a way that he sees you as being in charge. Then, you will also have to include some warmth and affection so that the child can both experience and begin to develop the next level of Needs. This is going to take some real skill on your part.

To sum up, the Four Rules for creating a therapeutic environment are the same for all TD children. How you as a caregiver implement the Four Rules to create that environment in your home is going to vary from one person to the next, and from child to child. I like the implementation suggestions that I give, but in all fairness, they work for me partly because of my personality, and they might not work for you. Providing you with specific strategies to implement the Four Rules is a secondary goal, not my primary objective. I want to be helpful, but I appreciate that my strategies might not be the best for you, and I encourage you to read other authors to put together a mix that works for you and your child. But as you formulate your plan for creating a therapeutic environment for your TD child, keep the Four Rules in mind and use them to balance the needed elements. I provide a model for evaluating existing and new ideas. Recognize that this book is mostly about understanding, not treating. Before I launch into the different treatment modalities I want to emphasize that my goal is not to provide you with specific techniques (that are already well-documented by other authors), but to create an understanding of when to use many of the available techniques, to create a rationale for the techniques that work, and a rationale for avoiding others that do not. This book is not intended as a replacement of the preexisting literature, but as a supplement to it.

Speculation on the Four Rules and the Causes of TD

Previously I said that TD is caused by a breakdown in Bowlby's attachment cycle. I claimed that what Bowlby calls attachment is really trust, and suggested that attachment disorder is really trust disorder. I went on to suggest Four Rules to repair the child. They are the elements you need in order to provide the proper environment for the child's emotional growth.

Let's have a little fun with this. I am going to take some liberties with my theory and my model, be a little bold and speculative, and perhaps stick my neck out to see if it gets chopped off.

Let's suppose that the Four Rules are not just rules for creating a therapeutic environment as I have previously stated, but that they are much more. Suppose that following the Four Rules is basic to raising *any* healthy child, that they apply to all children while they are being raised. What if the Four Rules describe the elements that are required for *all* children if they are to attain Transferal Trust?

What this would mean is that a child could develop TD if you violate any one of the Four Rules when raising him. It would mean that there are more ways to create a TD child (not that we would ever intentionally do so) other than a breakdown in the attachment cycle.

First, we have to take what we know to be fact and apply it to this theoretical model and see if it works. We know for a fact that attachment disorder is caused by inconsistent attention to the child's Needs during the first and second years of life. Rule number one says "Supply all his Needs." So far so good; Bowlby and Ainsworth have proven without doubt that if you do not supply all of the child's Needs, he will develop TD. There is no uncertainty in that not fulfilling rule number one will result in a child with TD.

What about rule number two, which says you must be trustworthy? If you routinely manipulate the child, lie to him, or try to trick him into behaving the way you want him to behave, the child will learn that you are not a trustworthy individual. Even if the behavior you are trying to elicit is in the child's best interest (eat carrots, not candy because they are better for you), I think the child will still learn to not place his trust in you as this is still seen as an attempt at manipulation. So rule two thus supports my theory.

Now for rule number three: be sure the child knows that he trusts you (i.e. be in control). This is the toughest rule of all to grasp intellectually, and I feel comfortable in saying that if this rule is not met, you will have a non-trusting (if not an overly controlling) child. Why do I say this? Because there are lots of examples out there to support my claim. Let me explain.

Let me go back to my bicycle analogy. Riding a bicycle can be much fun. Trusting other people with your Safety and Security can be very pleasant too, particularly because it allows you to focus on higher level Needs without anxiety and fear. So far the analogy works.

However, learning to trust, just like learning to ride a bicycle, can be a scary thing. Until you achieve some degree of skill and become somewhat accomplished at riding, there is a real danger of falling and hurting yourself. What actually keeps you from getting up on the bicycle and learning to ride is not the fall or the hurt, but the *fear of the fall and the hurt*. It is the same with learning to trust—it is the fear that keeps you from ever doing it. In both cases, with the bicycle and with trust, if the fear is strong enough you will simply refuse to do it. And in both situations, once you have mastered them, the fear disappears and they become wonderful additions to your life.

In both situations you may have to push the child to get him started on his way to mastery. Now some children will take to a bicycle without any apparent prompting, just as some children will develop transferal trust without any apparent effort on the part of the parent. However, other children need to be pushed and guided, and that is your job as the parent. You know what it takes to push and guide a child to learn how to master riding a bicycle, but what does it take to push and guide a child to learn to trust? This is where it becomes a little difficult conceptually, because it is obvious when a child is riding a bicycle, however, it is not so obvious when a child is trusting you.

Maybe it is simpler to identify when a child does not trust you and go from there. *A child does not trust you when he is in control.* That may be the best I can do for you in terms of helping to identify when your child trusts you and when he does not. If you have a difficult, defiant child who always seems to be testing you, then he is probably not trusting you. Just like the bicycle analogy, it is unlikely that he will ever learn to trust without your push.

I believe that it is possible for you to fulfill the first two rules and still have a child that is controlling and defiant. I believe that this happens because you fail to satisfy Rule number three. Furthermore, I am saying that there are lots of these children around, and their numbers are far greater than those of attachment disorder children. These children are self-centered, manipulative little brats, and they are often being raised by good and caring parents. These are parents who do not drink or use drugs, but instead go to church, attend every little league game, and save diligently for their children's college education. I have written more about this in Chapter 19 (The Brat).

There is much advice bandied about that directly supports my third rule. This is advice such as "do not be a friend to your child be a parent"; "set limits"; "do not be afraid to ask your child where he is going and who he will be with"; set up rules, employ consequences, and be in charge. I have never heard of any of these precepts being forwarded as a way to teach your child to trust, however, that is exactly what they help us to do. It is something that good parents have known intuitively since man has been around on this planet. What I am saying is that there is nothing new or revolutionary about my rule number three; good parents have been doing it forever. What is new is an intellectual understanding of what the advice is supposed to accomplish.

I would argue then, that a child cannot develop trust if you do not satisfy rule number three.

And now the last rule, number four: be emotionally strong. Will the child trust somebody who appears weak? Common sense tells us that we want our leaders to be strong competent individuals, that we will not place our trust in individuals who appear to be easily controlled by others.

What this means is that perhaps you can create a TD child by violating any one of the Four Rules; that maybe there are more ways to create a TD child than just a breakdown in the attachment cycle. It would also mean that maybe this book should have more universal appeal than to just foster and adoptive parents.

I know that I have been playing with the model, and that what I just presented is speculative and unproven, but I like it. I do not think that the children who are missing rule number four will be as severely lacking in trust as the children who are missing rule number one. I have placed the rules in order from what I feel to be most important (rule number one) to least important (rule number four).

Notes

[1] Keck & Kupecky, *Parenting the Hurt Child*, 2002, p. 42.
[2] Thomas, Nancy L., "What is the difference between Attachment therapy and traditional therapies?", http://www.nancythomasparenting.com/Attachtherapy.htm, March 1, 2004
[3] Thomas, Nancy L., *When Love Is Not Enough*, 1997. p. 21.

11

The Repair Cycle

How high do we set the bar for TD children? The bar is a helpful analogy derived from the high jump in track and field. As a jumper gets better he sets the bar higher, thus the expression, "raise the bar." Are we going to start with a low behavioral bar (lower behavioral expectations) for the TD child, or are we going to start the bar at what we might call "normal behavior" from day one? The answer to this depends on which expert you ask. Psychologists specializing in behavior, not surprisingly, tend to place a greater emphasis on behavior than other psychologists and would start the bar at a higher level.

It is improper to set the bar so high that the child is doomed to failure. A child who is always wrong, always failing, never receiving any positive feedback, always being chided for some infraction will not improve his behavior. Alternately, setting the bar too low, so low that even though the child misbehaves he is never consequenced, never corrected, never given negative feedback about his behavior also will not improve his behavior. For most people this is common sense.

Yet I cannot tell you how many times I have had experts insinuate that I am setting the bar at an inappropriate height: sometimes too high, sometimes too low. What's a boy to do with all this conflicting advice? Do I not pick any battles, or do I pick every battle?

The Cycle

What I am about to describe is a cycle that I observed happening over and over again with my TD children. I noticed that our relationship swung from periods when his behavior was exasperating to periods when I looked forward to his company. What I wanted was for the next good period to last forever, but that does not seem to be the way it happens. Analyzing the swings, I now appreciate that the swings themselves are part of the repair process, and I label it the "repair cycle."

The initial cycle normally starts with a good period called the honeymoon. During the honeymoon, because both the child and the caregiver are trying to get to know each other, the bar is set very low. I talked about this earlier in Chapter 6 (Behavioral Characteristics of Transferal Trust Disorder). There I suggested that one of two things causes the end of the honeymoon period—either we increase our expectations, or the child emotionally cannot keep up the "charming to strangers" act for very long. The honeymoon period is the only time you will directly benefit from his charming to stranger routine, so enjoy it.

Anecdote

A child with a high suspicion of having RAD is placed in foster care. The honeymoon period lasts for less than two hours. What went wrong? This is a true story and the child involved was not so badly damaged that the honeymoon period was doomed to be so short-lived. The foster parent did not take advantage of the honeymoon period. She rushed it going immediately into the next part of the repair cycle.

She was forewarned that this would be a defiant controlling and difficult child and that if she gave an inch the child would take a mile, so she came into the new relationship with her guns blazing and what she got was a battle from the very start. This was a big mistake, for she may never get the cycle moving again, she may be stuck in battle with the child forever.

As initially charming as TD children can be during the honeymoon it takes a lot of energy for them to keep up the act, so it usually is not long before their true colors show through. The other side of the coin is the caregiver. The charming act is designed to manipulate strangers. In the beginning the caregiver will and should bend over backward to make the new child welcome in their home, and the charming act will seem to work. After a while the caregiver will start to place demands on the child—that is to say, raise the bar. As soon as any significant demands are placed on the TD child his act will break and his everyday behavior will emerge. The act will break because the child will see the charming act as no longer working and will revert to the typical behavior that he normally uses around people in authority.

The honeymoon will be terminated by some misbehavioral incident that will invariably be caused by some demand being placed on the child by his caregiver. The caregiver's demand sends the message to the child that the charming act is no longer working. The caregiver, by asserting what most people would consider to be a natural parent's both privilege and obligation to set boundaries, limits, make rules and enforce all these things, has triggered behavior based on the child's deep-seated emotional belief that not being in control is dangerous. This need to be in control is not just superficial bratty behavior in the TD child but is the main tenet in his emotional belief system. After Physiological Needs, being in control is the number one thing motivating the child. OK, I have said this one hundred times before, I know I am repeating myself, but it is so important to appreciate why the child behaves the way he does. It is going to help in understanding and helping the child.

The nature of the child's misbehavior will vary from child to child and will change as the child gets older. Typical misbehavior is aggressive and can be physical or verbal attacks on the caregiver, or the property of the caregiver, or random objects, or even on himself. Tantrums, defiance, destruction, urinating where he should not, bad language, name calling, anything that makes him feel like he is asserting his need for control.

Typically when the honeymoon phase is over a control battle follows. What happens after that is really up to the caregiver. Some caregivers remain locked in a control battle and the cycle stagnates. However it does not have to end in a perpetual battle.

There are four phases to the repair cycle. There is the pleasant phase of the repair cycle which, for the initial cycle of the repair cycle, is called the honeymoon, but for each following repair cycle I call the connecting phase. Second there is the precipitating incident that ends the connecting phase and starts the next phase of the repair cycle. Then there is the third phase, which is characterized by anger, misbehavior, and control battles: I call this the battle phase. The fourth and last phase of the repair cycle is the reconciliation phase, where we banish our anger and return to the connecting phase.

If you are actively and successfully repairing a TD child, you undoubtedly will be able to look back and identify that there were good

Elements of The Repair Cycle

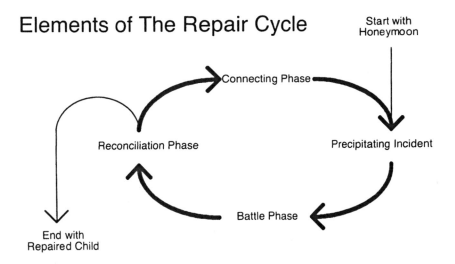

times and there were bad times, and something invariably triggered the bad times and somehow you transitioned back into good times. What you have been doing is going through the repair cycle. By creating my so called "Repair Cycle" I am not coming up with a new way to repair the TD child, I am describing a technique that people who successfully repair TD children universally use.

The most detrimental thing to the child is to become blocked in the battle phase. The next most detrimental thing would be to become blocked in the reconciliation phase or the connecting phase. If the child spends too much time in the battle phase he will regress, in the other two phases he will not progress. Of course it is better to stand still than to go backward, but for true repair we need to keep moving around the repair cycle. As repair advances the child should be spending more time in the connecting phase and less in the battling phase with each successive cycle completion, until on the final cycle the child just stays in the connecting phase.

The repair cycle is an effective way of implementing my Push-Pull technique and my Four Rules. Again, the Four Rules are:

- Rule 1–Supply all his needs
- Rule 2–Be trustworthy
- Rule 3–Be sure the child knows that he is trusting you (i.e. that you are in control)
- Rule 4–Be emotionally strong

The Push-Pull technique is where we push the child out of the Safety and Security level, the level where he seems to be stuck, by satisfying all his Needs at that level, while alternately pulling him into the Belonging and Love level. We do this while making sure that the child appreciates our being in control yet understands he is still safe with us in control.

The problem arises when we try to make the child both aware of the fact that we are in control (which is going to challenge them at the Safety and Security level, because they have a deep seated need to be in control and will not easily accept our being in control) and at the same time have the child experience Belonging and Love. The two emotions come from different levels and, as such, are not going to normally be manifest at the same time in the child. Humans generally have at any one point in time one dominate emotion that motivates their behavior. How do we solve this dilemma of conflicting emotions? The repair cycle of course. Since they cannot experience both Belonging and Love emotions at the same time they are experiencing emotions from the Safety and Security level, we cycle through their emotions. They cannot experience both emotions at the exact same time, but they can experience them relatively close together in time. We cycle the child through the different emotions and lessons, which is what the repair cycle does. Not necessarily ideal but the best we can do. Consider each phase of the repair cycle and what it contributes to the overall repair process of the child.

The battle phase of the repair cycle serves a very important function. It is the phase where we implement rule number three: be sure the child knows that he is trusting you. It is where you affirm to the child that you have rules, regulations, expectations, and you expect the child to meet them. Without battles the child will not know who is boss. It is important that you win the battles you accept (see Chapter 14–Battles). It is also the part of the repair process where the child can observe you as being emotionally strong satisfying rule number four. Early on in the repair process it is primarily through the battle phase of the repair cycle that the child is going to learn that you are in fact in control of his life, something he must appreciate in order to learn to trust. He must be forcibly placed into a trusting role for him to learn to trust because just like riding a bicycle you cannot learn to trust unless you do it, and he will not go into that submissive role voluntarily.

The reconciliation phase is where we move the child out of the battle phase and into the connecting phase. This is a deliberate process on our part, not something to be left to chance. During later repair cycles, as the child heals, he will initiate this phase; but in the beginning you must initiate it. This is the push part of the Push-Pull technique. Here we quiet the Safety and Security level emotions that were stirred up in the battle phase. Stirring up the child's Safety and Security need-to-be-in-control emotions are an undesirable side effect of the battle phase. There is a good side and a bad side to the battle phase, and it is very analogous to chemotherapy and cancer. In spite of the fact that chemotherapeutic agents do damage to the body we still give them to cancer victims because the benefit—killing the cancer cells—outweighs the damage. In spite of the fact that stirring up the child's Safety and Security emotions does damage to the child by heightening an awareness of something that we are trying to suppress, we still do it because the benefit (letting the child know that you are in control) is so important to the repair process that it outweighs the damage.

The connecting phase serves two important functions. First, it stimulates the child's need for love. Just as we know that if we challenge a child intellectually that he will become smarter, we can surmise that if we indulge a child in the good feelings of Belonging and Love that his capacity and desire for Belonging and Love will expand. Strengthen Belonging and Love enough, and the child will start to be able to transcend (be able to ignore lower unfulfilled lower level needs) some of his Safety and Security Needs. Secondly it is the other necessary element of trust building. There are two things necessary to build trust, we just discussed the fact that the child must be placed into a position of trusting but on top of that, things must simultaneously also go well in his life. It is this combination of, "Hey, my mom and dad really are running my life not me, I can see that ultimately they make the final decisions, but hey, my life is pretty darn good! So I guess I can trust them to be in control. They do not manipulate me to take advantage of me, they look out for my welfare so I do not need to focus and worry so much on that."

The very first connecting phase, the honeymoon period is perhaps the most important of all the connecting phases the child will experience. It sets a level of expectation that the child will always remember and will always want to repeat. The better it is the more easy it will be for you to keep the cycle moving.

Setting the Bar

The "bar," so to speak, which represents our behavioral expectations of the child should always be set at a level that is attainable by the child. When the bar is set too high, the cycle stops in the battle phase. The bar blocks the child's progress. The child can never get out of the battle phase because behavior becomes the major and only issue between the child and caregiver. True repair requires a combination of lessons learned from the different parts of the repair cycle, so we are going to overlook some misbehavior in order for the cycle to complete.

The bar will rise with each successive precipitating incident, and drop back for each ensuing reconciliation phase. However it should not drop back as much as its rise. In small increments with each cycle the net effect is that the bar will get higher and higher. When the bar reaches the level of "normal behavior" then repair is complete and the child can exit the repair cycle. What constitutes "normal behavior" will vary from caregiver to caregiver, but that is more of a comment on caregivers than on the child.

Everything is going fine, the child is in the connecting phase, and then the child behaves in an unacceptable manner. The behavior may have been behavior that we previously overlooked as part of picking battles and not picking all battles. We decide that the time has come for him to no longer drop his clothes anywhere he wants but to put them in the hamper, so this time we raise the bar. Remember that even though it is important and nice, and we do benefit from his improved behavior, the primary reason for the battle phase is as part of the trust building routine, not behavior modification. The child's basic problem is that he does not trust, it is not that he does not pick up his clothes or that he uses bad language. Any behavior improvement is frosting, correcting the underlying emotional deficit is the heart of the matter. If you stay in the battle phase too long, something a caregiver only intent on behavior modification might do, the trust lesson is lost. In the long run emotional growth is going to go a lot farther in improving behavior than teaching the child specific desired behaviors.

Move the bar up to create a precipitating incident, then move the bar back down in the reconciliation phase in order to get out of the battle phase. It is OK to do this in spite of the fact that you might think that you are being inconsistent. For example: one day you become angry at the child for not picking up his clothes and consequence him, the next day you ignore a similar incident. To get out of the battle phase of the cycle you may have to be flexible and lower the bar. Do not worry, you will raise the bar back up at the next precipitating incident. Keep the cycle moving.

Anecdote

Suzy lost pencils faster than her foster parents could supply them. Every night at homework time she never had a pencil. In the course of doing homework she would lose her pencil. The foster parents decided that they would give her two pencils at the beginning of each week and if they disappeared she would just have to suffer the natural consequences of not having her homework completed.

The plan backfired. Suzy continued to lose pencils but on top of it, she was no longer doing her homework either. After only a week her teacher, who originally endorsed the plan was expressing her misgivings about the incomplete homework and was withdrawing her support. The foster parents went to the web to ask for help. They felt that Suzy would see their rescinding the two-pencil rule as a win for her and a loss for them.

Suzy's foster parents certainly should have put more thought into the two-pencil rule before implementing it, but they did not, so what should they do?

Foster parents should never let a rule that they make be used against them. Suzy turned the two-pencil rule into a slick way to get out of doing her homework. The foster parents, who are supposed to be in control, can and should amend, or cancel any rule that is not working. Though this will not be counted as a win for the foster parents, it will not necessarily be a loss either. If they announce that, because they are in control, they can change rules whenever they want.

Far better than letting Suzy watch them squirm as she controls them with their own rule.

On a bigger scale, it appears that these foster parents are relying solely on behavior management to repair Suzy. Behavior management alone will not work.

Connection Phase

Love is truly a difficult concept to understand. If you were to approach a psychologist with the only request that he or she help you improve your ability to love you might end up with a polite referral to one of his or her colleagues. Originally, when I put to paper the concept of a repair cycle I called the Connection Phase the "Loving Phase."

However, love can be so many different things. Love of country is different from love of a best friend, or love of a child or of your spouse. The problem with love also is that love can be passive. You can love somebody and not show it. I realized that I needed a better word to describe the good part of the Repair Cycle, the part of the Cycle where the child learns that you care about him, and that your making the decisions on his behalf can be a good thing.

I needed a word that implied a more active relationship between the caregiver and the child and had a more specific meaning. I also needed a word that describes a relationship that can be turned on and off. A parent does not stop loving his or her child when they are disciplining them or even when they are feeling angry toward them. The feelings associated with anger and discipline are not warm and fuzzy. Warm and fuzzy can be turned on and off, love cannot.

Connection turns out to be the ideal word. It implies an active link between the caregiver and the child. It has an element of listening, respect, caring, concern, and communicating feelings. It can also occur between people who are not attached to each other or do not share a love based relationship.

The word "attachment" in the diagnosis "reactive attachment disorder" could just as easily have been "connection." It might be a better word choice. Connection is something that we can have with almost any person, whereas attachment is reserved for just a few special people in our lives.

Connection is not love, though it is certainly a healthy part of love. Another phrase that means connection is "being on the same wavelength." For guys it has been called "male bonding." Connection is an active process and takes work. Even though it is a healthy part of love, it is not necessary to love a person to connect with them. We connect when we become closer to another individual. Any lowering of our Safety and Security barriers and a concomitant increase in our Love and Belonging feelings can be defined as connecting. Using this definition it is possible to connect both with a loved one or a stranger sitting on a bus. The lower we make our walls the better the connection; consequently, it is easier to make a close and better connection with someone we know, trust, and love, than a stranger sitting on the bus.

People who connect to others easily do not dwell on Safety and Security. They go into new situations feeling comfortable that they can protect themselves if the need arises. They feel comfortable with who they are so they do not anticipate that they will be seen negatively. They expect the new situation to have a positive outcome so they enter it with their defenses down. They do not feel vulnerable. They do not feel the need to preemptively protect themselves.

There is nothing surprising about this. People with Safety and Security issues build and maintain walls. Walls keep people out. Once they get to know you—and only then—will they lower their walls, lower their guard, and let you in. A lot of people have trouble warming up to strangers, feel uncomfortable in groups, are slow to make friends, do not trust people who come on "too strong" and are always looking for a hidden motive in others. They are slow to trust, trust being right out of Safety and Security.

We need to form a connection with the child to promote his emotional growth. The connection is going to stimulate his feelings of Love and Belonging. In the Push-Pull technique this is the pull into the next higher level. However, before we can expect the child to drop his Safety and Security walls we need to drop ours. If you are trying to help a TD child and have trust issues of your own, now would be a good time to explore and resolve your issues. It is not going to work if both the child and the adult have deep-seated trust issues and are both struggling to be in control.

I have already said that the child's attachment disorder could have as easily been called connection disorder. These children do have difficulty connecting. However it does not matter how severely disabled we find the child's ability to connect, there are still going to be times when he is more connected than others. During the Connecting Phase we want to move him as close to his maximum ability to connect as we can. One of our goals is to teach him to be able to connect.

The very first thing we do to promote connection is to avoid anything that would stimulate his Safety and Security Need. Here is a list of suggestions to reduce the child's Safety and Security Needs:

- Be non-judgmental—setting yourself up as an authority is a sure way to increase the child's Safety and Security Need. Setting yourself up as an authority places you in control and will be sure to make him anxious.
- Be non-threatening.
- Give only asked-for advice—and give it with caution. Try to help the child come up with his own solutions. Do not tell him what you think, ask him questions about what he thinks. Give advice indirectly. For example, rather than telling him what to do, tell him how you handled a similar situation when you were young. (If you do not have a similar situation make one up.)
- Secede control of the conversation—control is important to the TD child. He will not open up and connect if he does not feel in control of the conversation. Giving him control does not mean asking him what he wants to talk about. That, in itself, is directing the conversation. Giving him control means being quiet and listening.
- Play a game or do an activity—this helps distract the child from his emotional fears. Boys in particular open up and connect better if they are engaged in an activity rather than attempting to just sit and talk with them.
- Use physical (holding) contact as appropriate—sitting on your lap, back rubs, pats on the back, and with the older child wrestling and horseplay can all be used to advantage. Boys wrestling with their fathers is a healthy activity. Physical contact becomes less appropriate after puberty.
- Make him feel safe—this is a time when the child should feel that his feelings are more important than rules. He will test you by saying bizarre things to see how you react. Do not take his bait. If he says he is going to do something horrendous, remember, he has not done it, he is just talking and talk is cheap. If he really were going to do it he probably would not talk about it.

The list above is what you do to avoid stimulating his Safety and Security Needs. Concomitantly, you also stimulate his Love and Belonging Needs. What do you do to make him feel love and belonging? Be friendly and be there. Be approachable. Listen and be interested. However, the most important thing is what you do not do, and that is to not stimulate his sense of being unsafe and insecure.

Generally you will know when you have connected with the child. The child will be listening. The child will not have the ability to make much of a connection when you first start his repair. Success is seeing him make better and better connection with each revolution of the Repair Cycle.

Realistically the Repair Cycle is not going to be a ping-pong from brutal control battles to deep heart-felt loving connection and back. For the seriously damaged TD child the cycle might be viewed by an outsider as just a lessening and increasing cycle of seemingly endless control battles.

In the beginning do not be discouraged if the best connection you can achieve with your TD child is at best shallow. It takes time to break down the Safety and Security walls that the child has built. It takes time for him to get rid of the pre-potent Safety and Security Needs that block the emergence of Love and Belonging Needs.

Be patient.

Enabling

Always remembering that all Four Rules must be satisfied in order to repair the TD child, and that showing acceptance and love toward the child is a major part of supplying all his Needs; there are times when you overlook behavior that you would find unacceptable in a normal child. So much of the child's behavior is unacceptable that if you try to correct it all from the very beginning you will be locked into such a prolonged battle phase that the repair cycle will be blocked; the child will never experience affection and love. Repair will stagnate. You know that he must have some affection and love, so you just choose to address only the worst of his controlling behaviors, and ignore the rest. This is all part of picking your battles.

With time and repeated repair cycles the worst behaviors should disappear and you progressively tackle the next level of misbehaviors and work through them. By repeating this cycle, eventually, the child heals.

Also with time you are going to form a bond with the child and the child will form a bond with you, his caregiver. He will start to trust. This is a good thing. The love and affection that the child needs in order to heal is going to be stronger and more genuine if it comes from a true bond between you and the child. The initial love and affection will not come from a true bond; it will come from the ability for you, the caregiver and surrogate parent, to generically love all children. Any caregiver who is lacking this admirable ability to generically love all children should not take on the task of repairing a TD child.

I have already pointed out the danger of the cycle being blocked in the battle phase. There is also a danger that the cycle can be blocked in the connecting phase as well; the cycle ironically being thwarted by the very desirable true bond that hopefully will form between you and the child.

What happens is that your love for the child will cause you to overlook the child's flaws. You and the child fall into comfortable behavior patterns. The child learns how far he can push you and stay within your limits; you become inured to the child's misbehavior, that is to say, over a period of time you become used to his unpleasant misbehavior, so that you are no longer bothered or upset by it. Have you ever seen a parent overlook behavior that you find unacceptable, that you feel requires reprimanding? Have you ever seen a parent seem oblivious to flaws in their children? The cycles of repair stop, and a status quo ensues.

The repair cycles should not stop until the child's behavior is totally acceptable.

Loving, caring parents have a tendency to overlook many flaws in their own children. On top of that, let's face it, the repair cycle is much work. It is easier to accept a comfortable truce than to work toward a complete repair.

Overlooking misbehavior in a child as part of the reconciliation phase in order to afford the child an opportunity to move out of the battle phase and into the connecting phase is appropriate. It allows the child to move through the repair cycle and experience belonging and love. However, it is not appropriate to overlook misbehavior in a child because you have lost the energy to go through another battle phase, or you have become inured to his misbehavior, or you have lost sight of his misbehavior due to your emotional attachment to the child. The catchword that we would use to describe this overlooking of misbehavior on your part is "enabling."

Enabling is when we passively allow a child to behave inappropriately. In this case we allow him to behave inappropriately by our not reacting to his misbehavior. By setting the bar too low we are allowing him to continue misbehavior without consequence.

Enabling, while not as emotionally damaging as blocking the child in the battle phase by engaging in constant control battles, does stop the repair cycle, which does then stop the repair process.

So how do you know if you are doing it right? It is actually quite simple; if you set the bar too high or too low you will not cycle. If you are cycling you are doing it right. In general the shorter the cycle time the better, but you cannot rush the cycle to make it short. Younger children need a short cycle time, perhaps a day or two. By age ten the cycle can take weeks. If the important lessons required to build trust are stretched too far apart as would happen if the cycle time is too long trust building will not take place. As the child improves, the amount of time spent in the connecting phase should increase while the amount of time spent in the battle phase should decrease. Also the child will start to initiate the reconciliation phase. It works.

Anecdote

My ten-year-old TD child and I had grown into a comfortable status quo. When he and I were together there were no outbursts, bad language, or blatant disregard of rules. If I told him to do something he might argue but he would do it. However I felt that growth had stopped. Furthermore he was not making the same progress at school where his relationships with his teachers were strained and contentious.

A vacation with its increased excitement levels (high arousal) made me acutely aware of my false sense of complacency toward his need for additional repair. The child and I were getting along but the child still did not get along with the world in general. Time was running out; when the child hits puberty it is natural for him to want more control of his life, repairing him then will be just that much more difficult.

I discussed with his social worker various ways to shake up the child, to give him a wake up call for change. The social worker suggested the following technique as the easiest to implement. I was concerned that it would not work. I was worried that the child would not take the threat seriously but just consider it as another manipulative maneuver on my part to control him.

In spite of apprehensions, the child provided me with a perfect opportunity to start the technique. I took him food shopping where he was allowed to purchase many items that he enjoys (no candy). On the way out of the store he asked me for fifty cents to put in a vending machine that sells small toys in plastic capsules. I refused him this request and he announced in turn that he would refuse to help me put away the groceries when we got home if he did not receive the fifty cents.

I said no more until we got home where I told him to get to work and help me bring in the groceries. He refused, and I chose this incident to create more than just a small rift between him and me. I raised my voice and spoke in a manner using body language that left no doubt that I was angry. I told him that his not helping to put away food, much of which was purchased solely for his pleasure, was very self-centered. That he showed no appreciation for the nice things I had done for him and just behaved in a manner to get as much for himself as possible. I announced to him that I considered his behavior very inappropriate and unacceptable. I went on to suggest that his self-centeredness was a personality flaw that needed correction, and I did not intend to continue tolerating it.

He set to work helping me but as he worked he was formulating his rebuttal. After about five minutes it came in the form of an award winning performance detailing all the bad things that happened in his life meant to evoke sympathy followed by his statement that he had no intention of changing and that he liked himself just the way he was.

I withdrew emotional support for about a week. I literally limited my interactions with the child to only those required to fulfill my obligation as a foster parent. Then after a week I just stopped being cold and distant and acted as if nothing had happened. Within a few days we had achieved a total reconciliation. What followed was by far the best connecting phase the child had ever had.

Three weeks into the connecting phase and I saw deterioration in the child's attitude. This time the battle phase lasted only an hour, reconciliation was effortless, and we are back in a connecting phase.

Locked in the Battle Phase

There are going to be people who read this book and just shake their heads at my statement that in order to repair the child we have to set the bar low enough so that the cycle will move. Their TD child's behavior is just so unacceptable that there is no way that they could ever overlook it, and their anger directed toward the child (anger caused by the child's continually draining their emotional resources, continually destroying their property, and continually tormenting and driving a wedge between family members), makes it impossible for them to even consider ignoring the child's transgressions and initiating having a fun happy time with the child. They do not see themselves ever being able to participate in a connecting phase with the child.

The best I can do for you if you are one of these people is just to offer some observations:

- From a practical point you cannot win them all. Some children are just too damaged to be repaired.
- Not everybody is suited to work with TD children, it takes much patience, love, and energy. These TD children are definitely special needs children requiring special parenting skills. These special skills do not come naturally to most parents, so do not beat yourself up if you find that you are not the right parent for a TD child.
- A good time for the child might not need to be as warm and fuzzy a time as you might think. Based on the child's past experience just ten minutes of being with you without your nagging, punishing, or criticizing him might seem like a good time to him. You may not have to do all that much to have what would be considered the connecting phase of the repair cycle.
- Have a good time with another sibling in front of the TD child. If he cannot experience it himself, then let him see what it looks like and experience it vicariously.
- Consider the boot camp approach to repair described in Chapter 9 (Introduction to Practice).

Anecdote

A family filed a petition to the court for an adoption dissolution. The child, adopted at age six, is now ten. The child's early history and lifelong behavior is very consistent with severe reactive attachment disorder. In the meantime, the family contacted their local child protective services and had the child physically removed from their home.

Whereas the state cannot make you raise your child, they can and in this case are penalizing the family significantly by charging them an exorbitant amount of child support while the child is out of their home and in foster care. The family now has to make the difficult decision of facing financial ruin (in order to make the child support payments for any length of time they would need to sell their home) or bring the child back into their home.

It seems unfair that good people who willingly take on the responsibility of caring for other people's children should end up with their lives and their finances so totally ruined. What went wrong with this adoption?

The family went into the adoption process blind. The adoption agency, most likely to make a placement, did nothing to open their eyes. Specifically the adoption agency did not:

Tell them the child had RAD,
Tell them the ramifications of a child being abused for the first few years of his life,
Give them a complete history of the child's early abuse,
Give them any training for raising a child with RAD,
Have them talk with other parents who had adopted abused children so that they might have an inkling of what they were getting into.

What the adoption agency did do was:

Sugar-coated the child's behavior,
Never suggested that the child might have RAD and that the family should read up on RAD and consider seriously if they would be willing to raise a child with RAD,

Downplayed the child's previous abuse and portrayed it in a way that made the family feel sympathetic and protective toward the child,

Gave the family the impression that a lot of love was all this child needed to be fine,

Subtly pressured them to take on the legal responsibility of a child that the agency knew was emotionally damaged.

If a family were adopting a child with a physical handicap, typically, the adoption agency would fully inform them of all the child's disabilities. Furthermore, no agency would mislead prospective parents by making false claims such as, "if you just love the child enough his eyesight will return." No; instead prospective parents would expect the adoption agency to spell out the exact nature of the handicap and most likely offer financial aid. Just because TD cannot be seen does not give adoption agencies the right to place TD children in homes without the same type of up-front discussion and awareness, and the same type of long term assistance and support that a physical handicap placement receives.

It is difficult to affix blame for the child's failure to heal while in the care of this family. Possibly the child is just too damaged to fix. If the child were blind no one would expect adoptive parents to make the child see. Perhaps the emotional damage, just like some physical damage, is just too severe to repair. The other possibility is that this family is not suited to be parents for a RAD child, that the right parents would be able to heal the child. Either way it still falls back to the adoption agency. If the child is too damaged to fix, that is exactly how he should be advertised. Furthermore, adoption agencies have a responsibility to match the child with the right parents.

Other Ways of Building Trust

The repair cycle is not the only way to build trust. For one, if the TD child is so locked in the Safety and Security level that he will not cycle, so locked that you cannot get him to move out of that level even for a little while, so locked that there is no honeymoon and that no reasonable amount of reconciliatory behavior upon your part can move the child—then nothing is left other than the boot camp approach.

I have previously mentioned an intellectual approach but this requires a willingness on the part of the child to change.

Within the Push-Pull technique there are strategies that do not require the battle phase of the cycle. Remember, the function of the battle phase is to let the child know that you are in control. Only then, with you in control and things going well in his life, will he learn to trust you.

In the beginning the repair cycle will probably be your only tool for repairing the TD child. As trust starts to form other easier and even fun ways to build trust will become available. The only reason you need to have a battle phase is because you recognize the absolute need for the child to see you, the caregiver, in control. If you can send that message without a battle, so much the better, everybody is happier. Consider some of the ways you can send that message without a battle.

You can have attitude. This is rule number four, be emotionally strong, expressed with cockiness and panache. If you are showing love and concern for the child and at the same time your general bearing and attitude sends the message that you are not the type of person that allows yourself to be controlled by anybody else, then your TD child can only conclude that you can be trusted, that if you wanted to you could use and abuse him to your advantage. However, you do not, so you must be trustworthy. The child senses that things are going well in his life without him being in control, and you did not have to have a battle to send the message that he is not in control.

You can refuse to engage him when you do not like his behavior. Cristine Chandler in her book *4 Weeks to a Better Behaved Child* strongly advocates only giving attention for good behavior and withdrawing attention for bad behavior. Yelling at a child is attention. She suggests something she calls "cool down." She describes cool down as, "First, parents make very clear to the child exactly which behavior has caused this consequence to be invoked. Second, they [the parents] immediately and completely withdraw their attention."[1] This cool down technique really is my repair cycle with a different twist on what happens during the battle phase. It gets you through the battle phase without much emotional turmoil while still sending the important message that you are in control. Understand, though, that it will only work if

146

the TD child has healed enough to care and be aware of the fact that you have withdrawn attention. Early on in treatment a badly damaged child might actually like being ignored.

Kidding is an interesting tool that allows you to assert control, avoid battles, and have fun all at the same time. See Chapter 16 (Kidding).

You should avoid letting the TD child have control of your hot buttons. His not being able to push your hot buttons is a passive yet effective way of denying him control without having to have a battle.

Final Thoughts

One of my claims is that there is nothing really new in this book. I also state that there are a lot of other good books written on this subject, and in any specific area there are quite a few that are helpful. For example there are books that cover, in greater depth than I attempt to cover—behaviorism, consequences, connecting, and so on. However, there is no other book out there at the time of this writing that tie all the elements together with an understandable and meaningful model. One that explains when and how to use all the elements and why they work and when not to use them.

I did not sit around wondering how to repair a TD child and one day come up with the idea of trying a repair cycle because all else had failed. On the contrary, I was having good success repairing the TD child without reading any books or taking anybody's advice. I disagreed with much of the advice I was given. This book represents an intellectualization of the techniques that people use who, like me, have instinctive skill in successfully raising the TD child. Though these skills are apparently not universal to all humans, they certainly have been around from way before recorded history.

In 4 Weeks to a Better Behaved Child the author writes that the primary thing a parent can remove from a child's life as a consequence of misbehavior is himself or herself. She calls it "the power inherent in giving and withdrawing [your] attention."[2] She is right of course, a well-attached child will miss the connection to the parent more than he or she will miss any toy or privilege. Understand, she is not recommending that you emotionally abandon the child. She is just saying that in order for the child to maintain a warm and supportive connection with the parent, the child must behave.

I could not agree more with her concept of withdrawing attention. It is by far the most common consequence that a child under my care receives for misbehavior. It is very effective, and it does not require much effort on my part. It is by far the easiest consequence of misbehavior to administrate.

Though she does not describe the process as a cycle, it actually is. The child misbehaves and what does Dr. Chandler do? She severs connection. All the elements of what I call the repair cycle are right there in her book. She has the good times and the bad times, and even if not explicitly stated, there is implied a precipitating incident and a period of reconciliation.

If you are successfully raising a TD child, or even in normal good parenting, you have been using what I call the "repair cycle." No matter how you dice it, there are good times and bad times, thus the repair cycle. So why do we need to analyze it, give it a name, and break it down into its phases? Because when the child misbehaves, it helps you understand that the ensuing battle phase is an opportunity to let the child know that you, not he, are in control. This understanding helps you to accept the bad behavior and deal with it without anger, since you see it as part of a constructive repair process. It helps you to understand the need for the battle phase of the repair cycle and the danger of letting the cycle stagnate. Furthermore, it helps you to insure that each phase of the cycle accomplishes what it is supposed to accomplish.

Notes

[1] Chandler Cristine Ph.D., McGrath, Laura, *4 Weeks to a Better Behaved Child*, 2004, p. 41.
[2] Pp. 29.

12

Touching and Holding

Several of the books on attachment disorder suggest touching and holding as a very effective procedure that should be employ as often as the child will allow.[1,2,3] Touching and holding appears again and again when researching treatments for attachment disorder. As such, the model that I develop here embraces this technique, and helps explain why it is therapeutic.

Broad ranges of holding modalities exist, from a simple and informal pat on the back, to far more complicated and aggressive holding techniques. For example, one expert suggests that the child be wrapped in a blanket and bottle fed up to the time he is twelve years old. I certainly would not want to try this technique on an eighteen-year old, and I doubt I would even attempt it on a ten-year old. I understand the goal, but more sophisticated techniques must be used on the older child. Besides, if the TD child is not repaired by the time he reaches adulthood, there probably is very little that we can do to help him, at least not with something as simple as a holding technique.

There are several extreme forms of holding therapy. One is a formalized version of holding treatment therapy known as the Holding Nurturing Process, originally developed by Marth Welch, M.D. Two therapists place the child over their laps, with the lead therapist placing the child's right arm behind his back. In this position, the child, who is also wrapped in a blanket, is forced to look directly into the eyes of the therapist.[4] Though this may be effective in strengthening attachment, therapists are not cheap; two increases the cost, and finding therapists who are trained in this technique is not always easy.

My model predicts that touching and holding are important elements in the treatment of TD children. It states that we need to fulfill all of the child's Needs, including Belonging and Love Needs, as well as all Physiological and Safety and Security Needs. Touching and holding is very effective because it simultaneously addresses at minimum two levels of Needs. When the child is held, he can feel safe, secure, and loved at the same time. It even addresses an Esteem Need in that the time spent holding the child sends an unspoken message to him that he is important.

Understand that you are not going to be able to take a child with whom you are unfamiliar, or a child whose needs are strongly rooted in the Safety and Security level, and expect him to sit on your lap and feel safe and secure. On the contrary, he is gong to feel restrained, and most likely become anxious and apprehensive. I would take exception with anyone who would force touch and holding on a child unless they were using a boot-camp technique. It would only serve to increase the child's level of insecurity (as evidenced by anxiety), which has no benefit in the Push-Pull technique.

Holding is a powerful therapy, but it needs to be introduced only as quickly as the child will tolerate, and it never should be forced beyond that. However, you can force it *up* to that level. You are going to discover his tolerance level by learning to read the child, and also by trial and error. Push a little, and if the child reacts negatively, back off. Over time, keep pushing and backing off. His ability both to tolerate and enjoy physical contact will vary by time of day and by situation. I have had children who like to be held in the morning, and I have had children who like to be held in the evening.

The healthy child might seek your lap as a safe haven when feeling threatened, the TD child will not. He does not see you (or others) as his source of safety and security. Instead, he has learned to trust himself (and only himself) as his source for satisfying this Need. If he is feeling threatened, the child will shun your lap. His primary goal for seeking your lap is going to be for Love and Belonging, and he will only seek this at times when he is feeling relatively safe and secure. Any child normally will not be functioning on two levels simultaneously. If the TD child is sitting on your lap, he probably already feels safe and secure, and is seeking Love and Belonging. Stated another way, the TD child already feels safe and secure with you, which is why he allows himself to be so physically close to you. Since he already feels safe and secure, then it follows that he is on your lap because he is seeking belonging and love, the next higher Need level. Though the only times the TD child sits on your lap are when he already feels safe and secure, with time he will learn to associate you with safety and security. He will thus be able to move from situational trust to interpersonal trust, which is exactly the goal of treatment.

With time, the child will eventually allow touch and holding, and once comfortable with it, will actually seek it out. This can happen pretty fast, and you will have to manage how much you think is enough. Having him sit on your lap while watching TV is convenient and appropriate, but having him sit on your lap while eating is a little awkward and forced. Also, as the child heals, you can substitute shorter duration, higher-intensity acts such as hugs, for longer duration, less intense acts like a gentle hand on the shoulder, and get the same therapeutic result.

If you cannot touch or hold the child, it is going to be more difficult (though not impossible) to help him. The child just might be too insecure to allow any touching, or he might be too old for any significant touching to be appropriate. Instead you are going to have to use verbal communication to relay the same messages to the child. As I mentioned earlier, it is very important that you are careful with the words you choose and just as important to say the right things so that the correct message is heard. Some psychologists dedicate their careers to learning how to say the right things so that they can effect the desired emotional changes in their patients. It is an art, and even with a lifetime of learning and dedication, not all of the professionals do it well.

Notes

[1] Keck & Kupecky, *Adopting the Hurt Child*, 1995, p. 171.
[2] Mansfield & Waldmann, *Don't Touch My Heart*.
[3] Thomas, Nancy L., *When Love Is Not Enough*, 1997, p. 21.
[4] Levy & Orlans, *Attachment, Trauma, and Healing*, 1998, pp. 114–117.

13

Behavior Management

Behavior management is a set of strategies used to manipulate or change a child's behavior.[1] If we are looking out for the child's welfare, we first seek behavioral changes that contribute to his emotional development. Next we seek behavioral changes that make him easier to live with, and contribute to his development. For example, we want to manage his behavior so that not only does the child use sociable language, but he also completes his homework.

The best behavior management technique is for you, the caregiver, to just communicate to the child how you expect him to behave. However, expectations require the child to be connected with you, and want your approval. You let the child know what is expected of him, and he tries to live up to those expectations. For expectations to work the child has to be able to read your cues. Because cues are often subtle and unspoken, the child must have a connection with you, and he must want to maintain that connection. He has to want to please, and the child has to be both sensitive to and bothered by your potential disappointment if he fails to meet your expectations. As any child's level of emotional maturity grows, as predicated by Maslow's Hierarchy of Needs, his awareness of your expectations grows.

The use of expectations will work with the child who is both emotionally connected and able to function at the Esteem Needs level. This is *not* the TD child.

It should be noted that your level of connectedness with a child should increase over time. It never hurts to express expectations, and to praise the child when those expectations are met. As the child's ability to trust grows, start to use more expectations. There will even be times with the TD child when expressing an expectation works.

More often the behavior management techniques used on the TD child rely on methods that do not require the child to care about what you think and feel; these techniques generally involve rewards and/or consequences.

Many books on reactive attachment disorder, much of the literature regarding raising difficult children, and many routine parenting books extensively cover behavior management techniques. I could not even begin to detail here all the techniques available that you might use.

As we even saw within the technique touching and holding, there exist a myriad of variations. I would consider some proposed techniques to be bizarre. One book suggested that when the RAD child is first brought into your home, he should sleep in a room with an alarm on the door that sounds every time he opens the door to leave the room. If you travel, say take a trip to grandma's house, then carry a portable alarm. The idea is if an alarm goes off every time the child leaves his designated area, he learns his boundaries, and eventually feels safe and secure because of those boundaries. An extreme technique.

It is not my intention to tell you which behavior management techniques you should use, but to alert you to the fact that there are many available. You should do some research to determine which ones might work best for you and your child.

Anything that attempts to change behavior technically is a behavior management technique; however for my purposes, I am using the term "behavior management" to refer only to behavior management techniques that involve the carrot and the stick approach—rewards and punishments (or consequences if you are truly skilled enough to keep a consequence from becoming a punishment, the difference will be describe shortly). Methods such as setting rules, adherence to artificial consequences, rewards, or charts where the child might get a sticker on the days he has been good. See Appendix D for an example of a behavior management goal-oriented sheet used by teachers to achieve whatever the goal-of-the-day happens to be.

I have trouble relying on behavior management for anything more than a way to tame the beast; to make it possible to live with the child while we are therapeutically developing his ability to trust.

Behavior management does not help the child to develop long-term and meaningful attachment—the kind we like to see in adults. It does not teach the child to trust, but it does teach him that it is okay to manipulate others. Being manipulative destroys trust. The carrot and the stick approach (rewards and consequences) is blatant manipulation, and it is manipulation that we adults tend to overlook. We become too focused on attaining the desired behavior to see our methods as manipulative. It is not so obvious to the child, as it is to us, that our goals as caregivers are in his best interest. He does not share our value system, and most likely he believes adults are trying to manipulate him for their benefit. It follows that if the child thinks it is acceptable for adults to manipulate him, it in turn should be acceptable for him to manipulate adults—it is to him the way of the world. The child feels that what's good for the goose is good for the gander, which is not true in this scenario.

Behavior management can be an onerous task to administer. Constant battles build walls. I want connection with the child, not just a behaved child. With too much reliance on these techniques, you are not going to develop that connection, you will only modify his behavior.

Often behavior management simply does not work. The TD child resists reward systems, thinking that he is being controlled if he cooperates. To him, being in control is a more urgent need than receiving the reward. He sometimes feels he can never achieve the reward anyway, so why should he even bother trying? He might think that the reward has a hidden hook, one that he will want to avoid. In addition, his lack of maturity can interfere with his perception of time, so unless the reward is immediate, in his world it does not exist. A reward he receives at the end of the week for good behavior he is supposed to exhibit now may be too distant.

Finally, with behavior management the primary lesson for the child can get lost in the ensuing battles. For example, the TD child curses. In response you consequence him by ordering him to go to his room. This makes the child angry and he argues with you. During the argument, he pushes several of your buttons, and you become angry. You then administer a second consequence, which is now a punishment because you have done so out of anger (I explain consequences versus punishment later in this chapter). But now, both you and the child have forgotten the initial infraction (cursing), because you both have become so wrapped up in the ensuing battle. Another example where behavior management fails (or at least your implementation of behavior management fails), as any chance of teaching him the original lesson was lost in the heat of the battle.

Despite my lack of excitement for behavior management, it does have a place other than just managing misbehavior or encouraging desired behavior in helping the TD child. Consider my third and fourth rules for developing trust: rule number three—be sure the child knows that he is trusting you, and rule number four—be emotionally strong.

When you set boundaries, you are displaying strength and control. If you are in control, then the child is forced to trust you. He will not learn to trust a person who is weaker than he, and why should he? So a well-implemented behavior management regime does contribute to satisfying rules number three and four of the Four Rules. This is not to suggest that you should be an overbearing ogre about putting limitations and regulations on the child. Do not go overboard with behavior management. You must do behavior management with both a forceful yet loving demeanor, or it is likely the child will learn to detest you rather than trust you. It is possible for you to respect the child and let him have some control over his own life, while at the same time setting boundaries and limits.

Earlier in this chapter I stated that behavior management techniques are bad, and here I say they are good, or at the very least that they have a rationale based in my theory and have empirical evidence from both me and others to support their use. So where is the middle ground? Behavior management is a way of showing the TD child that you are in control. Hopefully we are all in agreement that this is a necessary thing—showing the child that you are in control. An excess of behavior management is also a way to create a loveless, rigid environment that does not leave the child with positive feelings about somebody else being in control. We should all be in agreement that this is a bad thing—systematically teaching the child that losing control to his caregiver is synonymous to being miserable.

A middle ground is created by the fact that the control issue has two aspects: being in control of yourself, and being in control of the child. You do not need to have iron-fisted control over the child's behavior for him to be able to develop trust in you. If you overdo it with control, the TD child (or any child for that matter) will feel totally boxed in. He will become overly anxious, and you will only confirm his belief that when other people are in control, he is not better off.

You do, however, need to be unequivocally in control of yourself. That alone should be enough for the child to realize that he is not running the show. It should be enough for him to appreciate that things can go well in his life while somebody else is orchestrating it, or at least in a position to orchestrate it, and it should be enough for him to see that placing his trust and control in another person does not spell disaster.

TD children cannot be allowed to manipulate you. This does not mean that you need to rigidly structure their lives by removing all autonomy, such as their use of free time and use of personal resources. Some people think that the only way to display to the child that he is not in control is to be controlling. Not necessarily the case.

Force of Personality

Not everyone needs to work at appearing to be in control. There is an aura of authority that some people just emit; it is a personality thing. Certainly you have met individuals whom you instinctively knew were used to having their way. When placed in a position of authority, these individuals may inadvertently overdo it with control, even in situations where it would be better if they backed off and gave other people a little space. This is a facet of their personality they need to work on. They do not need to learn to act like a person in control because they already know how. If you think you may be one of these individuals, ask a friend. They know where you lie on the control spectrum. If you are very controlling, though, they may be afraid to tell you the truth.

Being in control does not mean you have to say no to every request that the TD child makes. Loving, caring people do consider requests from the people they love. While in control you do still need to show love as well. For example, the child asks, "Can we go to McDonald's for dinner tonight?" If you do not want to go say, "No, I am going to make dinner tonight." No more discussion, and ignore any whining or complaints. But sometimes you may respond, "Yes, I like that idea. I want to take you to McDonald's." There are other ways of saying it, but always pause and think about his request, making him wait just a moment so he will be aware that *you* are making the decision and that *you* will not be rushed. Then try to incorporate words in your response that indicate you are in control as in the example with, "*I like* that idea. *I want* to take you."

Behavior management techniques can work as part of a therapy program, but there are easier and more effective techniques that do not interfere quite so much with the execution of my first rule (supply all his Needs, which includes love). It is very difficult to fulfill his need for love while practicing behavior management.

If you think that you are going to repair this child through behavior management alone, you might as well give up right now. It will not work. The best you can hope for from only behavior management is just that: managing his behavior. It will not address all the underlying problems. If all you care about is dealing with his behavior, then by all means, go for it. I would like to add, however, that a happy, well-adjusted child is a lot more fun to be around than a well-behaved child. By using only behavior management without addressing the underlying issues, you will probably never get him to be a well-behaved child, anyway. The best you can hope for is one who just behaves in an acceptable manner.

Consequences vs. Punishments

All of the literature I have read on child rearing and behavior management agree—do not punish—instead, consequence. The problem is the differences can be elusive, and may be even altogether indistinguishable.

Before differentiating between consequences and punishment, consider that there are two types of consequences: natural and imposed.[2] Natural consequences are easy to define. It naturally follows that if you drop a glass, it breaks. It also naturally follows that if you forget to wear a coat in winter, you become cold. These are natural consequences; nature dictates the lesson. For this kind of consequencing, parental involvement is not required. Use natural consequences whenever possible. However, some natural consequences are dangerous and should not be used. For example, it follows that if you step in front of a moving vehicle, you get hit. When the child's welfare is threatened, obviously you do not use natural consequences to teach a lesson; for these situations use imposed consequences.

Imposed consequences are artificial because *we* determine the consequence. For example, if you do not eat your peas there will be no TV tonight. The imposed consequence is you will not be able to watch TV. As mentioned, use this type of consequence when no natural one exists, or the natural consequence is potentially dangerous.

Punishment, like imposed consequences, is also always artificial. If you do not eat your peas there will be no TV tonight. The punishment is you will not be allowed to watch TV. How does this differ from my previous example for imposed consequences? Why is this a punishment? Is not this exactly the same as the imposed consequence example above? On the surface, yes it is. So how do we differentiate between punishment and imposed consequence?

The difference has nothing to do with the consequence/punishment itself, but with your attitude. If you are angry, then it is a punishment.[3] This may not sound significant, but it is. If you are angry, the child knows from your tone of voice and focuses on your anger, not his infraction. The message you send him is, "push my buttons and I strike back." Not the message you want to send. The message you want to send is "eating your peas is important." However, that message is lost as a direct result of your anger.

However, maybe your real message when you start a battle is, "I am in control and you have to do as I say," (winning control battles does send the message "you have to do what I say"), and then the child, in the ensuing battle, succeeds in making you angry. The effectiveness of your communicating the "I am in control" message is diminished. Even if you successfully carry out the punishment (because you became angry it is no longer a consequence but a punishment) the message is diminished. The child pushed your buttons. Thus, the punishment does not work because the child, by making you angry, still feels he has control over you.

The more closely related the imposed consequence is to the infraction, the more it can be considered logical, and the more logical it is the better. "Don't eat your peas or there will be no TV tonight," is not as logical as, "Any toys you leave lying on the living room floor overnight will be picked up by me and donated to needy boys and girls." This example is more logical because the problem (toys cluttering the living room and lack of respect for his personal property) is directly connected to the imposed consequence (the toys will be removed from the household so they will never clutter the living room floor again, and they will be given to other boys and girls who may show more respect for them). This is logical in that the imposed consequence helps to resolve the problem; if the toys are removed from the household and given away, they will never be in the way again.

Maybe I should define a third group of consequences called illogical imposed consequences, where the consequence has little or no relationship to the misbehavior, as in my first example with the peas. It seems like an illogical imposed consequence because there is no logical connection between peas and television.

Do you always warn a child prior to invoking an imposed consequence? Yes and no. Natural consequences do not warn ahead of time; from experience we learn them. However, it is not fair to pop a new rule on a child and then immediately impose a consequence on him for breaking it. On the other hand, most misbehaviors, that your child commits, are repeats from the past. If you warned him when he was five years old not to write on the walls, there is no need to ever warn him again for repeats of that misbehavior. If you feel the child knows the difference between right and wrong in any situation, then it is always acceptable to immediately impose a consequence on him rather than give another warning.

If you think he is unaware that he has broken a rule give a warning, talk to him about the rule, and your expectations for his future compliance. Then if the child repeats the offense, you consequence without warning. So you always have to warn a child ahead of time for the first instance of a specific misbehavior before invoking an imposed consequence, but you only need to do it once in his lifetime. You may choose to re-warn the child of a rule rather than impose a consequence, often it is just easier and gets the behavior you want, without the hassle.

Unknown, unpredictable imposed consequences are better than known ones. When you tell the child what the consequence will be ahead of time, it gives him the option of choosing to commit the crime and take the punishment, or not commit the crime and avoid the punishment. If the child chooses not to eat his peas and consequently loses TV privileges for the evening (even if you never get angry), he still has controlled the situation and little good has come out of the encounter. You have lost the battle. Do not commit to an imposed consequence until after the child misbehaves. By not forewarning him of the nature of the imposed consequence, you do not have to make the consequence so onerous—you are not using the dislike of a particular consequence as the deterrent to keep him from the misbehavior.

If the child asks you what the imposed consequence is for a specific misbehavior, he is negotiating. Do not negotiate; when you negotiate the initial message is completely lost. We want the misbehavior to stop, not just be paid for by enduring the imposed consequence.

If you say to the child, "If you don't get ready for bed right now, young man, I will not read to you tonight," this is a good way to insure that the child takes as long as he possibly can take to get ready for bed. If, on the other hand, you wait until the child is in bed and just announce, "You took too long to get ready for bed, so no reading tonight," he will probably move faster tomorrow night. Do not give children control over choosing an imposed consequence. If you administer them after the misbehavior, make them as logical as possible, and always stick to them. They do not have to be harsh or difficult to administer. Make sure that the imposed consequence is not so onerous that you will later either regret it or take it back.

Why Not Use Rejection, the Natural Consequence of Social Misbehavior, to Teach the Child to Be Nice to Others?

One of the natural consequences of the child's social misbehavior is rejection. Natural consequences are supposed to teach a lesson. Here is a case where the very obvious lesson to us is totally missed by the child.

Natural consequences are what happen naturally when we do something, for example drop a glass and the consequence is that it breaks. The imposed consequence of a child's misbehavior would be something that we would think up that hopefully would be somewhat associated to the misbehavior, such as if he does not pick up his toys then I give them to charity. We shield our children from natural consequences when the natural consequences are dangerous. The natural consequence of not wearing a seat belt is great personal damage or death in an accident. This is unacceptable to us as parents so we substitute imposed consequences for the child's not wearing his seat belt such as the child cannot go with you to the store if he does not wear his seat belt.

For TD children, one of the natural consequences of their misbehavior is rejection. They often have few or no friends. Parents of potential playmates do not want their child associating with a self-centered, foul-mouthed, lying, stealing, and manipulating child (would you?) Teachers are turned off by the child's behavior and become at times hostile in spite of the fact that they are supposed to be professionals. In the end, teachers are human too. And ultimately foster parents may reject the child. A foster child may be bounced from foster home to foster home, institution to institution, not bonding to anyone where ever he goes.

The natural consequence of the TD child's misbehavior, rejection by caregivers, mentors, and friends, though not dangerous or life threatening in a Safety and Security sense, certainly cannot be considered beneficial for the child. Yet I stated earlier in this chapter that whenever possible, use natural consequences to teach the child lessons, not imposed artificial consequences. Why not, then, just let the child be rejected and learn from that natural consequence?

The TD child, who is functioning primarily in the Safety and Security level, interprets the social rejection as a Safety and Security level threat, not as a Belonging and Love level loss as would most adults. Thus, rather than feel sad, abandoned, and alone like we might feel if rejected; he feels threatened, insecure, and the need to become vigilant in his battle to take control of his life so others cannot hurt him.

He gets and understands the natural consequence just fine, he learns the lesson well, but because his view of the world is different than ours, he processes it differently and in the end the lesson he learns is not the lesson we want him to learn. He learns to become more self-sufficient, work harder for control over his life, trust others even less. This lesson takes him in the wrong direction, we do not want to reinforce this lesson—he already knows it too well.

Things That Do Not Work

The TD child's issues are strongly rooted in the Safety and Security Need level. He has learned only to trust himself and known situations (situational trust); he has not emotionally advanced up the Hierarchy to having interpersonal trust, so demanding it from him before any has developed does not work.

Unless you are prepared to go so far that the TD child is completely broken down (boot-camp approach), verbal reprimands and threats do not work. He resists you, and probably succeeds in doing so. He prevails because he cannot and will not accept your control. Given a situation where you think it impossible for him to argue his way out of criticisms regarding his behavior, the child can surprise you, and manage to invent a defensive argument to support his actions. This usually speaks highly of his intellectual level.

Like it or not, you are going to find that the direct approach to behavior management does not always work. You then have to have to find more effective ways to manage the child.

People flippantly use the term low self-esteem, especially in regard to the TD child, but it is not necessarily an applicable phrase. Here we need to differentiate between low self-esteem and no self-esteem. Low self-esteem occurs when the individual has a minimal opinion of himself, whereas no self-esteem is when an individual has not advanced to the Esteem Needs level of Maslow's Hierarchy. Because the TD child is not functioning on this level, it is not important to him how other people see him.

This is why embarrassment should never be used for behavior control; it does not work on the TD child. Often, he already behaves in ways of which he should be ashamed; but his immaturity, and his reduced awareness of the emotions of others, make him seemingly immune to embarrassment. Again, this is a direct result of his not having advanced to the Esteem Needs level. This is explained in greater detail in Chapter 17 (Esteem).

Things That Do Work

It is imperative that you have more than one strategy, and just as imperative that you mix them up. If you use one technique too often, it will become ineffective. The TD child is often manipulative, and is very capable of thinking up ways to outwit you to his advantage. By mixing things up, you keep him off guard.

"If-then"s stated in a non-threatening manner, often work with immediate results. The key word here is non-threatening, as anything said in a threatening manner may increase his resistance to cooperation by increasing his need for Safety and Security. For example, instead of saying, "If you don't finish your seat-work, then no recess," a teacher might say, "The policy around here is that if you don't finish your seat-work then you have to stay in from recess, and I'd hate to see that happen." It means the same thing, but also shows caring on the adult's part. It also focuses less on confrontation that invokes an immediate defensive reaction, and thus allows the child to focus more on the consequences of his actions.

The TD child may respond to rewards. If you offer him something he values in exchange for specific behavior, after a guaranteed round of negotiating conditions, he frequently becomes the perfect child. Personally, I find this paying for performance technique troubling and try to limit its use. I liken it to feeding a dog table scraps from your plate during dinner—he'll leave you alone while eating, but then returns begging for more. I have witnessed a TD child use this kind of phony good behavior in advance of any contract, in hopes that it will result in some reward, like a video game or money. After a while he points out his good behavior and demands the reward. Conversely, I have also been threatened with bad behavior if I do not offer or provide a reward. Do not suggest or propose payment for good behavior. It shows that children often are fully aware of what constitutes good and bad behavior, and they have the intellectual capacity to turn if off and on at will.

I suggest three main principles that underlie the effectiveness of rewards. First, rewards work better when the time period between the behavior and the reward is not too long. Secondly, your motivation for having him do whatever you are asking should be obvious to the child. Finally, your request should not necessitate that he relinquish too much control to you. Remember, the child does not trust, and is always suspicious of your motives. If he has to give up too much control, the price to pay for the reward will be too great and he will not cooperate. Rewarding him for cleaning up his room might work just fine, while rewarding him for sitting might not work. If these three conditions for rewards are met, then the end result will be cooperation from the child.

With time, the TD child will develop trust, and with trust his behavior will improve. It is possible that the improvements we see from a well-executed behavior management regime would have occurred anyway even without any behavior management. That is to say, building trust is the best behavior management technique.

Anecdotal Experiences with Behavior Management

A major concern by the foster care agency in the screening process for foster parents was to discover how they discipline children. I had trouble expressing my techniques for discipline because I was not sure what it really was. My wife and I rarely ever disciplined our two natural children. Just letting them know our disappointments and our expectations seemed to work fine. Over time, they both grew up to be competent, accomplished, self-disciplined adults with the ability to make strong emotional attachments. It was during my foster parent training that I was taught about discipline and not to discipline, but to consequence.

One day a friend of one of my foster children was grounded as punishment for something he did. My foster child asked me why I never grounded him. Admittedly, my reasons for not grounding him were partly selfish, as the mechanics of grounding him and enforcing his staying home would punish me, too. Quite simply, I did not want to sit around and supervise him to be sure he did not defy his punishment. Quick thinking had me answer his question with a question. I asked him, "Do you think that grounding you as punishment would change your behavior?"

"No," he replied.

"That's why I don't ground you." We went on to talk about behavior, punishment, respecting each other, and expectations. It turned into a nice discussion.

It seems that most children watch a lot of TV, and my impression is that foster children watch more than average. Since poverty is a common thread in the background of many foster children, for them TV becomes a major form of entertainment; it is free, readily available, and has an addictive effect that distracts the child from having to deal with harsh realities. In my experience, foster children dislike your limiting their TV watching. I have taken away TV, computer games, and DVDs on a few occasions. Their reaction was always intense. Without TV they did not know what to do with themselves. I liken their reliance on media to an addiction (see Chapter 8 on Addictive Personality Paradigm). One book on reactive attachment disorder suggested that they should not be allowed any television at all for the first year in your home. I do not know if this would be helpful or not. There is nothing in my model that suggests it would be beneficial other than it would show that you are in control, and I do not think that you need to make life quite so harsh to get that message across.

Last Thoughts on Behavior Management

If you are looking for good discussions on behavior management techniques, almost all of the books on parenting difficult children and books about reactive attachment disorder have information on the topic. I suggest that you use behavior management techniques on an as-needed basis, and you should also not expect much more from them than basic management of behavior. Read all of the available books that give a myriad of different techniques; pick out the ones that might work for you and try them.

You do not need to be in constant control of the child, but it is important that you make sure he is not in control of you. It is possible to be a warm, loving person who does not take any guff from others—in a nutshell, that is what you want to be. You do not want to be stiff, rigid, or authoritarian, but instead be a kind and warm person who will not tolerate being abused. You want the child to know that you respect yourself.

In summary, I dislike behavior management techniques for the following reasons:

- They distract the child's attention from the lessons you wish to teach by focusing more on the consequence than on the misbehavior.
- They are not the best way to show the child that you are in control.
- They can interfere in your fun with the child if the techniques are too complicated.
- They often give the child an opportunity to defy you by purposely going for the consequence. The original lesson gets completely thrown out the window, and managing the consequence becomes a control battle.
- They require proper administration, and the prospect of additional control battles arises as a result.

- If your consequences are not well thought out, they can penalize everybody, for example "if you don't do this, then nobody gets to go to the mall."
- They can turn into the primary focus of your interaction with the child, leaving little room for other treatments.

Notes

[1] This is just my assessment, and admittedly is a somewhat negative definition.
[2] Cline & Helding, *Can This Child Be Saved?*, 1999, p. 175.
[3] Cline, Foster M.D., *Parenting with Love and Logic*, p. 97.

14

Battles

TD children want to be in control all the time, it is very important to them. Rule number three of the Four Rules (be sure the child knows that he is trusting you), basically says that he must see you as being in control. When two people want to be in control at the same time there invariably are going to be battles. If you take on the role of caregiver to a TD child and if you want to create a therapeutic environment, one that follows my Four Rules, you are going to have control battles.

You cannot raise a TD child without control battles

You do not have to be in control all the time, you do not have to run every part of the child's life, you just need to exert enough control over the child that he sees you as a strong person who routinely makes decisions on his behalf; and when he is in control, it is because you allow it. With time, like it or not, he will appreciate that he is in a trusting position. Then, assuming that things also go well for him, he will learn to trust you, that it is not so bad. A person, who trusts, worries less about Safety and Security and is able move up Maslow's Hierarchy to higher levels—which is good.

In Chapter 11 (The Repair Cycle), I suggest that a precipitating incident will initiate the battle phase of the Repair Cycle. I spoke about raising and lowering the behavioral bar. Choosing when to raise or lower the behavioral bar is just another way of saying, "pick your battles."

Pick Your Battles

All the literature and all the specialists who deal with "difficult children" state that you should pick your battles. This is universally accepted to mean that we should not fight with the child over every infraction, but instead select the most important ones while letting others slide. This is clearly good advice. After all, you cannot always be fighting with the child; there must be some good times, too, for both your sanity and that of the child. I have already discussed the need to win every battle that you *do* pick, which is another good reason to be selective in choosing your battles. Pick only the battles that you can win, because it is better not to engage the child at all than to engage him and lose.[1]

The Chauffeur

When he first came to me my foster child always wanted to ride chauffeur style in the back seat. For almost a year I allowed it but then decided that he should ride shotgun. From then on he was told he had to sit in the front seat and be sociable with me. One day in an attempt to deliberately defy me he got into the back seat. I was going to pick up somebody else so I did not think much about it, he was going to have to move back there anyway. I said nothing. As we pulled out of the drive he announced, "I am not going to sit in the front seat!" I kind of nodded my head and remained silent. He repeated, "You can't make me sit in the front seat." I said, "It's OK, I don't want to fight." When he could not get a fight out of me on the seating arrangements he changed the topic. He said, "How come we always have to listen to your music, you never let me pick the station." He was just begging for a fight. Eventually that evening, he got one.

As you become familiar with the child you will know when he needs a battle. Sometimes it is just obvious that the child is itching for a fight. A child can become like a volcano ready to erupt. A precipitating incident is imminent and the next battle phase of the Repair Cycle is about to start. If you know that a battle is inevitable, then why not plan to have it at a time that is convenient? It sounds a little strange, I know, but having the battle at a time when you are not rushed and when you can devote your full attention to the battle will reduce your stress and allow you to more effectively manage the battle. If a battle presents itself at an inopportune time, ignore it, even if ignoring it might cause you to appear inconsistent.

You do not want the child to be the one who has control over which battles you fight, or again he has won. I have discussed that a battle, which becomes the precipitating incident that starts the battle phase of the Repair Cycle, has an almost necessary therapeutic effect. These battles are your opportunity to remind the child that you are in control, and only by his knowing that you are in control, and also that you are fulfilling his needs, will the child learn trust.

The Bath

A prime example of picking battles would be when one evening I decided that my foster child needed a bath. I knew that he would balk, but he really needed one, and it was a convenient time for me. As expected, he did not want a bath and I found myself locked in a power struggle. Rather than argue, I picked him up and took him into the shower stall. I did not even bother to remove his underwear, and I just put him in the shower and washed him. He certainly did not like it, but he got a bath. My point is this: I did more than pick *my* battles, I picked *a* battle.

Consistency

Much of the literature has suggested (and I have no basis to disagree) that consistency is less important with TD children than demonstrating that you are in control.[2] What this means is that you can pick a battle over a certain behavior one time and ignore the same behavior the next time. This contradicts advice that you would give to a parent raising a more trusting child. In a trusting child, consistency is going to be helpful because he already trusts you as the parent, and it is when you become inconsistent that you run the risk of shaking your child's trust.

With the TD child, however, there is no trust to begin with. The TD child will use consistency on your part to their manipulative advantage. If they know you are always going to get angry when they do something they will use that behavior to push your buttons. It is better to be unpredictable in the battles you pick.

Admittedly there is a upside and a downside to inconsistency. Consistency does build trust, but consistency at the expense of losing control does not build trust. It is the concept of do you set the rules and the rules control the situation, or do you control the situation.

Pitfalls

There are pitfalls you may want to consider before you pick certain battles, battles you may want to avoid because they are very difficult to win. On the other hand, if you feel the need to have a battle with the child, and one of these potential pitfalls comes up, I say go for it. Any precipitating incident will do in a pinch. But if you are going to set hard and fast rules and commit yourself to always enforcing them, then be careful before you set rules for the following.

Food

Number one in this category is food. You just cannot control what the child puts in his mouth without crossing the abuse line, and even if you can force it down, he can always throw it back up.

Food can have special significance for the TD child for two reasons. First, it is possible that food was one of the Needs sporadically supplied during infancy instead of being provided consistently as it should be. Secondly, food is very symbolic of the fulfilling of our Needs. The TD child does not want you to be the source of his food because if you supply it, then he feels dependent upon you. Since he already feels that he cannot trust you, this makes him anxious. As I have mentioned, he does not want to be dependent upon anybody outside of himself, because when he is in control, he feels safe.

Food would seem to be a wonderful tool because if you supply it, the child is forced to accept you as the supplier of his needs. The problem with food is that unless the child wants to eat, you cannot force him do so without bordering on child abuse. You can lead a horse to water . . . Even if you can get the food into the child, he can always spit it back up. Once the power struggle starts, any lesson is lost.

The TD child wants to have a house filled with snack foods that he controls. He prefers to eat out rather than at home because, for some reason, when you buy food, it is not the same as when you prepare and serve it. You can even make the exact same thing he would get at a restaurant, and he will not eat it. The mere fact that you make it puts you in control.

It is surprising how little food the body really needs to thrive on a strictly nourishment basis. With this in mind, I cook meals but I do not worry about how much the child eats, and I typically do not even pay attention. I have just learned not to worry about it: it is a non-issue; I refuse to force a battle over food.

On the other hand, I absolutely insist that the child attend at least the start of each regular meal. We always sit down at a table for dinner as a family, and never with the TV on (except the few times a year when the Philadelphia Eagles have a night game). I always place some food on his plate even if he objects so that even if he does not eat much, he is at least participating in a social event. Though I will not fight about the child eating, I will have battles over attendance at the dinner table. I had a child sit angrily with his back to the table during the meal—but he was there. This is a good battle to pick because it is easy to supervise since you are going to be at the dinner table anyway. Once the meal is over, there is no way the child can undo having attended.

I cannot emphasize enough how I feel about the importance of daily family meals with no TV. This is healthy for all children and adults, too. If the child has a friend over, I insist that the friend either eat with us, or leave. If the friend says, "No thank you, I have already eaten," then I set a place for him at the table, put a little bit of food on the plate, and say that it is rude to sit and watch others eat. If he wants to stay, he will have to pretend to eat.

My point in making an issue of the TD child (or any child for that matter) being at the table for meals is twofold. First it is to demonstrate that food can serve a social function. More often than not, in the TD child's past food was simply a tool for survival, but for the majority of us, that is not the case. Many a night is spent socializing with friends and family for a few hours eating at a restaurant, which is clearly not necessary to survival. Secondly, this is a control battle that you can win. As I have stated, you cannot always control what goes in their mouths, but you can exercise control over them being at the table. For these reasons, I feel it is important for the TD child to engage in family meals.

I do not make much of an attempt to stop the child from snacking between meals. I do try to avoid taking him shopping at the supermarket where he will try to load the cart with all kinds of junk food. My control

171

technique over junk food is to limit the amount available, not to try to regulate it.

Clothing

Another one is clothing; it is really hard to keep clothes on a child if he does not want to wear them. As soon as your back is turned, he can take them off. If the child wears too little clothing in the winter natural consequences will let him know he made a mistake. If he picks clothes that look silly, so what. Skip this battle.

Bad Language

What comes out of a person's mouth is very hard to control. On the other hand, how those words affect you is totally in your control. I have learned to ignore foul and denigrating language from a TD child. I am only bothered by it when it is done in the presence of strangers who do not know the child or the situation. Basically I get embarrassed, for both the child and me. The child does not seem to get embarrassed or understand my embarrassment, something we have already discussed.

Sitting at a nice restaurant with other adults and having the child call me f——face did get a rise out of me.

Bedtime

Bedtime is also tough because unless you are willing to sit there every night and enforce it, the child can always get out of bed. If this is the case, then how are we supposed to get him to go to bed? My answer is that if it is important enough to you that the child sleeps, and you can find the energy to stick with the fight, go ahead and do it. The child is trying to take control to reaffirm to himself that he is in control. At the same time, he needs to be shown that the opposite is true and that you are in control. Again, this is a difficult battle but if it is important enough to you and you think you can win, pick this as one of your battles to fight.

A possible compromise would be to just insist that the child go to his room at bedtime and not worry about what happens when he is there.

Money

We are taught to place great value on money, to save it, to work hard for it, never to waste it, and so on. We grow up placing such importance and emphasis on money that it never occurs to us that money is an artificial concept that never existed until quite recently in the history of man (about the last few thousand years, which is insignificant in the development of our species).

Because money is an intellectual concept, and its value is artificial (manmade and based on trust in the government that prints it), it does not have the symbolic component of food. Money is not one of the basic needs.

Our culture, though, believes that money is important, and that the child should be taught to respect, earn, save and value it. Frugality, deferred gratification, planning, and differentiating needs from wants are all lessons tied into money. These are all very valuable lessons that the child needs to learn in order to grow into a responsible adult. However the child with TD is often not emotionally ready to learn these lessons. This child is still stuck on the issue of trust. Consequently, moving on to latter issues, even though they would seem appropriate given the chronological age of the child, can subvert our plan to develop trust.

If the child earns his money, then he sees himself in control. This would be good in the typical ten-year-old, but bad in the TD ten-year-old. In the typical ten-year-old child, we are working toward building self-confidence and independence, both desirable goals for adulthood. For this normal child, trust is an old issue that was established early in life. In the TD child, anything that empowers him to be independent and in control is going to undermine our program of building trust. After all, you do not need to trust other people if you do not need other people, and you do not need other people if you are in control.

Giving the TD child money when *you feel* like giving it to him, not when he wants it or earns it, makes you the symbolic source of his Needs. Since money is not a real Need, you can be a little erratic about it. Remember the Four Rules necessary for the TD child to develop trust are (1) supply all his Needs, (2) be trustworthy, (3) be sure the child knows that he is trusting you, and (4) be emotionally strong. Any opportunity to reinforce one of these rules takes precedence over other lessons, even though we know that other lessons are important and will eventually have to be taught.

Money should be just given to the child with words such as, "I just want you to have this because I love you." No strings attached, no reason given. This is not to say that a certain amount of the money that the child receives cannot be in the form of a bribe in the form of payment for doing simple chores. However a child should not always be paid to do simple chores. He is receiving room and board already, and payment to do daily chores simply deludes him into thinking that he is totally entitled to all the material things you provide for him. He will also feel that he does not have any obligation to pitch in and help out unless he is paid, which is wrong. In this way, paying him to do simple chores is really a bribe. This again relates back to my comment about inconsistency: If the child cannot figure out when you are going to give him money, then you have the upper hand in determining whether or not money becomes an issue for control battles.

Furthermore, a child who thinks that he has earned money is going to believe that he has the right to spend it any way he wants, which should not be true. You are still going to place restrictions on what he can have, regardless of where the money comes from. For example, buying too much candy or buying a pocketknife should be your choice, not his.

Relapse

The relationship between my foster child and me is going very well. I feel good about everything, and he also seems to be happier and even accepts my overtures for closeness and affection. And then wham! He will not ride in the car. I put him in the car, but he will not wear his seatbelt. He swears, becomes angry, belligerent, and basically a monster. What happened to all of our progress? Why is he suddenly so defiant over something as trivial as a car ride? And why in the world would he want to jeopardize a good relationship over something so unimportant?

Relapse is all part of the Repair Cycle. It starts with a precipitating incident and proceeds through the battle phase. The relapse ends with the reconciliation phase.

As I have previously stated, the child has learned not to trust through repeated experiences. He has also learned to take care of himself. Being ever vigilant in a hostile world and watching out for one's own welfare is a valuable survival skill (Safety and Security Needs). In the extreme case, survival skills can mean the difference between life and death.

When things are going well and the child becomes more relaxed, it is only natural that his defenses will drop. Then some trigger will remind him that he has lowered his guard. Perhaps if I had given him more time to think about the trip, I would not have reminded him that he was relinquishing control. Perhaps I forgot that he was not just another child, and that I needed to prepare him for even minor schedule changes.

Sometimes when the TD child has been good for a while, he then feels the need to be bad, to make up for the control he gave up when he was well behaved. Being good usually translates into being cooperative, which translates into giving up control. Praise for good behavior can backfire.

The whole issue turns into a control battle, that is to say, who is in charge and who makes the decisions. The TD child needs to feel in control because he does not trust others. If others are in control, then he is vulnerable. If he is in control, he can protect himself. If others in his world are in control, they can take advantage of him. He assumes that they will be taking advantage of him even if he does not see or understand how they are doing it. You can argue with him until you are blue in the face, but no matter how strong your argument, how obvious your position seems, it will not work. This is because he realizes that you have the superior intellectual capacity as you are the adult and he the child. So winning the intellectual argument only means that you are good at hiding your manipulative intentions. In the child's mind, no matter how sound your argument, he still feels he needs to be watchful, a vigilance that appears irrational to the adult.

Once a control battle starts it is desirable that you win it. Remember, it is not really control that he wants so much as it is being less vulnerable and being in a position where he will not be used or be hurt. Being in control is just a mechanism to achieve that goal. If he wins the battle, there is no lesson learned. If you win the battle, there is the potential for the TD child to learn a major lesson. He needs to figure out that he can relinquish control and still be safe, be taken care of, and have his needs met. If he wins battles, then he will just assume that his needs are being met because he is in control. This does not do anything to help him change, and it reinforces past experiences. If you win control, then he has the opportunity to associate your being in control with his needs being met, and this is the lesson that we want him to learn. Also remember that if he makes you angry, he has won the control battle, even if your will prevails. You must not become angry to win the battle.

The relapses serve a purpose, an opportunity to remind the TD child that while life has become less stressful, things are going better. He is becoming more connected and possibly experiencing love for the first time in his life, and it is all happening while he is not in control. If he is not in control and things are going well, he can trust after all, and this is the only way I can think of that he ever will learn to trust.

Also remember that he has a basic need to be connected to others (Belonging and Love Needs), so that deep down, he wants to trust you. As you assuage his Safety and Security Needs, his Love and Belonging Needs will pull him further toward trusting.

Looking at the relapses as a necessary and beneficial part of his recovery also helps you to handle them effectively. The TD child is very good at pushing buttons to make people angry. If you can stand back a little, keep yourself from getting angry, and see his behavior as just another opportunity to reinforce a positive lesson (that you are in control and his needs are being met), it makes it much easier to tolerate another battle without despairing what appears to be a step backwards in behavior.

Conclusions

So how does one define winning or losing a battle? In short, you have lost the battle if the behavior you want from the child does not happen.

You may also have lost if in the process of the battle you become angry. If the child has made you angry he has controlled your emotions. He has won that round, and at best, you have a draw.

Understanding

Understanding the emotional state of the child helps me to see through the angry words being spewed at me, and makes me feel more empathetic to his situation. I feel more in control, and that helps me to stay calm.

Before I achieved understanding, I found my anger was not so much with the child but, rather, with my inability to control his misbehavior. I was upset with the prospect of my being trapped in an intolerable situation with no apparent end. I was fighting against the possibility of failure.

Understanding his emotional state removes much of that frustration and replaces it with hope. Understanding for me also turns the battles from being emotionally charged to being intellectual, further reducing my anger because I am thinking rather than getting mad.

There are undoubtedly going to be compromises with a TD child. One such compromise is balancing what is best for the child with how much energy you as the caregiver have to expend on him. Better to stay in for the long run than to burn out. It is better to make mistakes, even knowingly so, than to wear yourself out. In the end it is the war, not the battles, we want to win. So do not worry too much about what you cannot do, or what others might consider to be a bit of sloppy parenting along the way.

Notes

[1] Cline & Helding, *Can This Child Be Saved?*, 1999, p. 139.
[2] Keck & Kupecky, *Parenting the Hurt Child*, 2002, p. 67.

15

Structure (Situational Trust)

A friend was telling me about an experience she had with her son while he was in elementary school: He had started to write letters backwards. Her son's teacher called her to report the regression and asked if anything unusual was happening at home. My friend reported that her husband had recently left her. The teacher had correctly surmised that the child's letter writing regression was caused by an emotional setback in the child's life.

The teacher said that mom needed to structure her son's life highly, that everything should be done on a rigid schedule. So she did everything the teacher suggested, and sure enough, her son stopped writing backwards.

So the question here is what role did structure play in fixing this particular situation? Did the structure fix the situation, or was it more like a Band-Aid. Is structure good as a general rule? Or is it more like vitamins in the sense that it cannot hurt and may possibly help? Just what is structure?

Structure, or as we would probably say, "creating structure" within the context of this chapter and child raising in general, means to create an environment that is highly predictable; the child gets up at the same time, eats at the same time, studies, naps, all his daily activities are planned and scheduled such that the child always knows exactly what is going to happen next. There are no surprises and the routine should neither be overly stimulating nor should it be frightening or dangerous. Structure and situational trust are closely related. The repeated routine that structure provides lulls the child into trusting his environment, which is by definition situational trust.

I have defined two types of trust, transferal and situational. Transferal trust is when one's faith and confidence are placed in another person. If someone I trust tells me something, I believe it. If they lead me into a new situation, I feel safe and secure because I am confident they would not intentionally place me in harm's way. Situational trust, on the other hand, is a knowledge that specific situations are safe and secure. Situational trust is based on experience, and grows with repeatedly good outcomes of the same situation. Bowlby's attachment cycle first uses situational trust to move the child up into transferal trust.

The two types of trust, together, encompass the Safety and Security Needs. Within the Safety and Security Needs I have ranked situational trust as being below transferal trust. This means situational trust must be fulfilled before the individual can move on to transferal trust; the ability to have and enjoy transferal trust does not emerge until one has developed and enjoys situational trust.

I have also talked about transcendence, and I would suggest that an individual, including a child, can transcend situational trust if transferal trust is strong enough. I have suggested that individuals who have achieved higher levels may choose to transcend lower level Needs that become unfulfilled.

So in this case, when the boy's father left, both his emerging transferal trust and his situational trust were shaken. Would he have weathered the emotional storm of divorce if he had held a firm, deep seated belief that no matter what happened between his parents that both of them would never abandon him, that they would guarantee that he was safe and secure and provided for emotionally and physically. In other words, had he had firm deep-seated transferal trust? Without a doubt. But he did not have that deep-seated transferal trust; he was at an age where children are developing that trust, and the impending divorce caused him to regress back to situational trust. He could not transcend the level that immediately preceded his current working level.

The child falls back into the situational trust level. The teacher recommended that the mother use an excess of structure, basically an environment that engenders situational trust, to create the stability the child needs to end his slide backward and begin moving back up toward higher levels. Situational trust is based on the known and familiar. Safety and security is derived from the predictability of a familiar situation. Creating a rigid routine increases predictability, and thus creates trust. Children need a world that they can trust, so in this case, increasing situational trust to compensate for the shaken situational and interpersonal trust helped the child.

Maybe the child would have healed anyway and time was all he needed. Of course, sometimes there is no way of knowing until we try it. Just because the problem might go away on its own, however, does not mean we should not try to rectify it rather than play the waiting game.

Structure can and does play a large role in the development of any child and continues to be important in the life of the TD child. The child's need for fulfilling situational trust starts developing within weeks (if not days) of birth as per Bowlby and the attachment cycle. It must be satisfied for the child to move on to transferal trust. The TD child has attained little if any transferal trust and for him creating structure is going to be an important way for us to create a stable safe and secure base for him to use to satisfy his situational trust so that he can move on to work on and learn transferal trust.

How many children out there do you think are struggling with mastering transferal trust? A lot more than just the TD children. Consider the situation when you introduce a new food to a child, you might say something like, "I know you will like this," and of course you mean what you say (I assume that anyone reading this would never manipulate or lie to a child). The child might balk, and if he does, it is for two reasons: his lack of transferal trust, and his lack of situational trust. In simpler terms, he does not trust you (transferal), and he does not trust that he will like the new food that is being introduced to him (situational).

Our immediate goal for the TD child is transferal trust. We want the child to trust his caregiver, his teachers, authority figures—and later in life, his spouse. We do not want the child to have to live in a rigid, structured world where he cannot enjoy new experiences, people, places, and things. But we appreciate with the TD child that achieving this goal is going to take time. In the meantime, we will use structure as needed to help the child feel safe and secure.

16

Kidding

Use kidding as a tool to help the TD child? *You're* kidding, right?
No!

Kidding tends to be one of my primary tools for working with the TD child; I use it whenever appropriate, and that is often. Consider the following scenario:

You and the child are watching TV, and the child says, "Go get my can of soda. I left it in the kitchen." When his attitude is pushy and demanding, you are not going to be bullied into getting the child his can of soda. But what are you going to do? Punish him for being disrespectful? Lecture him on who is in charge? If it is not already obvious to the child who is in charge (and it should be you), you have already lost the battle, maybe the war—so hopefully you should not have to lecture him on that.

So instead you respond, "While I'm up, would you like ice with the soda?" and return your attention to the television. If he says nothing more, then the exchange is over. If he says, "No, just the soda will be fine," you respond with something like, "Are you sure? Some ice and maybe some chips sound like they may be mighty nice with your soda." If he says yes rather than no to your instigations, you might add other things to his request, and keep adding them until the request becomes totally absurd. You might end your conversation with something like, "Ha, you just want too much. It's too much for me to carry, and I need to sit here and build up my energy. But if you go get it, while you are up can you bring me a soda, too? I would like mine with ice."

At some point the child realizes, that rather than getting angry or taking his attempt at manipulation seriously, you are going to play the same game right back at him. If he can get you to respond, "No, I think you are old enough to get it yourself!" he has won, because he has gotten an angry response from you. He has pushed a hot button. Repeatedly responding in an angry fashion wears you down, lowers your patience, and eventually you risk your anger becoming rage.

In addition to all of this, lecturing the child by telling him "you are old enough" sends the message that what you do for the child is only because he is not capable of doing it for himself, and I hope that is not the case. I do many little things for my foster children that send the message that I care about them. Since they are emotionally younger than their chronological age would indicate, they need little things done for them like helping them dress or tying their shoes. There is nothing wrong with doing these little perhaps age-inappropriate things for them as long as you both enjoy it.

Kidding is like a little verbal con game where you make a bizarre, unbelievable, or ironic statement in a serious way and try to convince someone you really mean it. The fun then, is seeing how far along you can take your victim before he catches on to your attempt at playful manipulation. He in turn can respond by pretending to take your statements seriously, and adding even more bizarre elements to the tale, in essence kidding back. Kidding includes an element of closeness and even respect, as we never kid with somebody that we do not like, or somebody we think cannot handle it.

When I did not answer with an angry, serious, or judgmental response to his request to get me his drink, but with the flippant comment about ice, I sent him the message that I had interpreted his original request to me as him just kidding me. I trivialized his request by kidding back, thus eliminating any need to get embroiled in a manipulative and controlling verbal exchange.

Believe it or not, this is powerful stuff. Anytime the TD child tries to gain control of you by manipulating you, treat it as if he is just playing a game with you, just kidding with you. Of course when someone kids with you, you are fully justified and within your rights to kid back. If he wants to maintain that his request is truly a serious one, he will be put on defense and be forced to prove it.

There is no need to punish a person who kids. In fact, having a sense of humor is a good thing. Tell the TD child how witty he is—it is much more effective than getting serious all the time when he makes an attempt to manipulate you or others.

It is a lot more fun too, I enjoy the repartee with the child, and even though he knows he has been had (so to speak), he laughs too when the absurdity of his request is exposed.

He learns that you will not be conned, that you can play the game, and that if he wants to be taken seriously, then he had better make reasonable requests. He learns that you do not rise up to any request that you think is out of line, but treat it as if he is just begging for fun. He learns all that, while having fun.

Then at the end of the repartee you might finish up by saying something really serious to him, but still in a kidding manner. Look him straight in the eye, put on your best serious face, and say, "I just want you to know that I value the time you spend with me."

As much as I advocate kidding with the TD child, you should only use this technique if he is old enough and smart enough to understand it, otherwise the sarcasm will simply be lost on him. Unless you and the child really enjoy kidding around, you should also only use this if the child initiates it. This way you can use it as a tool to control the child by turning the tables on him, thus winning another control battle.

Examine your options. The child makes a statement, and no matter what the statement is, you do need to respond. Of course if the statement is reasonable, you should respond in a reasonable fashion. If the statement is not reasonable, that is, confrontational, manipulative, controlling, and so on, how are you going to respond? Ignoring it, not responding at all, is an option, but that too is going to be a thought-out process, so I would consider that to be a kind of response in and of itself. Of all the possible ways of responding, interpreting his original statement to be kidding and an invitation for you to be just as unreasonable is the only way you can achieve all the elements needed for him to heal.

You have done everything needed to help the child, you have taken over complete control of the conversation, you have made it quite clear that you are in control, and you have made him feel connected and fed into his need for love. Wow! What started as a control battle ended up into a little therapeutic moment. What an opportunity.

Here is what you have accomplished:

- You have trivialized a ridiculous request such that you need not respond to it directly, or let it progress to a control battle.
- You have taken over control of the conversation.
- You have given the TD child an answer to his request while avoiding direct confrontation.
- You have had some fun.

- You have turned it into an opportunity to tell the child how important he is, how much you love him, or whatever your message de jour may be.

17

Esteem

Thus far I have by and large disregarded Maslow's fourth level Needs: Esteem. This has been intentional. As Maslow predicted, and as I concur, esteem is not really an issue for the TD child. I appreciate that this may be a controversial statement for some people, and may represent a significant shift in the way they see the TD child. Based on my research, it seems that I am one of few who downplay the significance of esteem. I do feel uncomfortable taking a stand that seemingly contradicts conventional wisdom, but if you consider this statement anecdotally it will help to clarify my position.

Let's say that you are out in public and your child starts behaving in a bizarre and totally inappropriate way. He starts acting like a baby, making loud, imitative crying noises followed by shouting hateful comments, and then screams profanities. You become overcome with embarrassment and want to shrink into your chair, or point to him and say, "Whose child is this?" In other words, you wish to disassociate yourself publicly from any ownership of him and his behavior. In the privacy of your own home, you might just shrug off the same behavior, but in public it is upsetting.

It was just such an experience that first turned me on to the idea of using Maslow as more than simply an interesting paradigm that we learn and quickly forget, but instead as a paradigm that can have everyday implications and usefulness. Why I was thinking of Maslow at that time I do not know, but I distinctly remember putting the child's behavior and Maslow's model together, and suddenly it was as if Maslow's model took on life.

So why is it that the child is not embarrassed with the way he acts when that same behavior embarrasses you? And why does not embarrassment inhibit his public behavior like it does yours and mine?

Maslow proposes that higher level Needs do not emerge until lower level Needs are satisfied, and as previously stated, the child with trust issues is stuck in the Safety and Security level. Esteem is two levels higher than Safety and Security with Belonging and Love in between. Embarrassment is an Esteem level emotion. If the child is stuck in the Safety and Security level then he is not working at the Esteem level, so it follows that he is simply unable to be embarrassed. At the very least, he is not able to be embarrassed at that point in time.

And there you have it. The child was behaving exactly as Maslow would predict. The child's Esteem Needs had not yet surfaced, he did not care what other people thought about him, he was insensitive to criticism, and therefore the child could not be embarrassed.

Before I go any further I think I should back away from my statement that the TD child is unable to be embarrassed. I admittedly made that statement more to get your attention than because I truly believe it.

I have previously discussed that the TD child, or any child for that matter, has the ability to function on multiple levels, but at any given point in time will only be functioning on *one* level. At the point in time when he was acting out in public in a very upsetting manner, he was probably unable to be embarrassed. At another point in time, perhaps when he was less tired and operating on a higher level, the child would be able to feel embarrassment. I would never say that we could flat out ignore the Esteem Needs of the TD child. I would say that focusing on his Esteem Needs as a primary focal point in therapy makes little sense.

Maslow further subdivides Esteem into two categories: self-esteem and esteem of others. He defines self-esteem as "the desire for strength, achievement, adequacy, mastery and competence, confidence in the face of the world, and independence and freedom." He defines the esteem of others as "the desire for reputation or prestige, status, fame and glory, dominance, recognition, attention, importance, dignity, or appreciation."[1]

Praise

The TD child's need to be in control, and all of the behaviors associated with his need for control (belligerence, defiance, lying, manipulation, etc.), are behaviors motivated by Safety and Security Needs. The child cannot trust others and feels the necessity to be in control is essential to his own safety and security, and possibly essential to his Physiological Needs being met as well.

I have previously suggested that the child's developmental progress toward higher level Needs is not a smooth linear process, but is characterized by moving up the Hierarchy and then relapsing back down. You should not view the occasional relapse as anything more than part of the normal healing process, and should not worry that it means all your attempted work at healing the child has gone down the drain.

Along with relapse, though, will also come the opposite. There are going to be times when the child moves ahead of his normal position along the Hierarchy, and even if he is not overtly motivated by Esteem Needs, he will certainly enjoy recognition, attention, dignity, and appreciation. I would never withhold deserved praise and adulation, but be aware that it is not usually a strong motivator for the TD child.

Have you ever received compliments or praise that you felt were underserved or unearned? If so, you know what it is like to receive a phony compliment. You feel that the person complimenting you is just trying to butter you up, maybe to get something from you. Immediately your defenses go up, and you try to figure out what it is he or she wants.

This is how the TD child feels when you praise him. Regardless of your intentions, he often sees praise as an insincere, manipulative maneuver on your part to obtain good behavior. He does not believe your compliments, so rather than enjoying them or benefiting from them, he looks for your ulterior motives. When you raise somebody's defenses, you increase their Safety and Security level awareness and decrease their trust. This works against you and your goal to develop trust. Be careful with praise and complements, and expect to be challenged. Make sure that:

- The child is emotionally ready to receive praise. This means that at the time you give the praise the child's behavior is motivated not by Safety and Security Needs, but by Love and Belonging Needs or Esteem Needs.
- The praise is warranted. If you make up things to praise him about, he will probably see right through that.[2]
- If he challenges you, you can support your contention that he has done something praiseworthy.

187

Embarrassment

Embarrassment is the feeling you get when you have lost esteem big time. For people who function strongly on Maslow's fourth Esteem Needs level, embarrassment and the fear of embarrassment are primary motivators in their lives. This explains the classical behavior of teenagers who are motivated by peer pressure, like the need to wear the right clothes, be seen with the right people, or say the right things. They are afraid of what others will think of them, and they are right in the midst of working through their own Esteem Needs.

Our TD child is not worried about esteem. Telling him to "sit still and be quiet because you're embarrassing me," does not work. Telling him not to do something because of "what other people will think," also does not work. You have to deal with your embarrassment on your own; your TD child is not going to alter his public behavior to help you. Do not reject your TD child for displaying embarrassing public behavior. Embarrassment is not an issue with him yet: he does not understand it, so he also will not understand why you are pushing him away. After all, you have the issue with embarrassment—he does not.

When you feel he is trusting you, which varies from hour to hour and day to day, and when he is working on a Belonging and Love level (no control battles going on), which varies as well from hour to hour and day to day, that is when to give him some compliments, and that is when he has the potential to respond positively to those compliments. If you push him too quickly with compliments, he may feel manipulated and retreat further into the Safety and Security Need level.

A prime example of what I am talking about can be seen in the TD child's attitude toward schoolwork. Why does he do sloppy work in school, quickly completing assignments, not paying attention to quality or detail and just doing what he has to do to get the requirement out of the way? Because impressing others with a good job and looking for the praise that comes from doing a good job is a function of esteem.

So in summary, why does the child not care about what you or others think? Because these are Esteem Needs and he is simply not there yet. If you do your job well, esteem will become an important part of his life to be eventually replaced by Maslow's fifth Need level: Self-actualization. Do not worry about Self-actualization. You cannot teach it—you can only model it.

Notes

[1] Maslow, *Motivation and Personality*, 1970, p. 21.
[2] Eshleman, *Becoming a Family*, 2003, p. 99.

18

School Issues

School is a huge part of your child's life. His teacher may even spend more time with him than you do. Ideally, the therapeutic environment that you create for the TD child by implementing the Four Rules in your home can also be implemented for him at school. It can happen and luckily it does happen. Sometimes a teacher is the one responsible for creating the environment that changes a child's life. However, due to class size, the demands to accomplish curriculum goals, and a myriad of other demands placed on teachers, it is unlikely that he or she can create the quality of therapeutic environment that you can in your home.

I have discussed the TD child's unwillingness to take directions because he sees any attempt to control his behavior as manipulation, and he has not been manipulated positively in the past. It is a trust issue. Most teachers do a good job of treating all their students equally. If the child were to just trust the teacher, follow his or her rules, and cooperate, things would go smoothly and everybody would be happy. The likelihood that the teacher would take advantage of a cooperative child is rare. If anything, the cooperative child probably gets favored, but the TD child does not see it this way.

The TD child, with his limited experience, only knows that people have not been trustworthy in the past and believes that he must be vigilant. Since he cannot trust others, he wants to be in control. With the ongoing rotation of adults and peers that the child interacts with at school, his level of anxiety is going to rise. Furthermore, being in an environment that requires strict adherence to rules, by its very nature, highly structuring his life, removes a significant amount of the child's control over his own life. With loss of the child's cherished control, there comes even more anxiety.

We demand that the TD child sit still in his seat and listen attentively, but teachers and administrators rarely appreciate the level of stress and anxiety he is experiencing. Anxiety is built into his life, and it is a constant byproduct of not being able to trust. The TD child always has to be on guard, but he hides the fact that his misbehavior is triggered by anxiety, and he does this by acting cool as if he is in control. "Any child who feels anxious or threatened can manifest extreme behavior"[1] Asking the TD child to sit still and be quiet in school is akin to asking the typical adult to sit quietly on a chair placed in the center of a heavily trafficked intersection. Being stressed and anxious is not an emotional state conducive to learning.

In dealing with teachers and administrators, you are going to encounter a large range of empathic ability to understand and work with your TD child. Some teachers will instinctively know just what to do to help your child. Others will enter into control battles from day one, and things will only seem to go downhill from there.

Not much needs to be said about the teacher who possesses the skills to successfully tame and teach your child while juggling all the other demands and requirements of maintaining control and structure in a full classroom, except to express admiration and thanks. Hopefully your school administration is aware of the TD child's special needs and will match him with the appropriate teacher. It is naïve to think that this is always going to happen. Eventually your child is going to be assigned a teacher that just does not get it. Then what should you do?

When faced with this situation, people with resources typically pull their child out of that school and find another, often a private school. This is probably the best solution as it gives you control over selecting the right teacher, and in the end finding the right teacher is going to be a lot quicker and easier than trying to convert a bad teacher into a good one.

If you do move the child from one school to another, leave him at the new school until he graduates, if possible. Do not put him into a new school for one year, and then move him back to his old school (or to any other school for that matter), unless things at the new school do not work out and it becomes necessary. The TD child does not move well. As I have stated, his trust is primarily situational, and as such, once he becomes comfortable in a situation it is really better to not move him unless it is essential. Moving a TD child is like giving candy to a diabetic child; do not do it if not necessary. My point in saying this is that private schools are expensive, and unless you have the financial resources to keep the child in the private school for his entire academic career, then consider some of the other options I present here.

Behavior

If you get a call from the child's school that there is a behavior problem, his teacher or some other school representative might request a meeting. Hopefully the calls and meetings are informational in nature and are only meant to keep you aware of what is happening in school, both because you really should be kept informed, and so that you can also knowledgably talk to your child about what he did or what is happening. As a general rule though, the more administrators and experts that they bring to the meeting, the more you can expect that they are preparing to transfer responsibility for managing the child's behavior from them to you. This is not a good thing.

If it does get to this point, you are going to have to answer whether or not your child is so bad that his misbehavior falls outside the range that we would expect an experienced teacher to handle. Or is it a case of his teacher just not having the skill level to deal with him, skills that we reasonably expect a teacher to have? If the school suggests (and you agree) that the child does not belong in a traditional classroom setting, then of course you and the school will pursue appropriate alternatives.

The public school systems are required by law to give your child an "appropriate education." Special educational programs are quite expensive, so you can expect school officials to want to maintain him in a traditional classroom setting if possible. This works to your advantage because you should also want him to stay in a traditional classroom if possible.

You can pretty much expect the school to focus more on the misbehavior of your child than on the inexperience or lack of skills of their personnel. They might try to transfer their problem with your child at school to your home.

The school might ask you to take an active part in controlling his behavior in class by having you administer consequences at home for his misbehavior in school. They might ask you what some of your child's favorite activities or pastimes are, and then ask you to take them away from him on daily basis when he misbehaves in his classes. You must resist this. It is the school's responsibility to deal with your child's school misbehavior at school, not to pass the responsibility on to you. You already have the responsibility of dealing with behavior problems at home.

But you might ask that if you do not discipline him for misbehaving at school, will not that send him the message that you are accepting of his misbehavior at school, so long as he does not do it at home? Not at all. He should be disciplined for misbehavior at school, and the school should administer the discipline.

If you take on the responsibility for discipline both at school and home, you become the bad guy, as in the statement "wait till your father comes home." This is wrong. You also lose some of your tools for behavior management at home by giving control of them over to the school, which makes your job just more difficult. But the most important reason to resist becoming the main disciplinarian for your child is that it makes it much more difficult for you to follow rule number one of the Four Rules.

Rule number one—supply all his needs, which includes his need for love. You cannot make a child with whom you are constantly battling feel that he is loved. You can be pretty sure that if the school is unwilling or unable to handle his misbehavior, that his time spent there is probably somewhat contentious. Since he is not getting his Belonging and Love Needs satisfied there, it is even more important that you make him feel loved at home. You cannot allow a bad environment at school to poison your environment at home.

You and the school should work in a joint effort with a common goal—to help your child grow both emotionally and intellectually. Just like you need to do your part, they too have an obligation to do their part as well.

Every child is going to be a behavior problem at some time. Elementary school teachers are trained to handle behavior problems. Of course, some are better than others. If your child's teacher is not coping with your TD child, there are other options.

Develop a Relationship with His Teacher Early

There are many reasons why having a good relationship between a parent and a child's teacher are beneficial, and they hold for the TD child as well. There is one reason unique to the TD child that people generally do not consider: your behavior can speed the process of building trust between the child and teacher. If the child sees you as accepting, respectful, comfortable, friendly and considerate toward his teacher, he will be more likely to drop his guard thus becoming more trusting. The child already knows you (and hopefully trusts you), and he can transfer some of that trust from you to his teacher. The quicker he becomes trusting of his teacher, the sooner his levels of anxiety drop, and the sooner he will be able to sit still, concentrate, and cooperate.

Maybe you can avoid his ever becoming an unmanageable behavior problem. Talk to his teacher early in the school year. Your visits can be short, but make sure the child sees the two of you talking. Be upbeat, but not critical or defensive. Save any negativity for when your child is not around. Not only will this help your child, but the teacher will also feel better about having your child in class if he or she feels there is an interested party with whom to communicate possible problems.

Special Services

There are individuals and organizations that specialize in childhood behavioral management. These range from services that provide a few hours of observation and offer teachers and parents some advice, to a full-time aide who sits in the classroom the entire time the child is in the classroom and manages the child's behavior.

CAIS (Wrap Around) involves having a specialist observe the child in a natural school setting who then gives advice to the teacher about how he or she can better manage the child. Note—this same service is available for parents and foster parents, and generally the specialist will work with both you and the teacher, wherever the problems lie. (See appendix A.)

Individual Education Plan

An Individual Education Plan (IEP) is a legal document that mandates schools to provide for your child's specialized needs. These needs can range from requiring the school to provide a gifted educational program for your high IQ child, special support for a slow learner, or emotional support for a child with behavioral problems. The advantages

194

of having an IEP are: (1) it provides for outside evaluation of the child by a psychologist at the school's expense, which may be more objective than the school's analysis, (2) if you do not like the evaluation of the child, which is usually done by a psychologist who was chosen by the school, it allows for you to challenge their evaluation and have it redone by another psychologist at the school's expense, (3) it requires that a formal plan be developed for your child, (4) it provides for greater input on your part in formulating the plan, (5) it requires that the school implement and follow the formal plan, and (6) it gives you certain legal remedies if the school fails to follow the plan.

If you are unhappy with the way your school is managing your TD child's behavior or education, and you feel the school needs a push to change, consider an IEP.

Homework

I personally cannot see any reason why the TD child should be treated any differently than any other child when it comes to homework. My policy with any child is to have them do and be responsible for whatever homework they can manage on their own, and help them when they need it. If they are struggling with a subject, give them help, or even get a tutor, like a reading instructor who you might hire over the summer for the child who is behind in that particular skill.

If you value education, this might be one of the battles that you pick. The typical TD child has a low esteem need (not low self-esteem, but a low *need* for esteem-based support). What this means is that he is not going to be embarrassed by low test scores, and will not be motivated to be a high achiever in order to impress anyone.

Surveying some of the books on raising difficult children give a slightly different approach from mine:

> School work is 100% the child's responsibility. Do not interfere in any way with the child's studies. Do not check homework or even ask if he has homework.[2]

If you take this approach, your emotionally immature TD child, who is lacking Esteem Need level motivation, will most likely not do any homework at all. Going to school every day unprepared is certainly going to add to the friction between him and his teachers. School is a large part of his life, and success there is going to be valuable in speeding the child toward healing. It is true that you should pick your battles, but this one-hour battle at night has the potential pay-off of giving the child six hours of success the next day at school. It is a worthwhile battle to pick not only because it makes all the time spent at school less stressful, but also because the addition of falling behind in his intellectual development to his already retarded emotional development is certainly not in the child's best interest.

If the child is already behind in his reading, writing, or math skills, ignoring his schooling will make it even harder for him to catch up later.

Summary

The child's intellectual growth and his emotional growth are both clearly important. If you are lucky enough to have a good, competent teacher, between the two of you, you should be able to provide the child with a joint school and home therapeutic environment that provides for growth in both emotional and intellectual areas.

Unfortunately, you may have to make a choice between concentrating on his emotional growth or his intellectual growth. If the battle to get your child to do his homework becomes too consuming, you might have to choose to temporarily put his intellectual development on hold while you concentrate on his emotional development. There are people out there who have never learned to read who live full and happy lives. There is nobody out there who never learned to be happy who went on to live a full and rewarding life. His school will not like this, but if the battle over schoolwork effectively destroys the therapeutic environment the Four Rules are meant to create, then the school has to take second place. It is going to be easier to catch up intellectually later on than to catch up emotionally.

Do not let the school ruin the good work that you are doing with the child at home. Do not let them "bully" you into a situation where precedence is placed on homework and intellectual growth rather than on emotional growth. If you cannot do both well, then place your emphasis on the emotional component and just do it well.

Often, though, you can manage both. Knowing that some battles with the child are not only inevitable but necessary (see section on relapse)—and if you have the skill, the tenacity, the wits, or whatever else it takes for you to win the homework battle—homework is a worthwhile battle to undertake. Homework can be a major and difficult battle to win because often the child has had some truly bad experiences in school and wants to have nothing to do with anything that has anything to do with school. If you win the homework battle the child ultimately benefits a great deal because, not only do you win a battle which we have previously discussed as being necessary and important, but it will contribute toward the child succeeding in school which makes life easier for everybody.

Notes

[1] Turecki, *The Difficult Child*, 2000, p. 85.
[2] Quote from Thomas, Nancy L., *When Love Is Not Enough*, 1997, p. 78. Also see Cline, *Parenting with Love and Logic*, 1990, p. 165.

19

The Brat

There are many children in our society that I might label "brats." These are strong willed children who seem to mostly care only about themselves. They talk back to their parents, they are very opinionated, they whine or throw temper tantrums when they do not get their way, and they are often fussy eaters. They sound a lot like the TD child but the interesting thing is that they come from stable, loving, traditional two parent families with no history of abuse or neglect. If anything, they come from the other end of the spectrum, their Needs were assiduously attended to from the moment they popped into this life until the present.

The "brat" is a controlling child. He uses all his manipulative strategies to get his way. Many books have been written about these children to help parents co-exist with them, book titles such as *The Difficult Child, The New Dare to Discipline, The Explosive Child*, and *The Challenging Child*. Most of the books have one thing in common, they mostly present strategies for wrestling control away from the child and back to you, the parent.

There are clearly different levels of "brats." Some children behave bratty all the time, while others are bratty only part of the time, or only for certain people or in certain situations. It would be the exceptional child indeed that never has a bratty moment. Raising a child who routinely defers to others and never makes any demands to have his own way would not be quite right either. But within a culture and within a society there are levels of acceptable behavior for children and when in the presence of a "brat" you can just feel that this child is outside that norm: that the child is running the show too much; that the parents are somewhat being held hostage to his demands; and that you want to tell the parents to just say "no" to the child, set some boundaries, let him know who is the parent and who is the child.

I have seen a public service announcement on TV where the parents are told not to "be a friend" to their child but to "be a parent" with the message that children do not need you as a friend, they need you as a parent. It is primarily to the parents of "bratty" children that these announcements are directed.

As an aside, I have also seen public service announcements (that appear to have been created by the same advertising agency) that suggested that the parent read and spend more time with their children, not be so distant, be more of an accepting accessible friend to their child. So what is the bottom line—do we become more authoritarian, strict, and controlling, or do we become more friendly, accepting, and accommodating? The answer again, of course, is that one size does not fit all when giving such advice, it depends on the child and the parents. Some parents need to be more authoritative, and others need to be less authoritative and more supportive and accessible. One of the tenets of my book is that you *can* be both, though maybe not at the exact same time; it is a balancing act. In the case of the public service announcements, I worry that the already too strict parents are going to use the "be a parent not a friend" message to justify their already too controlling approach to parenting, ignoring the other message to which they really should be listening; while the parents who need to set some limits will only hear the "be a friend to your child" message and use it to justify not setting firm limits. People have a tendency to hear only the messages that support their beliefs. I laud the intent behind the announcements but worry about their actual effect.

The brat and the TD child seem to exhibit many of the same behavioral characteristics. It begs the question, do they share the same underlying emotional makeup, an emotional makeup that in turn drives their behavior? Do they both lack trust?

The answer to that question is, I am not quite sure, but I think it an interesting concept to consider, after all, since there are so many similarities in their behavior and since much behavior is motivated to satisfy emotional needs, and since we all share the same basic set of emotional needs, it follows that there is likely a common thread of shared unmet emotional need between the brat and the TD child which may be responsible for the similarities in behavior.

It really should not be a trust issue with the brat; the brat has no reason not to trust, all of his needs have been routinely met. What about the fact that the brat appears to be stuck in the Safety and Security level. Why do I say that? Controlling behavior implies an inward self-centered orientation. The higher Maslow levels are outward oriented. The brat is definitely a controlling individual. The brat is also self-centered. So I aver that the brat is functioning primarily in the Safety and Security level. Maybe saying the brat is stuck is too harsh, maybe Maslow is wrong, maybe there is no natural tendency for human beings to move up this Hierarchy, maybe the only impetus to move up comes from the parenting we receive from our caregivers. Maybe the brat is not so much stuck as he just is not receiving any impetus to move up.

Whether there is a natural tendency to move up the Hierarchy or not, either way I suspect that parenting plays the dominant role in determining the emotional growth of the child, a role that is more important than any possible internal impetus; and it is the primary caregiver implementing my Push-Pull repair technique utilizing my Four Rules that I expect to be responsible for the bulk of the repair we will see in a TD child. So maybe the problem is that the brat is just not being pushed or pulled up the Hierarchy.

Infants are very controlling. They cry when they want to be fed. They cry when they are uncomfortable. They let their needs be known without any regard for the feelings or needs of others. It is interesting that we as humans go from being in complete control as infants, to being controlled as children, and then to being in control again as adults. Life is not simple.

I suspect that the brat is created by his caregivers not pushing him up the Hierarchy, but instead letting him languish at the Safety and Security level. By their not forcing the child to relinquish control after his brief but powerful stranglehold rule over all facets of his primary caregivers' lives during his first year of life, where the caregivers, from the baby's perspective, live only to serve, a brat is made. The caregivers keep performing the first year of the attachment cycle, the "healthy attachment cycle," long after it should be over, and never move on to the second year, the "secure attachment cycle."

The first year "healthy attachment cycle" is where the child's needs are repeatedly fulfilled by the primary caregiver and the child learns trust. The "secure attachment cycle" is the second year where the care-giver starts saying "no" and teaches the child the differences between wants and needs.

So the difference between the TD child and the brat is, the TD child is created by a breakdown in the first year "healthy attachment cycle" while the brat is created by a breakdown in the second year "secure attachment cycle." Either way the result is similar behavior, at least as a child. I have seen many self-centered bratty children just seem to outgrow it and become very nice adults. On the other hand it is not so easy for the TD child to outgrow his trust deficiencies.

Whereas the reason for the TD child to be controlling is different from the reason for the brat, the resulting behavior is similar. In both cases the child is not good at trusting others. The TD child because he sees real danger in trusting others, the brat only because he has had limited experience in trusting others, as his caregiver does not expect or demand it of him. My analogy that learning to trust is a little like learning to ride a bicycle still holds, you have to do it to appreciate it.

It appears that if given a choice, we human beings would prefer to never give up the self-centered controlling life that is automatically conferred upon most of us as infants. It would also appear that once we as human beings learn to trust and move up to higher Maslow levels, given a choice, we never go back to being a controlling self-centered individual. And finally it appears that the emotional movement from the first state of controlling self-centeredness to the emotionally mature state of caring outward-centeredness requires the nurturing of a competent caregiver or it likely will not happen.

My main point in this chapter is to argue that children do not automatically trust even when there is absolutely no reason why they should not. They cannot see the benefit until they have tried it and they will not try it until they see the benefit. Because we as caregivers are more mature, more emotionally advanced, and have experienced trust in our own lives we can see the benefit, so we must teach them to trust.

As caregivers we teach trust without conscious awareness. How many times have you heard a child argue, "Why can't I do or have this or that, you do or have it?" Your answer is, "Because I'm an adult!" Saying I'm an adult is not really a reason, but it gets across your underlying message which is, "Because as an adult and your caregiver I am in control and you need to obey me without question and that learning to obey without question is a good lesson for you, it teaches you to trust." Some caregivers will make the mistake of never invoking their right as the adult to make unilateral decrees, but will always allow the child to engage them in debate over anything and everything. Never making a unilateral decree never gives the child the opportunity to see that he can still be safe and secure while giving up control.

In the name of balance I need to point out that as a child grows and matures it is also our job to teach him to make good healthy choices and eventually take control of his life. This means that there are going to be times when you do seriously consider his objections, ideas, and concerns and if they are reasonable, incorporate them appropriately into your thinking. It is a balancing act but good parents do it without any conscious effort, they just seem to have a sense of when to listen and consider the child's opinions and when to cut off debate and make a one-sided ruling, when to be hard and strict and when to be soft and accommodating.

There is a paradox that I will call the "control paradox." The more the child demands control of his life the less control we willingly grant to him. The more compliant and obedient the child behaves the more we push for him to take control and make choices. To us adults we understand why this happens, but to the child, it seems backward. I could have just as easily named this book, *Understanding and Overcoming the Control Paradox in Raising Children.*

Here is a test to insure that you have been paying attention while reading this book. Why must we teach the lesson of trust first and complete that lesson before we then go on to teach the lesson of making good choices? Why is the order that these lessons are taught important? Answer: trust is a Safety and Security level issue. Without learning to trust, the child will perpetually function at the Safety and Security level and will not appreciably rise beyond that level. Though we do not define the word "good" in the phrase "good choices" we can probably agree that good choices more often than not involve an element of Belonging and Love and Esteem. Good choices are being polite, being respectful of yourself and others, being helpful, being mindful, etc. Some good choices do arise out of the Safety and Security level such as not walking down a deserted alley in a dangerous neighborhood—but for the most part, they arise out of higher levels. How can we expect a child who is battling for survival at his Safety and Security level to internally recognize on an emotional basis what good choices are? In other words, is it realistic to expect a child to use a full range of emotions to make good choices when his emotions are limited primarily to Safety and Security? Of course we can intellectually teach them through behavior training to do and say the right things for different situations, but how much better it is if the child's behavior is motivated by a mature emotional base. We must teach the trust lesson first because Safety and Security is lower on the Hierarchy, more pre-potent, than Belonging and Love and Esteem and we need the child to get through that level and start developing emotions in the higher levels. The child needs a complete emotional base before he can be expected to make good choices.

Remember my Four Rules for developing trust:

- Rule number one: supply all his Needs
- Rule number two: be trustworthy
- Rule number three: be sure the child knows that he is trusting you (i.e. that you are in control)
- Rule number four: be emotionally strong

Just as Maslow ranked his Hierarchy, I too have ranked the Four Rules in pre-potency from number one being most pre-potent to number four being least pre-potent. This concept of pre-potency implies that it does not matter how well you satisfy rule number two, three and four if you fail to satisfy rule number one. If you are going to fail to satisfy rules, it is better to fail the higher numbered rules than the lower numbered rules.

Consider the child who comes from a strong stable family that provides a good house, consistent food and other material necessities, has rigid rules never allowing the child to question who is in control, with strong dominant parents, but is missing only one element, and that is love. Everything in rule two, three, and four is completely satisfied, and everything in rule number one is provided except love and esteem. The child grows up with emotional problems. You cannot skip important elements when attempting to satisfy the Four Rules.

We have already established that the TD child is created by violating rule number one. Now I would like to establish that the brat is created by violating rule three. If I am right, then because rules one and two are more pre-potent than rule three it follows that the TD child will have more emotional damage and be more difficult to repair than the brat.

The "secure attachment cycle" should occur during the second year of life. The "secure attachment cycle" has the caregiver setting limits, developing boundaries, saying "no" and teaching the child the difference between wants and needs. But on top of the child learning the difference between wants and needs, the child also learns that the primary caregiver is ultimately in control and makes the final decisions. When you say "no" you are denying the child's demand, and effectively transferring control from the child to you. The child then learns that all the good things that happened to him and for him during his first year of life were really not happening because he demanded them, they were happening because the primary caregivers chose to provide them. This is where he learns that he has been trusting and can continue to trust his primary caregivers, and that their performance in the past proves that they can be trusted now and in the future.

The second year "secure attachment cycle" is where we implement rule number three. For the first year of life we have not been implementing rule number three. Note that going down the list of rules they progressively require greater intellectual capacity on the part of the child, so we hold off implementing rule three until the child is mature enough to appreciate that a want and a need are not the same thing, and has the intellectual capacity to get and understand the "no" message we are sending. We can hold off even longer in implementing rule number four, be emotionally strong, as pre-school children are not that aware of personality strength of character and sometimes are even frightened by it. Sometimes implementing rule number four has the parent with the stronger personality take over a greater share of the parenting responsibilities when the child grows older.

The Four Rules have become more than a set of rules for repairing TD children, they are actually rules for raising all children, and we have considered that many emotional development problems of children can be attributed to different permutations of the ways that the Four Rules were violated. Different rules are violated to create a TD child as opposed to a brat, but the outcome seems to be similar, not trusting but being controlling—with the difference seeming to lie in the depth of the damage and the difficulty of the repair.

Contradiction

I have created a contradiction within this chapter in some of the statements that I have made. I have suggested that children often do not move up to higher levels without the parenting of their caregivers. I have suggested that one major element of parenting is the implementation of my Four Rules and that these rules are important for creating a trusting individual that can go onto developing their Belonging and Love emotions and their Esteem emotions. I have said that brats are created by caregivers who fail to provide rule number three; be sure the child knows that he is trusting you. And I have said that brats often seem to just outgrow their brattiness, and often become fine adults.

The contradiction, of course, is the child outgrowing his bratty behavior without the caregivers changing their parenting style and implementing rule three.

Remember that I labeled my overall technique for repair of the TD child as the Push-Pull technique. I have the caregiver implementing the Four Rules. The Four Rules part of the Push-Pull technique addresses the "push" part. The push part pushes the child out of the Safety and Security level. It is meant to satisfy the child's Safety and Security Needs reducing the grasp that Safety and Security has on the child's emotions as much as possible. Because of the real Physiological level deficiencies (for example not getting fed) that occurred in the TD child's early history his Safety and Security level emotions are going to have a very strong grasp on him; beyond rational, often an irrational grasp, and even implementing the Four Rules will not be enough to push the child out of the Safety and Security level.

We also need the pull part. The pull part is your feeding into his Belonging and Love Needs that we argued were still there buried somewhere in the child even if overshadowed by the more pre-potent Safety and Security Needs. We are going to find those Needs and we are going to stimulate them, and we hope that the push and the pull together will move the child up the Hierarchy.

The brat does not have such strongly entrenched Safety and Security Needs and he typically has caring and loving parents; even without the firm push that totally implementing the Four Rules provides, as he grows older and his higher level Needs become stronger, the pull of his Belonging and Love Needs will often be enough to overcome his brattiness.

What happens to the brat that does not spontaneously overcome his brattiness or is not actively repaired by his caregivers? See Chapter 8 (Addictive Personality Paradigm). If I had a brat for a child I would not leave his repair up to fate—I would intervene. It would not hurt for parents of brats to do a better job in implementing rule number three. Not all brats go on to become healthy adults and clearly the better you parent your child, the less you leave things up to chance.

20

Misconceptions Revisited

In this chapter, I am going to repeat myself somewhat, but with a different approach. I want to talk about statements that people flippantly throw out in conversation and treat as little pearls of wisdom. I am talking about the one thing that more people in the entire world have in common than anything else: everybody is an expert at raising children, and everybody has an opinion. And even though ostensibly the topic of this book has been "trust disorder," it has really been "good parenting." Every good parent or caregiver really treats his or her child for trust disorder. If they succeed, their child does not have it, and if they fail, the child gets it. It is as simple as that. It is not as if some children are immune so that they would not need the kind of parenting that emphasizes developing trust as a first step toward forming lasting bonds. All children need to learn to trust.

With so many "experts" out there, you are going to get a myriad of opinions and many of them are going to be either wrong or misguided. Advice that over-simplifies, misdirects or ignores the true problem can be dangerous. Not all of the misstatements that follow come from non-professionals.

A partial list:

"The Child Just Needs to Work His Anger Out."

My point on discussing anger before in this write-up was to demonstrate that anger is a symptom, not an underlying problem. Use anger to identify the need for help on some problem, then identify and treat the underlying problem. Anger, in and of itself, is a good thing (when it does not lead to rage) because it is an agent for change, and change is generally what is needed for TD children.

"He Has Been Burned by Being Rejected Before so He Is Afraid to Attach Now."

It is true that the TD child has been hurt by rejection, and there is no doubt that rejection does hurt, but it is usually not the hurt of rejection that it causing him to avoid future attachments. The child with TD is very fearful of losing control.

When a person attaches to another individual, regardless of age or the depth and nature of the attachment, there is going to be a loss of control. This is true whether it be a relatively casual friendship, a marriage, or an adopted or foster son or daughter's relationship with their new parents. No matter what the situation, there is going to be some loss of control. It just has to happen. Ideally, the loss is shared by all parties, rather than one side becoming a slave to the other.

As an example of what I'm talking about, consider a chance exchange of pleasantries with a stranger on a bus. Even with this most trivial relationship, you may be asked to look at pictures of the stranger's grandchildren, when you really want to read the newspaper. You could be rude and tell the person you have no interest in his grandchildren, and ask him to stop bothering you; or alternately you could submit to the boring pictures. You could look at the pictures for what you consider an appropriate amount of time, and then assume control by expecting your new acquaintance to look at your grandchildren's pictures in turn. You would each have a turn at controlling the topic of discussion. Or you might insist that your grandchildren's pictures be the only topic of discussion, in which case there is still a loss of control. It is just one-sided, all on the other person's end.

From the deepest to even the most trivial of relationships, there is loss of control, but there is also a gain. One gains a greater sense of belonging and love, and I have already discussed when and how important this might be for human beings. For most people, the gain of belonging and love far outweighs the loss of control, making most relationships a positive experience in their lives. The main reason human beings do not move quickly into relationships is to insure that the net gain from the relationship is positive. That is why relationships start slowly and build with time, it is not that people do not want belonging and love, rather it is that they want to make sure they do not give up too much to get it. That is why relationships may fall apart; after time one person may feel that their loss of control has become too great for their gain of belonging and love.

When children commit to you, when they say they want to be your son or daughter, when they say they want to be part of your family, they give up some control. Implicit in agreeing to be part of a family is an unspoken commitment to abide by the rules, values, traditions, and culture of the family. Abiding by the family rules, values, traditions, and culture constitutes a loss of control. TD children are really afraid to give up control, and this is the reason they are reluctant to attach. It is not because they have been burned in the past or because of past rejections.

"Have You Considered Military School?"

This generally comes from the kind of person who would rely heavily on behavior management as the fix for the TD child. Military schools are probably very good at setting limits, boundaries, discipline, respect for authority, etc. What they lack, however, is the caring and loving that needs to be a part of the less harsh aspects of raising a child. In military school, one can expect most of the child's need to belong (Maslow's third level Needs) to be supplied by peers and not by adults, and very little of the child's need to be loved to be supplied by anyone. I do not see military school as a good match for the child with trust disorder. Unfortunately, probably too many of them are sent there.

"Children Need Boundaries. Even Though They Fight Them They Really Want Them. They Feel Safer When They Have Boundaries."[1]

The problem with this statement is not the part about children needing boundaries, which is true. The issue is the lack of insight behind it. It becomes a "one size fits all" approach to child rearing. The truth is the TD child does not want boundaries; he feels less safe when he is not in control. If you are setting boundaries and making them work, it sends a very clear statement that you, not he, are in control. If you send a clear message to him that you are in control, and at the same

209

time fulfill his Physiological, Safety and Security, and Belonging and Love Needs in a way that he is aware that those Needs have been met, then he can develop trust. If he develops trust, then he can relax and not be so vigilant. If he relaxes, he is happier and enjoys life more, and that is what he (and everybody else on this planet) really wants. So if lack of boundaries is all that is missing then, yes, setting boundaries will be the fix. But it is only half the picture, and if you do not consider the whole picture your chances of success are drastically reduced. Years ago doctors used to bleed patients; some got better, some got worse. We are smarter than that now.

"The Children Are Testing You, or Will Test You."

The actual model for this "testing you" theory is analogous to the reason that cities in medieval times built strong walls. You are those strong walls, and only when the TD child knows that the walls are intact can he relax. In order for him to feel safe and secure, the child needs for you to be a strong person, which translates into a strong protector. He is ready and willing to place his trust in you if only he can be sure that you are strong enough to be a true protector. He is not sure, however, that you are strong enough to protect him, so he "tests" you regularly just to reassure himself. In order to gain his trust it is very important that you always be strong, and that you pass the child's tests. Only then can the child trust you, relax, and feel safe and secure.

The child pushes at the boundaries (the walls) to assure himself that they are there, and he usually appreciates it when you set limits and boundaries even though he might not show it. You should ignore his protestations because he really does not mean it; he just does not know he does not mean it. I have also heard statements like he feels out of control and wants you to set limits because he does not think he can do so for himself.

This model has real appeal, and we all can relate to the strong wall analogy since we all lock our doors and windows every night. We want our walls, doors, and windows to be strong to protect us as we sleep and are vulnerable. However, the model has one major flaw: it dismisses any major trust issues, and it assumes that the child is ready and willing to place his trust in you in exchange for safety and security.

The model as I stated it above is wrong. The undermining and challenging of your authority, the control battles, the defiance, the manipulation, lying, stealing; these are not tests of you to see if you are strong. They are just simple survival skills that any person placed in a hostile uncaring world would learn in order to survive. In no way, shape, or form is he ready and willing to place his trust in you. He is not just testing to see if you are strong enough to be a protector. He does not see you as a potential protector that just has to pass a simple strength test, what he sees you as is somebody that can hurt him. It is not going to be as simple as setting boundaries to get his trust.

In order for him to feel safe and secure, he tries to stay in control. In order for him to get his needs met, he tries to control you. He does not feel safe when you are in control of his life, and he does not want you setting limits. He is not testing you; he is trying to feel safe by being in control, and he is trying to get his needs met by manipulating you.

You are not being tested—you are being challenged.

The "testing you" model places great importance on winning control battles and suggests that winning is basically all you need to do to heal the TD child.

I have said that in order to heal the TD child, you must be sure the child knows that he trusts you. He must realize that you are the adult running the show, that he is dependent on you, and that you are in control. However, he must also be happy and sense that his life is going well. Then over time, in a reactive sort of way, he can learn to trust.

It might seem that the outcome is the same, you do need to set boundaries, so why make a big deal over a flaw in the underlying traditional theory behind the "testing you" model.

There are two reasons. First, the "testing you" model does not include all the elements required to help the child, and it can lead to a false sense that you are doing all the right things to repair the child—which is not true. It leaves out a very important part of the repair effort, love. In fact, it is a model that almost invites you not to love, since being a strong authoritarian is somewhat at odds with being warm and loving.

The second reason is that my model differentiates between two types of control battles: the battle for the child to control his own life (defiance), and the battle for the child to control your life (manipulation). My model says that for healing to occur, you must be emotionally

211

strong, you absolutely have to be in control of you own life, at least most of the time (all the time is ideal, but come on, it's a real world). However, it is OK for you to relinquish some control to him so that he can direct some of his own life. I place the emphasis on *relinquish* to stress that even in areas where he is running his own life, he should have the feeling that whatever control he has is because you are giving him permission to be in control. He should not feel that he is taking it. The good things in his life, the freedoms, the control he has, the privileges, all these things come from you. You are a benevolent dictator, not a rigid strong one. Of course, you are still a dictator.

My model is much easier to administer because it not only allows but also encourages you to let him have control over stuff that does not really matter to you (like whether or not he eats, or what he wears). This allows you to fight the battles that are important to *you*. My model also suggests that you do not have to act strong all the time, only when he is challenging you, because your strength is not really the issue. My model acknowledges that you will have to act strongly and fight battles, but not every minute of the waking day, which I sense some people are doing with TD children. My model encourages more warmth and love, and is a lot more fun day to day.

"Children Don't Need You to Be Their Friend; They Need You to Be Their Parent."

Just like most pearls of wisdom, there is truth in this one, as well as the potential for misuse. I remember seeing public service spots on TV that sent this message. It really brought to question the fact that I liked spending time with my children and doing things with them. Sometimes we would kid each other, rough-house, or do things that were cooperative in nature rather than authoritarian. Was I being a bad parent because I liked doing things with my children that they might also do with a friend?

The answer, of course, is no. I was not doing anything wrong at all. The problem is that the statement is meant to be directed at a subgroup of parents who do not clearly communicate to their children that they are in control. This is a subgroup that is so desperate to be loved by their child that they will even do so on the child's terms. It is not that being friends with the child is the issue, it is that doing it *at*

212

any cost is the problem. It does not help the child to learn trust; the child will never trust somebody he does not respect.

I have many friends that I hold in high regard. Being a friend does not mean that I do not respect them, as the above adage might imply. If you are my friend it means I care about you, I trust you, I respect you, I look out for you, I enjoy the time I spend with you, I want to do more things with you, and I do not abuse you. There is nothing about the parent-child relationship that precludes being close and connected, and all the other good attributes of a friendship type relationship.

"He Just Has Low Self-Esteem."

A variant on this would be to say the child has "poor self-image." Maslow states that higher level Needs do not significantly emerge until lower level Needs are essentially satisfied. If the child were struggling fulfilling Safety and Security Needs, why would you expect him to also have Esteem Needs? He does not. He cannot be embarrassed, he does not worry about his reputation, he is not out to impress anybody with his good grades, and you cannot shame him into better behavior. I have spoken about this earlier, but, there is a difference between low self-esteem and no self-esteem. He has no self-esteem. It is simply not an issue.

Say an older child acts out in public in an age-inappropriate, aggressive, socially unacceptable way, spouting profanities and climbing on and over furniture knocking things down. This child is functioning at the Safety and Security Need level. His total lack of concern over making a public spectacle of himself tells us that the child is not functioning at all at the Esteem level. The child feels no embarrassment over his behavior. If you ask him if he is ashamed of himself, the answer will be that he is not. Embarrassment and shame are not yet part of his emotional framework.

Before someone can have low self-image, he has to be functioning at least a little on the Esteem level. If not, then self-image is a foreign concept. Another example would be the young teenage girl who sleeps with any boy that makes a pass at her. Adults might wonder where her pride is, and why she does not care about the kind of bad reputation she is creating for herself. In this case, the girl is not functioning at the

Esteem level; reputation and pride just are not important to her as she is still searching for Love and Belonging, the third Need level.

"Lap Sitting Is Regressive Behavior."

It was suggested that an older TD child regressed by wanting to sit on a lap. When I heard this I questioned whether a TD child's wanting to sit on an adult's lap should be considered regression. There are two reasons that a child might seek out an adult lap. The first reason would be to seek shelter, safety and security. The second reason would be to be close, to seek love and belonging.

We have already established that the TD child is locked in the Safety and Security level. Any behavior motivated by the Safety and Security level should not be considered regressive behavior for him—it is typical behavior. The child can only regress after he has progressed, and our TD child has not progressed. However, it would be accurate to say that he has exhibited regressive behavior compared to the average child his age, but this is going to be true for much of his behavior and is not going to be helpful in helping the child.

If the TD child seeks out a lap to find shelter, safety, and security, we consider that progress, not regress. Looking to somebody else for Safety and Security requires trust. That the child can trust means that he is growing emotionally. The child who seeks a safe haven on an adult's lap is satisfying his need for Safety and Security by employing transferal trust (If I sit on your lap and you protect me, I can then relax and you will keep me safe).

Alternately, the TD child might be seeking out a lap to find love and belonging. Anytime a TD child exhibits behavior motivated from the Love and Belonging level, and of course assuming the behavior is not too inappropriate for the specific social setting, we are going to consider it as progress, not regress.

Consider that the severe TD child is likely to find an adult lap a dangerous place, not a safe place. Adults are not to be trusted; after all, they did not keep him safe in the past. Being on a lap confers a certain amount of control to the adult, a loss of control which for the child is frightening. The TD child's being able to comfortably sit on an adult lap can be considered a major milestone in his emotional healing process, and his being able to sit on a lap and enjoy being on the lap is huge progress.

So regardless of which Need level motivates the child's lap seeking behavior, the behavior is not regressive, at least not for the TD child. It is important that we avoid the regressive behavior label because it is a negative label, and will cause us to discourage a behavior that can be very positive for the child. We want to encourage the child to use transferal trust to satisfy his Safety and Security Needs and we want to encourage the child to develop his Belonging and Love Needs. In an appropriate social setting (while he is with a group of peers is not an appropriate social setting because his peers will make fun of him) we will not discourage lap sitting. See Chapter 12 (Touching and Holding).

"The Child's Acting Up Is a Cry For Attention."

So many times I hear from people that a child's acting out (his demands and his misbehaviors) is a cry for attention. Ask the question, what Need level requires attention from others for fulfillment? The most obvious answer is the Esteem level. Next in line would be the Love and Belonging level. Last would be the Safety and Security level and I cannot make much of an argument for attention from others satisfying any Safety and Security Need. Saying that the child is crying for attention is to say that the child's emotional motivation is either derived from the Esteem Needs or the Love and Belonging Needs, and we have already established that that is not the case.

Acting up is not a cry for attention, it is a simple and clear statement that you cannot control me, I can do what I want, and I will and can ignore your rules. Misbehaving is not an attention getting mechanism, it is a controlling mechanism.

"Do You Know How Lucky You Are to Be Living with John?"

This is not so much a misconception, but rather something that people say to the child that they should not be saying. "Do you know how lucky you are to be living with so and so?" The truth of the matter is that the child's life sucks. A harsh word but it is true. Do not expect the child to feel lucky, fortunate, or anything else good about being rejected by his natural family and forced into foster care, regardless of how nice or how many opportunities the child receives from his foster home. When he is older and hopefully healed, he may appreciate the good care that he received, but while he is going through it he will not. Telling him something like this clashes with what he is feeling, and it only serves to make him feel worse. It reminds him of the terrible situation he is in, and it makes him think something is wrong with him for not seeing the wonderfulness of being rejected and being forced to live with strangers.

The person who says something like this is usually well intentioned and often means, "Given your rotten situation, it could be a lot worse, so you should be thankful for that." This is not something that you want to say to the child either, so it is just as well to say nothing.

"Things Were Better When I Was a Child!"

This one is really way off topic, but since you have gotten this far through my writings maybe you will tolerate my ramblings about something that bothers me (and it does involve trust).

So many people that I talk to are very convinced that things were better when they were children and I cannot help but ask why. What causes a person to feel so strongly that the world is turning bad when I can point to obvious indications otherwise? Proving that the quality of life in general, on this planet, or at least in this country, has improved over the last one hundred years would be a monumental task and would take up much more time and space than I have spent or want to spend here. It would not matter anyway, because if your feelings are that things are getting worse, you are probably going to trust your feelings over my intellectual arguments anyway. Just to mention a few social improvements in the last century; at the beginning of the twentieth century there were child brothels in New York City, children worked in factories, women could not vote, blacks had separate and unequal school systems in parts of the country, separate bathrooms, and rode in the back of buses. A parent could beat a child mercilessly and nothing would happen, but you get my point.

I am saying the world is better now than one hundred years ago. It is better place to live, it is safer and more secure. I can think of two reasons why the reverse, though, may seem the case.

One reason the world may seem less safe now is our greater collective awareness of social problems. Television, electronics, communications, radio, newspapers, media, and the Internet all have contributed to provide far more information to us than we got in the past. Much of that information is negative.

The other reason has to do with trust. If you were raised by a primary caregiver who did a good job, early on in your life you would have no reason to mistrust anybody. As you mature, there is only one way the world can go, and that's down. The unconditional trust that you developed in your first year of life is bound to be followed by disappointment and disillusionment when you find that the world is not quite as worthy of trust as your childhood experience was. With age and maturity comes increased awareness of the true state of society, an awareness misinterpreted as society changing for the worse.

You might have been safer back then, but *society* was not.

"Keep the Birth Mom from Getting too Close to the Child, Because if She Leaves, It Will Damage the Child."

This statement refers to a foster care visitation program and a policy of limiting visitation length and frequency for the natural parent(s). This is an emotionally charged statement, and one with a strong historical basis. Understand, there is no supporting evidence to back it up, and there is emerging a body of very strong evidence to the contrary.

In the early part of the twentieth century, newborns without parents were routinely placed in institutions before being placed into adoptive homes. The feeling was that it was desirable to let the baby mature a few years in order to better determine his or her physical, mental, and personality characteristics so that a better match could be made with an adoptive family. These newborns languished with death rates between twenty to a high of seventy percent.

By the 1950s, Bowlby, Robertson, and others were making strong arguments against the prevailing policies, and by the late 70s and early 80s, the attachment cycle theory and its suggested importance of the mother-child bond became accepted as fact.

It was not that long ago that foster parents were instructed not to get too close emotionally to their foster children, especially if the foster placement was known to be temporary. It was felt that the separation

217

loss when the child left the home would do emotional damage to the child. We now understand the absolute importance of the child forming bonds with his or her primary caregivers. The damage from not forming attachment does more emotional harm than the ensuing damage from separation.

Today's foster parents are asked, encouraged, and expected to bond with their foster children. There is the realization that children, if they are to emotionally grow, must form some kind of attachment. This is said over and over in the literature, and it just feels right. It is hard to believe that only thirty years ago this was not policy. The emphasis then was placed on the damage from losing an attachment, not the benefit derived from forming an attachment.

The accepted thinking today is that the benefit from any attachment outweighs the damage from the eventual loss of that attachment. Thus, experts encourage foster parents to bond to their foster children. Experts encourage this even knowing that the foster relationship is often a temporary arrangement with an almost guaranteed separation loss facing the child in the end. But thirty years ago was not that long ago, and some of that old thinking still creeps in. I have seen a mother's access to her child restricted because of a fear that she might not fulfill all the requirements to regain custody, when all the evidence seems to support allowing access, even in the face of a guaranteed subsequent separation loss.

We are in a transitional thinking period and it has produced somewhat of a double standard, the new one for the foster parents but the old one for the birth parents. The old one—that is, do not get close to the child because of the potential damage of separation loss—needs to be discarded, and the new one, that the benefit from any attachment almost always outweighs any subsequent separation loss damage.

So the old saying is true: It is far better to have loved and lost than to not have loved at all.

What actually do we lose when we are faced with a separation from someone we love or need in our life? When someone leaves our lives, for whatever reason, by choice, by circumstances, or through death, we can lose more than just Love and Belonging. A child who loses his primary caregiver also loses Safety and Security, and probably Esteem too if the parents were doing a good job. The loss can leave a deficiency in any one of Maslow's Hierarchical levels.

If a child experiences a loss on multiple Maslow Need levels, the loss on the lowest Need level is the one that has the greatest potential for motivating behavior. For example if a child loses his parents, he could easily sense a loss of Safety and Security, Belonging and Love, and Esteem all at the same time. Help for the child should start on the Safety and Security level. It would not make sense to tell that child how proud you are of him when his immediate issue is not Esteem but Safety and Security.

Since trust is our measurement of Safety and Security, putting it into trust terms, we might say that the child gains more trust from seeing that there are people in the world that he can trust even if they may disappear after a while than not having the attachment experience at all.

A loss is a loss is a loss, regardless of its being because the parent screwed up or because an agency moved the child. Removing a child from a good, caring, loving, quality foster home is just as damaging to the child as the natural parent dropping out of the picture because of recidivism. Yet we encourage the bond with the foster parents while discouraging it with the natural parent(s) when we think that the natural parent(s) have a high probability of not becoming a permanent fixture in the child's life. This just does not make sense.

"The Child Just Needs to Learn to Trust You."

Now here's one that I do not think I have heard much, but I like it.

Notes

[1] Keck & Kupecky, *Adopting the Hurt Child*, 1995, p. 69.

21

Conclusions

A criticism that I would make of many books on reactive attachment disorder is that they tend to use a shotgun approach to theory rather than a surgical approach. I suspect that the reason for this is because for the most part they are practitioners, not theorists. The advice that they are forwarding is empirically derived. That advice is good, what they say does work, they are getting results and I think that is great; that is why I do not try in this book to give a comprehensive treatment agenda, but encourage you to read the other books.

My problem is that they feel obligated to support their empirically derived treatment modalities with theory on why their treatment modalities work, and that therein lays a major weakness. They throw out every plausible reason why the child may be behaving the way he does. Here again all the reasons that they throw out are undoubtedly valid for some particular child someplace in the world, but by giving you twenty-five potential reasons why your TD child just called you a smart-ass obfuscates what the main reason may be, which is hopefully one of the twenty-five.

Too many choices just confuse us. It would be so much more helpful if they gave us fewer choices plus a method for determining which one applies to our child; or, alternately, would indicate the most likely cause of the child's problems along with their laundry list of possibilities.

If I, as a self-proclaimed expert, were to tell you gentle reader, that your TD child was suffering from both trust issues and low self-esteem, which one would you work on first? Trust is a Safety and Security level issue; low self-esteem is an Esteem level issue; the techniques for addressing one are different from the techniques for addressing the other. You need to be told which one is more important right now, which one needs your attention first—then you know where to direct your efforts.

I am saying in this book that in most instances Safety and Security Needs are the primary Needs that need to be addressed first, and that they are characterized by a lack of trust which in turn beget a myriad of negative behaviors. Honing in on a specific starting point should really help in creating the appropriate therapeutic environment for healing the TD child.

This writing is intended for use by foster and adoptive parents who take into their homes and hearts children with trust issues, trust issues which range from mild to severe. Trust issues are common to many children, not just foster children. The Four Rules proposed to help TD children heal are good rules for raising any child.

Disease, colic, chronic ear infections, anything that causes the baby to live in constant pain can potentially cause the baby to perceive that his or her Needs are not being met. Poverty, having children too close together in age, or both parents having to work can make it near to impossible for all the Needs of all the children to be consistently met. Children do not come with an owner's manual, and what we call intuitive parenting techniques may just be techniques we learned from our own parents, and they from their parents, and so on and so forth, and they may be faulty.

TD leads to delinquency, addiction problems, and ultimately the high divorce rate seen in our culture. Looking at it this way, TD may directly touch up to fifty percent of the American population and indirectly almost everyone. There is a good chance that many of the people reading this will in some way be touched with TD. TD is a big deal and not passing it on to our children is a very good place to break the negative chain.

Maslow spoke about something that he called a "peak" experience, when the individual is hitting on all cylinders. We need to work so that more people can have "peak" experiences.

Nothing New under the Sun

There really is nothing in this book that is new. I have not discovered or invented a new way to treat TD children, nor have I come up with any new parenting techniques for damaged children. No, not at all. I am clearly not the first person or the only person to help TD children (or RAD children if you prefer). And if this book were never written, there still would be people out there taking damaged children into their homes and successfully helping them to overcome their fears and anxieties and teaching them to attach and emotionally mature into healthy adults.

This also is not the first book to give good advice on how to repair TD children. Lots of other books written by competent parents and clinicians give very helpful advice. Nor is this the first book to discuss the underlying causes of TD. Nor do I disagree with or propose errors in the existing theories.

In general all the other books are fine. This book does not propose any major thinking shift in the treatment of TD children. It does not propose any radical new or bizarre way of repairing the children. Unh-uh. Not at all. No way.

What this book does is take existing theories and existing empirically derived practices and tie them together. This book promotes understanding. After reading this book the children's caregivers should understand why they are using behavior management at one point in time, and why they are overlooking misbehavior at another. They will have a rationale for all they do.

For some this book will be unnecessary, for they already have an intuitive feel for the repair process. For them this book will just serve to reinforce what they are already successfully doing. It will also help them to stand up to critics, because for some strange reason, even people who are successful at repairing a TD child get criticized. Others miss the obvious improvements in the TD child and only focus on the remaining need for improvement, and for that the successful caregiver will get criticized.

However I am the first person to both write down what successful people are doing and relate that to the theory. If this book is successful, then perhaps what has been intuitive to a select group of caregivers can become intuitive to all the caregivers who help TD children.

Remember, although you can feel your own emotions, you can only see behavior in the child, and from that behavior you must guess at the underlying emotions that motivate the child. The biggest mistake made in understanding the TD child is using yourself as the emotional model for his behavior. But it is understandable; after all, for most of us—with no formal training—it is all we have to go on.

Who are the individuals that seem to have an intuitive feel for repairing the TD child? My experience so far has found them to be individuals who have had experience with TD as a child. Some claim they had TD themselves, and perhaps still have TD. Others claim that a sibling or parent with TD heavily influenced them. Is this surprising? No, not really. These are the people who have an intuitive understanding of the real emotions that motivate the child's behavior. For them, understanding the emotional makeup of the TD individual was often a survival skill, especially if the TD individual that influenced them was a parent or older sibling who had the ability to terrorize them if they did not step carefully.

For those caregivers who did not experience TD as a child (and it is my hope that someday nobody will ever experience TD as a child), you need to internalize a different emotional model than the one you grew up with if you are to help a TD child. It needs to be internalized because the decision making process in determining how you handle situations with a TD child on a day-to-day basis has to be quick and accurate. The child says something provocative. Do you react angrily, turn it into a joke, reprimand quietly, or ignore it? Each response has its appropriate place. Where you are in my Repair Cycle will dictate a different response to the same infraction. There is no time to pull out a manual or consult an expert.

This is the first book that pulls all the elements of TD together with the intent of giving caregivers who did not have the benefit (or the misery) of first-hand childhood experience with TD the intuitive understanding that seems so important to knowing how to repair TD children.

There is nothing new in this book. It just puts all the existing elements together and promotes understanding.

What Does the Proper Approach Feel Like?

It seems like there is a little bit of a balancing act between too much in the way of control battles and too much in the way of avoiding control battles. It is natural that each individual is going to have a different idea of what is right. My guess is that there is a range within which all will work out fine. Still, I can offer some guidelines that might be helpful.

If you are feeling used by the child, you probably need to be more aggressive in taking control or at least in setting boundaries. You are avoiding too many control battles. If on the other hand you do not seem to enjoy the child, never feel close to the child, you may need to work more on that issue.

You need to look at yourself and figure out your strengths and weaknesses. If you are good at controlling the TD child but not good at showing feelings of affection and closeness you will not be a good match for nurturing these children. Conversely if you avoid conflict by ceding too much control you will not be a good match for nurturing these children either.

Control does not necessarily translate into your dominating the child either; it can be modeled as well. Your setting limits and boundaries for yourself that the child can see in your interactions with others also demonstrates to the child that you are an individual that is in control without the need for any control battles.

How Do You Measure Success?

Not as slow as you might think. My experience with preteens has been good results in nine months and a child that would be considered to be within normal limits at eighteen months. Admittedly my sample population is small. I think that if it takes longer then there is probably pathology involved.

The ability to trust is not a constant thing; it swings back and forth within the child depending on many things both external and internal. You will have good times when the child seems normal, bad times when the child seems out of control. The good times get better; the bad times do not seem so bad. The child starts looking to you more for emotional support. He will search you out when he is feeling threatened. You will start feeling more and more attached to the child. The lying and swearing abates. He will look to you rather than to himself for problem solving.

Ultimate success is going to be when the child grows up and develops meaningful and trusting relationships with other adults. Right now we are happy if the child is tractable and moving toward our definition of maturity. Right now that is success. It does not matter if his emotional developmental schedule is a little behind his peers, just as long as he gets there.

In Chapter 5 (Evaluating Behavioral Motivation), I prepared a list of the Need levels with an indication of behavioral responses for each unfulfilled Need level. At any one point in time you will generally see behavior from only one level. Over a period of time you will probably see behavior from adjoining levels. Use this list to track the child's progress.

Some Suggestions:

- Have hope that success is possible, which translates into a more positive attitude toward the child. He can be helped.
- Provide all his needs including Love and Belonging and even some Esteem Needs.
- Have a policy of never violating a trust. If you say you are going to do something, do it regardless of it being a reward or a consequence. Try to be totally honest with actions and words.
- Be sure he knows you are in control. Of first importance is that he not be allowed to run your life, if you concentrate too much on running his life you may end up locked in one long continuous battle.
- Being in control means only holding discussions on things that you choose to discuss. Do not argue with him.
- Be sure that there is some good in his life. If he hates the life he has it will only confirm that he must be in control for life to be tolerable.
- Be a strong personality type, the type that he can trust.
- Use the Repair Cycle.
- Balance the use of behavior management with showing genuine concern and caring. Use behavior management as needed as a tool of behavior management, not as therapy.
- Balance the use of structure with spontaneity. Structure is a tool like behavior management, not therapy. Work toward transferal trust as the child's basis for safety and security.
- If you want him to do something partly or totally for your benefit, tell him openly how it will benefit you so that he does not

have to spend energy on trying to figure out how you are trying to manipulate him.

- Use holding and initiate intimacy (which in his case is often nothing more than a passive touch on the shoulder). Do back off if his anxiety level goes to high, but do not give up.
- See his immature behaving as part of his healing process and not as part of the problem and do not chastise him for it. Use it as an opportunity to provide nurturing that was previously withheld.
- Pick your battles and win the battles you pick. The importance of winning battles is basic to the trust development process.
- Use kidding as a response to unreasonable statements and requests. Do not let yourself be caught in a power struggle over words and ridiculous requests.

Here's an interesting thought. An individual like Dr. Spock comes along and writes a book that becomes a bible for child-rearing. In the book he suggests that you do not pick up the crying child, that manipulating the behavior of the child for the parent's convenience is more important than fulfilling the need that is motivating the child to cry. A whole society buys into the message, partially because the society has moved away from the extended family model and there are fewer adults around to care for the child. Because of the demands of a more complicated, less supportive social system, anything that makes the child-raising job easier is embraced. In addition both parents might work with no stay-at-home caregiver, giving efficiency in child rearing even a greater priority. We are told to check to see if there is anything obviously wrong with the infant and if not, to let the child cry. Not picking up the crying child teaches it not to trust you to fulfill its needs, and to look to itself for the fulfillment of its needs. This, of course, would not be such a bad thing if the child had the emotional and intellectual capacity to raise itself successfully, but, unfortunately, children still seem to need to be raised by adults. Children left to raise themselves generally mess up the job. Harry Potter did a wonderful job of raising himself, but I wonder if John Wayne raised himself?

One seemingly harmless well-meaning individual, with one simple well-intentioned statement, can drastically change the course of an entire culture. The word is truly more powerful than the sword.

If you are raising a boy, or if you are a teacher, counselor, case-worker, or any other professional with boys in your care, I strongly recommend you read *Real Boys* by William Pollack, Ph.D. It talks at great length about connecting with boys and dispels some of society's myths about boys.

Good luck on raising your TD child.

Appendixes

Appendix A:
CAIS

CAIS stands for Child Assessment and Intervention Special Team. The following is a copy from a descriptive write-up provided to me by Magellan Behavioral Health, dated 5/31/02.

This program is available to children and families presented with complex needs which may be difficult to fully assess in the context of an office setting. The goals of this service are twofold. First to provide immediate stabilization of the child during the assessment period through the consultative support and interventions of the clinician. Secondly, it will determine the most appropriate level and intensity of care needed through a comprehensive evaluation of the child in all life domains.

A Child Assessment and Intervention Special Team (CAIS) is a program that provides three functions: a clinical assessment, a case management role, and an evaluation and prescription for services. At a minimum each team will be comprised of a licensed psychologist or psychiatrist (the Evaluator and team supervisor) and a master's level Child Assessment and Intervention Specialist. Some teams may also include a separate Case Manager.

The CAIS team will be authorized for 24 hours of service to be provided in the child's home/school/community as needed. The clinician will meet with the child and family in the above settings and complete a functional Behavioral Assessment of the child.

A functional Behavioral Assessment is a process that attempts to identify and understand the function of a child's behavior. It assists in the identification of triggers for these behaviors and the consequences as well. This tool is useful in specifying what may be sustaining the behaviors, which then assists in targeting the treatment interventions and increases their effectiveness. The clinician will also provide the family and school staff with some preliminary treatment intervention strategies that may be useful in stabilizing the child.

The Case Management function, which may be completed by either the clinician or another staff member, will assist the family and school staff in identifying some family and community supports and resources which may be available to assist the child and family. Examples of this may be to assist the family that is accessing a local after school program, identifying family supports that are not currently involved, and assisting the family with any and all necessary referrals to programs.

Throughout the CAIS program there will be on-going assessment of the child's mental health needs and gathering of necessary data. An evaluation (psychiatric or psychological) will be scheduled which will prescribe the necessary services based upon all of the information collected by the CAIS team. The CAIS team will then assist the family in getting authorization for these services and remain open with the family until the new services begin.

The CAIS team will be authorized for up to 60 days of service, but will often be completed before this time period expires.

Appendix B:
Model Factors Overview

Any model is going to be a simplification of the real world, necessarily leaving out many variables and constants that go into making up the actual situation being modeled. But that does not lessen the value of the model. The model serves many very important functions.

First and foremost it forces us to think in a clear and logical way about the situation. It forces consistency; it helps us to understand inconsistency. It aids in communicating our ideas to others. It gives us something against which to test our real life experiences, and when the model is not as accurate as we would like, it still gives us a framework to incorporate new ideas into our existing set of ideas. Lastly, it helps us to balance and choose between many of the conflicting methods, techniques, and suggestions that people proffer as gospel for the management of these children.

In selecting the variables for the model we want them to be independent of each other—mutually exclusive would be nice. We obviously can only select ones that we can identify, and we select only ones that we think have significance. Insignificant variables, things that rarely are different between all children, and things that we identify as beyond the scope of our model we ignore. For example, our model will not include intellectual ability and will probably not be valid for the mentally retarded.

If you are into mathematics, you can look at paradigms as functions with independent and dependent variables. (If you are not into mathematics you can skip this paragraph.) All independent variables are by definition mutually exclusive (otherwise they would not be independent). A function is a defined relationship between dependent variables and independent variables that is characterized by having only one dependent variable result (never bi-variate) for any set of independent variables.

Factors

A. Intrinsic Independent Variables (placed on an orthogonal axis)

  1. Deficiency Level Needs

      a) Physiological Needs
      b) Safety and Security Needs
      c) Belonging and Love Needs
      d) Esteem Needs

  2. Growth Needs (Cognitive, Self-Actualization, etc.)
  3. Sex
  4. Intelligence
  5. Transient Instincts
  6. Personality?

B. Extrinsic Variables (Environment, way nurtured, etc.)

  1. Quality of first year nurturing

      a) Caregiver attention to physiological needs
      b) Caregiver attention to safety security needs
      c) Caregiver attention to love—socialization needs

  2. Quality of second year nurturing
  3. Quality of current care

C. Intrinsic Paradigms

  1. Maslow's Hierarchy of Needs (Modified)
  2. Anger
  3. Attachment (Modified)

Appendix C:
The Related Disorders

The American Psychiatric Association has identified three disorders that are highly inter-related and perhaps should be classified as one disorder. Let me list all three here with their associated diagnostic criteria, since, anybody who ever works with attachment disorder children should be familiar with these named disorders as they will come up time and again in conversations. These are copied from one of the American Psychiatric Association's manual *Diagnostic and Statistical Manual of Mental Disorders.*[1]

Diagnostic Criteria for 313.89: Reactive Attachment Disorder of Infancy or Early Childhood.

A. Markedly disturbed and developmentally inappropriate social relatedness in most contexts, beginning before the age of five, as evidenced by either (1) or (2):

1. persistent failure to initiate or respond in a developmentally appropriate fashion to most social interactions, as manifest by excessively inhibited, hyper vigilant, or highly ambivalent and contradictory responses (e.g., the child may respond to caregivers with a mixture of approach, avoidance, and resistance to comforting, or may exhibit frozen watchfulness)
2. diffuse attachments as manifest by indiscriminate sociability with marked inability to exhibit appropriate selective attachments (e.g., excessive familiarity with relative strangers or lack of selectivity in choice of attachment figures)

B. The disturbance in Criterion A is not accounted for solely by developmental delay (as in Mental Retardation) and does not meet criteria for a Pervasive Developmental Disorder.

C. Pathogenic care, as evidenced by at least one of the following:

  1. persistent disregard of the child's basic emotional needs for comfort, stimulation, and affection.
  2. persistent disregard of the child's basic physical needs.
  3. repeated changes of primary caregiver that prevent formation of stable attachments (e.g., frequent changes in foster care).

D. There is a presumption that the care in Criterion C is responsible for the disturbed behavior in Criterion A (e.g., the disturbances in Criterion A began following the pathogenic care in Criterion C). Specify type:

Inhibited Type: if Criterion A1 predominates in the clinical presentation

Disinhibited Type: if Criterion A2 predominates in the clinical presentation

Diagnostic Criteria for 301.81: Narcissistic Personality Disorder

A pervasive pattern of grandiosity (in fantasy or behavior), need for admiration, and lack of empathy, beginning by early adulthood and present in a variety of contexts, as indicated by five (or more) of the following:

  1) has a grandiose sense of self-importance (e.g., exaggerates achievements and talents, expects to be recognized as superior without commensurate achievements)
  2) is preoccupied with fantasies of unlimited success, power, brilliance, beauty, or ideal love
  3) believes that he or she is "special" and unique and can only be understood by, or should associate with, other special or high-status people (or institutions)
  4) requires excessive admiration
  5) has a sense of entitlement, i.e., unreasonable expectations of especially favorable treatment or automatic compliance with his or her expectations

6) is interpersonally exploitative, i.e., takes advantage of others to achieve his or her own ends
7) lack empathy: is unwilling to recognize or identify with the feelings and needs of others
8) is often envious of others or believes that others are envious of him or her
9) shows arrogant, haughty behaviors or attitudes

Diagnostic Criteria for 313.81: Oppositional Defiant Disorder

A. A pattern of negativistic, hostile, and defiant behavior lasting at least 6 months, during which four (or more) of the following are present:

1. often loses temper
2. often argues with adults
3. often actively defies or refuses to comply with adult's requests or rules
4. often deliberately annoys people
5. often blames others for his or her mistakes or misbehavior
6. is often touchy or easily annoyed by others
7. is often angry and resentful
8. is often spiteful or vindictive

Note: Consider a criterion met only if the behavior occurs more frequently than is typically observed in individuals of comparable age and developmental level.

B. The disturbance in behavior causes clinically significant impairment in social, academic, or occupational functioning.
C. The behaviors do not occur exclusively during the course of a Psychotic or Mood Disorder.
D. Criteria are not met for Conduct Disorder, and, if the individual is age 18 years or older, criteria are not met for Antisocial Personality Disorder.

Other related disorders would be Attention-deficit Hyperactivity Disorder and Conduct Disorder.

Notes

[1] American Psychiatric Association. *Diagnostic and Statistical Manual of Mental Disorders*, Fourth Edition, 2000.

Appendix D:
Goal Sheet

SHOOT FOR THE GOAL!

	Monday *Field Trip*	Tuesday	Wednesday *Thurs*	Thursday *Wed*	Friday
Math	③ 2 1	③ 2 1	③ 2 1	② 2 1	③ 2 1
Soc. Studies	③ 2 1	3 ② 1	3 ② 1	② 1	3 ② 1
Grammar	③ 2 1	3 ② 1	3 ② 1	② 1	3 ② 1
Science	③ 2 1	3 ② 1	3 ② 1	3 ② 1	③ 2 1
Lang. Arts	③ 2 1	3 ② 1	3 2 ①	③ 2 1	③ 2 1
Totals	15	11	10	12	13
Comments	Super Job! Keep it up!	Keep working on being on task. ★	11/11 needed many reminders to get on task today.	11/12 Please work on staying on task. keep working towards that goal.	Very chatty. Let's work hard on staying on task. 60 for the week
Initials					

Student: _____ Week of: _11/10 – 11/14_

GOAL: _Stay on task_   Reward: _Candy jar pick_

Point System:
3 = No reminders needed or only 1 reminder needed
2 = 2-3 reminders needed
1 = more than 3 reminders needed

Points needed to earn reward at end of week: _____ 70

Goal sheet must be initialed by parent/guardian daily.

Bibliography

Ainsworth, Mary D. Salter, Blehar, Mary C., Waters, Everett, Wall, Sally. *Patterns of Attachment: A Psychological Study of the Strange Situation*. Hillsdale, NJ: Lawrence Erlbaum Associates, 1978.

American Psychiatric Association. *Diagnostic And Statistical Manual of Mental Disorders*. Fourth Edition—Revised. Washington D.C.: American Psychiatric Association, 2000.

Bjork, Daniel W. *B. F. Skinner: A Life*. Washington D.C.: American Psychological Association, 1999.

Bowlby, John. *Attachment*. New York: Basic Books, 1982, 1969.

Bowlby, John. *Loss: Sadness and Depression*. New York: Basic Books, 1980.

Bowlby, John. *A Secure Base: Parent-Child Attachment and Healthy Human Development*. New York: Basic Books, 1988.

Chandler, Cristine & McGrath, Laura. *4 Weeks to a Better Behaved Child*. New York: McGraw Hill, 2004.

Cline, Foster W., M.D. & Fay, Jim. *Parenting with Love and Logic: Teaching Children Responsibility*. Colorado Springs, Colorado: Pinon Press, 1990.

Cline, Foster W., M.D. & Helding, Cathy. *Can This Child Be Saved?: Solutions for Adoptive and Foster Families*. Franksville, WI: World Enterprises, 1999.

Dobson, Dr. James. *The New Dare to Discipline*. Wheaton, Illinois: Tyndale House, 1970, 1992.

Dobson, Dr. James. *The Strong-Willed Child: Birth through Adolescence*. Wheaton, Illinois: Tyndale House, 1985.

Eldridge, Sherrie. *Twenty Things Adopted Kids Wish Their Adoptive Parents Knew*. New York: Dell Publishing, First printing 1997, 1999.

Forehand, Rex, Ph.D. & Long, Nicholas, Ph.D. *Parenting the Strong-Willed Child*. New York: Contemporary Books, 1996, 2002.

Goble, Frank. *The Third Force: The Psychology of Abraham Maslow, A Revolutionary New View of Man*. New York: Pocket Book, 1971.

Gray, Deborah D. *Attaching in Adoption: Practical Tools for Today's Parents*. Indianapolis, Indiana: Perspectives Press, Inc., 2002.

Greene, Ross W., Ph.D. *The Explosive Child*. New York: Harper Collins, 2001, 1998.

Greenspan, Stanley I., M.D. *The Challenging Child: Understanding, Raising, and Enjoying the Five "Difficult" Types of Children*. Cambridge, Massachusetts: Perseus Books, 1995.

Gulden, Holly van & Bartels-Rabb, Lisa M. *Real Parents, Real Children: Parenting the Adopted Child*. New York: The Crossroad Publishing Company, 2002, 1993.

Gurian, Michael. *The Wonder of Boys: What Parents, Mentors and Educators Can Do to Shape Boys into Exceptional Men*. New York: Jeremy P. Tarcher/Putnam, 1996, Trade Paperback Edition, 1997.

Hughes, Daniel A., Ph.D. *Facilitating Developmental Attachment: The Road to Emotional Recovery and Behavioral Change in Foster and Adopted Children*. Lanham, Maryland: Rowman & Littlefield, 1997.

Jewett, Claudia L. *Adopting the Older Child*. Boston: The Harvard Common Press, 1978.

Karen, Robert Ph.D. *Becoming Attached: First Relationships and How They Shape Our Capacity to Love*. New York: Oxford University Press, 1998.

Keck, Ph.D., Gregory C. & Kupecky, L.S.W., Regina M. *Adopting the Hurt Child: Hope for Families with Special-Needs Kids*. Colorado Springs, Colorado: Pinon Press, 1995.

Keck, Ph.D., Gregory C. & Kupecky, L.S.W., Regina M. *Parenting the Hurt Child: Helping Adoptive Families Heal and Grow*. Colorado Springs, Colorado: Pinon Press, 2002.

Kurcinka, Mary Sheedy. *Raising Your Spirited Child*. New York: Harper Collins, 1992, reissued 1998.

Levy, Terry M. *Handbook of Attachment Interventions*. San Diego: Academic Press, 2000.

Levy, Terry M. & Orlans, Michael. *Attachment, Trauma, and Healing: Understanding and Treating Attachment Disorder in Children and Families*. Washington, D.C.: CLWA Press, 1998.

Mansfield, Lynda Gianforte & Waldmann, Christopher H., MA, LPC. *Don't Touch My Heart: Healing the Pain of an Unattached Child*. Colorado Springs, Colorado: Pinion Press, 1994.

Maslow, Abraham H. Ph.D. *Motivation and Personality*, Third Edition. New York: Addison Wesley Longman, Inc., 1987.

Maslow, Abraham H. Ph.D. *The Farther Reaches of Human Nature.* New York: Viking Press, 1971.

Maslow, Abraham H. Ph.D. *Toward a Psychology of Being*, Third Edition. New York: John Wiley & Sons, 1999.

Molina, Brooke S. G. & Pelham, William E. Jr. *Childhood Predictors of Adolescent Substance Use in a Longitudinal Study of Children with ADHD.* Journal of Abnormal Psychology, 2003, Vol. 112, No. 3, PP. 497–507.

Neff, Pauline. *Tough Love: How Parents Can Deal with Drug Abuse.* Nashville: Abingdon Press, 1982, Revised 1996.

Pollack, Ph.D., William & Cushman, Kathleen. *Real Boys Workbook, The Definitive Guide to Understanding and Interacting with Boys of All Ages.* New York: Villard Books, 2001.

Pollack, Ph.D., William. *Real Boys.* New York: Henry Holt and Company, Inc., 1999.

Sansone, Carol & Harackiewicz, Judith M. *Intrinsic and Extrinsic Motivation.* San Diego: Academic Press, 2000.

Skinner, B. F. *About Behaviorism.* New York: Vintage Book Edition, 1976.

Skinner, B. F. *Beyond Freedom & Dignity.* Indianapolis/Cambridge: Hackett Publishing Company, Inc., 1971, reprinted 2002.

Thomas, Nancy L. *When Love Is Not Enough, A Guide to Parenting Children with RAD-Reactive Attachment Disorder.* 1997.

Turecki, Stanley, M.D. *The Difficult Child.* New York: Bantam Books, 1985, Second revised trade paperback edition 2000.

Watson, John B. *Behaviorism.* New York: W. W. Norton & Company, Inc., 1970.

Watson, John B. *Psychological Care of Infant and Child.* New York: Norton, 1928.

Welch, Martha G. *Holding Time: How to Eliminate Conflict, Temper Tantrums, and Sibling Rivalry and Raise Happy, Loving, Successful Children.* New York: Simon and Schuster, 1988.

9 780533 153220